Against Death

THEORY AND PRACTICE IN MEDICAL ANTHROPOLOGY AND INTERNATIONAL HEALTH

This book is part of a series. The publisher will accept continuation orders which may be cancelled at any time and which provide for automatic billing and shipping of each title in the series upon publication. Please write for details.

Against Death
The Practice of Living with AIDS

Robert M. Ariss[†]

Macquarie University
Sydney, Australia

with Gary W. Dowsett

Gordon and Breach Publishers

Australia Canada China France Germany India Japan
Luxembourg Malaysia The Netherlands Russia Singapore
Switzerland Thailand United Kingdom

Amsteldijk 166
1st Floor
1079 LH Amsterdam
The Netherlands

Parts of an early version of chapter 11 originally appeared under a different title in *The Australian Journal of Anthropology* (TAJA), vol. 4(1) (1993), and are reprinted here with permission.

Cover photo by Yair Metargem

British Library Cataloguing in Publication Data

Ariss, Robert M.
  Against death : the practice of living with AIDS. – (Theory and practice in medical anthropology and international health ; v. 5)
  1. AIDS (Disease) – Patients – Australia   2. AIDS (Disease) – Treatment – Australia
  I. Title   II. Dowsett, Gary
  362.1'9'69792'00994

ISBN 90–5699–564–2

And death shall have no dominion
Dead men naked they shall be one
With the man in the wind and the west moon;
When their bones are picked clean and the clean bones gone,
They shall have stars at elbow and foot;
Though they go mad they shall be sane,
Though they sink through the sea they shall rise again;
Though lovers be lost love shall not;
And death shall have no dominion.

— Dylan Thomas

CONTENTS

INTRODUCTION TO THE SERIES

Theory and Practice in Medical Anthropology and International Health seeks to promote works of direct relevance to anthropologically informed international health issues, practice, and policy. It aims to bridge medical anthropology — both biological and cultural — with international public health, social medicine, and sociomedical sciences. The series' theoretical scope is intentionally flexible, incorporating the most current advances in social science theory, while its topical breadth ranges from specific issues to contemporary debates to practical applications informed by current anthropological theory. The distinguishing characteristic of this new series is its emphasis on cultural aspects of medicine and their links to larger social contexts and concrete applicability of the anthropological endeavor.

FOREWORD

Dr. Robert M. Ariss died on May 9, 1994 from an AIDS-related condition. He was thirty-two years old. He had all but completed the final draft of this book, based on his doctoral dissertation, and on the morning of his death had decided on a new working title, *Playing Patients: The Practice of Living with HIV in Sydney, Australia.* The considerable irony of that title was not lost on those friends with Robert when he died; nor was it a choice unexpected by his colleagues at Macquarie University in Sydney, who had watched, helplessly, Robert's deteriorating health over the previous six months. Unfortunately, Robert's careful pun — "Patients"/"Patience" — loses something in offering his book to an international readership, which perhaps better knows the cardgame "Patience" (as it is called in Australia) as "Solitaire." Thus, the present title.

In chapter 9 of this book, Robert writes of the death of another activist, Terry Bell, in circumstances uncannily prophetic of his own:

His death shocked many who were unaware of the severity of his illness toward the end of that year. Terry was working on a draft of a treatment information news-sheet in bed on the day of his death. Terry Bell worked relentlessly to the last day to improve the predicament of people with AIDS.

Robert's fight with HIV infection was valiant and exemplary. And this book represents and documents much of that fight. But this is not a biography; nor is it a documentary of the struggle by People Living With HIV and AIDS (PLWHA). Rather, as an anthropologist, Robert Ariss was the ultimate participant-observer of a cultural and political phenomenon that he, in fact, helped create. His eye, always critical, scanned the sexual and social lives of his community, namely the Sydney gay community. In his activism, Robert was among the central few who created PLWHA culture and politics in Sydney and in Australia. Yet, he was keenly aware of the pitfalls of activism, the experiences that sharpen perception, the passions that cloud judgment, the courage of collective struggle.

This book is a critical work, engaging experience through the rigorous deployment of social theory. As such, it provides a significant analysis of a central period in Australia's experience of the HIV pandemic. As this country moves into a new phase, marked by the development of its third national HIV/AIDS strategy that aims to guide Australia through to the year 2000, Robert Ariss's book is a provocative reflection on the previous decade. His keen, analytical observations will be important in the time ahead, and those of us who mourn his passing will, through this book, have him with us always.

A number of people, Robert's friends and colleagues, worked to ensure that this book was completed, with the full support of Robert's family. I would like to acknowledge the assistance of the National Centre for HIV Social Research, Macquarie University, especially its director, associate professor Susan Kippax, and the contributions of Jo Elliot and Chris Lyttleton. And many thanks to Graeme Skinner, who undertook the copy-editing of Robert's text for publication.

Gary W. Dowsett

ACKNOWLEDGMENTS

This book is substantially based on my doctoral thesis, *Against Death: The Sydney Gay Community Responds to AIDS* (Department of Anthropology, University of Sydney, 1992). Funds for that study were provided by a Commonwealth Postgraduate Research Scholarship. Additional travel funds were provided by a Carlyle Greenwell Bequest.

My foremost thanks to my supervisors, Michael Allen and Jeremy Beckett, for their gentle and insightful guidance throughout that project. Thanks, too, to the staff of the University of Sydney's Department of Anthropology, in particular Vivienne Kondos, Marie de Lepervanche, Peter Hinton, Paul Alexander and Jadran Mimica, and also to my fellow postgraduate students for their interest and comments. The research team of the (then) National Centre for HIV Social Research, Macquarie University, has been an invaluable source of inspiration, support and encouragement; I thank in particular Gary Dowsett, Mark Davis and David McMaster.

I am indebted to the many staff and volunteers of the AIDS Council of New South Wales (ACON), in particular to Ken Davis for his penetrating insights, Kosta Matsoukas for his comments on early chapter drafts, and Brett Tindall for information and support throughout. From the Wollongong AIDS Research Project, thanks to Linda Viney for granting me permission to use interview material, Levinia Crooks with whom I worked, Beverly Walker and Rachel Henry. I am grateful to Paul Grguric, Michael Rawlins, Bill Robinson and Gray Sattler, who all helped me with proofreading the final draft of the dissertation.

Finally, thanks to all those people with HIV and AIDS whom I have known throughout my involvement in the area, to those who agreed to participate in interviews, and those who have shared with me their fears and hopes.

I dedicate this book to the men with AIDS who contributed but who died before its completion. It is their courage, creativity and humour in the face of death that were my inspiration.

Part One

The Anthropology of AIDS

CHAPTER 1

Introduction

In the final years of the 1980s, an anthropologist undertaking an ethnographic study of the AIDS epidemic in Australia often felt out of place, was held to be somewhat eccentric and was certainly misunderstood. Yet, barely a half-decade further on, anyone wishing to investigate AIDS from a social science angle will find a research environment somewhat, though not dramatically, more favorable. This shift has resulted from the changing interests of social researchers themselves, a broadening of the AIDS research agenda generally, and from the changing position of non-government AIDS organizations that have established for themselves a critical role in the international response to HIV/AIDS.

That is not to say that AIDS is no longer a medically defined problem. However, AIDS as experienced by a gay man, by a person infected with the virus and facing an early death, has earned a more determining position in the overall field of competing discourses through which we know this disease. We no longer rely exclusively on the authority of the medical physician and researcher. Now we are more likely to be confused by the clamor of competing voices, each claiming some position of authority, each denouncing the others, each clinging to a particular truth of AIDS.

This is not a book that offers, as many proclaim to, a truth of AIDS. What the reader will find here is an anthropologically informed perspective on a local AIDS epidemic. It is about a place: Sydney; and a people: gay-identifying men with HIV/AIDS. For all that this study focuses on the details of life in this epidemic, it is my intention that it, like all good ethnographies, speak about a wider cultural predicament.

Anthropology requires that the ethnographer simultaneously immerse him- or herself in the life of a community under study while ceaselessly problematizing that experience. This method positions the researcher *within* and *without* a community simultaneously and it is from this

3

perspective, as difficult as it may often be, that an anthropological view on a phenomenon such as an AIDS epidemic derives. The ethnographer must struggle for a balance between participation and observation. In the course of work, I took on a great many agendas, at times becoming more participant than observer. This frequently led to a fear that I was losing an objective perspective on events, and that I would be unable to construct an account that was more than descriptive, or a reproduction of local belief systems. Withdrawal from the field site returns the writer to some position outside the field of action and it is from here, one hopes, that a rigorous critique can be constructed. This withdrawal can be a painful experience, as it was for me, as one severs regular links with the many institutions and individuals that provided not only a source of interesting material for a social study of an epidemic but also love, friendship and support.

The boundaries of the gay community or of a population of people with a disease are highly problematic, and yet the nature of the field of the epidemic in Sydney, and more broadly in Australia, became clearer in time. In the course of my fieldwork, I endeavored to locate myself in a wide range of positions within the field of the epidemic, to speak with as many different kinds of people as possible, and to engage in a range of different activities. As the study progressed, this endeavor took on a momentum of its own. I started out volunteering my time for community-based AIDS organizations, a relatively easy entry into the heart of the community-based response to AIDS. I took on tasks of public speaking, education and policy formulation, counselling of the distressed, caring for the sick, political lobbying, consultation with federal and state governments, journalism in the gay community press, and, probably most importantly, became friend to a great many people with HIV and AIDS.

I have written about issues that arose, sometimes quite unexpectedly, during the course of fieldwork. This is the very strength and integrity of the anthropological method: faithful attention to the flow of everyday life while retaining a consciousness of the place of the researcher in the course of events. I am thus writing about my own recent life experience as much as about the experience of others.

I have experienced the deaths of many individuals since I began this study. Like many others living in urban gay communities struck by AIDS, I no longer have the courage to count my losses. To quantify, somehow, does not seem an appropriate means of conceptualizing the close experience of death. I stopped trying, just three years into the study, when the number of losses exceeded thirty individuals. Such loss leaves its imprint on a young man. Writing about AIDS in the way I have chosen has been difficult but the experience was anticipated and, I dare say, sometimes with curiosity. The experience has been a major influence both on how I understand this epidemic and the way this text was finally written. In order to understand AIDS one must experience death, and so that experience is largely what this study is about.

Moreover, this is a study about a struggle *against* death. Those who work with people with AIDS sometime classify this struggle, rather callously I think, as denial. But a will to live is *not* an inability to face the inevitable, even when that inevitability is as frightening as annihilation. The will and the struggle are an affirmation of life, a refusal to leave this earth before one's time, before one has taken one's fill of what it has to offer. The determination to refuse death has had some extraordinary effects, and to have participated in that struggle leaves one tired but nonetheless full of hope for the human condition.

THE ANTHROPOLOGY OF ILLNESS

Anthropology provides an alternative perspective on AIDS to those offered by the disciplines that dominate the field of knowledge about the disease: biomedicine, behaviorism, and psychology. Anthropology has a history of interest in questions of health, illness, healing, and death that is as old as the discipline itself. In recent decades this interest has solidified into the sub-discipline of medical anthropology, which has framed its own set of research questions, methodologies, and applications (for a recent review see Johnson and Sargent 1990). What is becoming clearer through such work is the significance of the body, health, illness, and healing to an understanding of societies. Consider this observation by Lévi-Strauss, one that could describe the predicament of the person with AIDS as much as it describes the victim of sorcery:

> An individual who is aware that he is the object of sorcery is thoroughly convinced that he is doomed according to the most solemn traditions of his group. His friends and relatives share his certainty. From then on the community withdraws. Standing aloof from the accursed, it treats him not only as though he were already dead but as though he were a source of danger to the entire group. On every occasion and by every action, the social body suggests death to the unfortunate victim, who no longer hopes to escape what he considers to be his ineluctable fate. Shortly thereafter, sacred rites are held to dispatch him to the realm of shadows. First brutally torn from all of his family and social ties and excluded from all functions and activities through which he experienced self-awareness, then banished by the same forces from the world of the living, the victim yields to the combined effect of intense terror, the sudden total withdrawal of the multiple reference systems pro-

vided by the support of the group, and, finally, to the group's decisive reversal in proclaiming him — once a living man, with rights and obligations —
dead and an object of fear, ritual, and taboo. Physical integrity cannot withstand the dissolution of the social personality (Lévi-Strauss 1979:167–8).

This description of the lot of the sorcerer's victim bears so much resonance
for the experience of having AIDS that the reader cannot help wondering
what hidden structural universals are being acted out. I am, however, less
interested in cultural universals than the notion of the self under attack
from the society in which personhood is defined and nurtured in the first
instance. Lévi-Strauss's observation reminds us not about the universality
of sorcery but of the fact that human existence is defined, structured, rendered meaningful and ultimately destroyed through cultural processes. In
short the body and the phenomena that modify it, in this case diseases, are
socially constructed.

This study is an exploration of this concept through an examination of
the experience of HIV infection and AIDS. Unlike most social studies of
AIDS, I do not concern myself with issues of HIV transmission, education, and prevention. These concerns are being addressed by a growing
multitude of social researchers working in a wide range of social-science
disciplines. Such research is unconcerned with the experiences of people
with HIV other than as vectors for transmission of the virus to the
uninfected. The exception to this is the growing body of psychological
literature which seeks to define the nature of the experience of HIV/
AIDS through accounts of coping strategies and responses to diagnosis
and health changes (see, for example, Catania et al. 1992; McKegney
and O'Dowd 1992; O'Brien 1992). These accounts psychologize the
experience of HIV infection by focusing on the individual and his/her
cognitive and behavioral responses. While relationships to "significant
others" are a consideration in these accounts, they fail to go beyond such
immediate social relationships to consider the wider social and cultural
contexts in which the individual experiences and constructs meaning out
of ill health.

This is the task of medical anthropology: to weld local experiences of illness to broader social, economic, political, and cultural contexts. At the
micro level, this study explores specific experiences of HIV infection, the
detailed everyday practices of living with HIV or AIDS. Emerging from these
practices are processes of collectivization among people with HIV, a collectivization that constitutes a counter-discourse to that of biomedicine. This
counter-discourse takes various forms: a literary genre of self-documentation (see Callen 1990; Grimshaw 1989; Michaels 1990; Navarre 1988;
Nungesser 1986; Phoenix 1989); organization-based leafleting and newslet-

ter production; and a progressively systematizing political discourse centered on the concept of empowerment and civic rights for the HIV-infected.

This counter-discourse is in a dialectical relation to the master discourse of biomedicine. Drawing upon discourses of civil rights, welfare, and social movement activism, it challenges, contradicts, and sometimes succeeds in transforming the medical construction of the AIDS experience. Simultaneously, this anti-discipline is framed by, is dependent upon, and draws its language and concepts from biomedicine. The practices, documented here, of people diagnosed and living with the condition — health strategies, relationships, the reconstruction of identity, the management of death, and the politicization of diagnosis — reveal the authority of medicine as well as its fragility as a social practice. An anthropological gaze exposes cracks in the hegemony of biomedical science and a field of possibilities for resistance and life-reconstruction available to those who constitute its subjects.

METHODOLOGY

Chance had it that this "People Living with AIDS" project coincided with my period of involvement with Sydney's community-based AIDS organizations. And this coincidence determined the focus of my study.

The study derives from ethnographic fieldwork undertaken between January 1988 and May 1991 in Sydney, capital of the eastern seaboard state of New South Wales, and Australia's largest city. Prior to beginning research activities I was cursorily familiar with Sydney's gay community, having already lived in the city for two years. It was in those two years that I was first exposed to the problem of the AIDS epidemic in Sydney, an epidemic concentrated within its large and visible inner-city community of gay men.

My formal AIDS work began on the day, in November 1987, that I telephoned the AIDS Council of New South Wales (ACON) and inquired, with this project only very loosely formulated, as to how I might become involved as a volunteer in the activities of the Council. I announced my research intentions, though I suspect those intentions were not well understood and it was not long before my project became subsumed, in the minds of my colleagues (and often myself), within the more immediate and urgent problems presented by the epidemic. Over the next three-and-a-half years I became engrossed in tasks that often seemed consuming and a long way from the objectives of an anthropological study of a disease.

In time, others' trust and dependence on my growing skills and expertise positioned me in increasingly determining roles. At times I wondered if this activity went beyond the reasonable bounds allowed an ethnographer. Identities slipped, the observer became the participant, and I the observed. However, it is these epistemological and ontological shifts that drive an anthropological perspective. Those working in AIDS, whether they be educators, lobbyists, or bureaucrats also frequently bear more than one role or identity. It is not uncommon for individuals to be highly conscious of this multiplicity of self. One frequently hears allusions to the wearing of different "hats" in different circumstances and sometimes, with the most politically astute, simultaneously. In adopting many different positions within this field of study I was able to gain access to some experience of a wide range of phenomena. This is crucial in seeking to understand a community's response to AIDS, because that response is so multifaceted and dynamic.

In 1989 I suspended independent research activity and joined a team of psychologists at the Department of Psychology at Wollongong University. Our team project was an investigation of the problems experienced by people with AIDS and HIV and their care providers. While involved with the Wollongong AIDS Research Project (WARP), I conducted up to 250 interviews with approximately one hundred different infected gay men and their care providers. I have selectively used some of that material in Part Two.

Some of the individuals I interviewed for WARP were already known to me when we began the study and some became friends and informants in the course of that work. Subsequently I have been able to continue documenting the stories of some of these men through interviews, conversations, and observations that place their narratives in a broader timeframe. In some cases, I was able to document the life of man right up until the time of his death and to interview surviving friends and family. In addition to the men recruited through WARP, I came to know many other people with HIV and AIDS through my contacts with AIDS organizations, in particular those community-based self-help groups that began to emerge at the time of my entry into the field. These are men who are relatively well connected to the institutional infrastructure of the gay community and the new health organizations and services it has established and developed.

I have endeavored to re-present the narratives and conversations of my informants with as little editing as possible, allowing individual personalities to speak through idiolect. These narratives represent the view of the social actor: the "patient's point of view," to play with Geertz's phrase. Narrative solicitation is a dialogic process, providing circumstances for the production of meaning through the interviewer/interviewee relationship. The narratives of the gay men presented in Part Two represent the collaborative textual presence of the research participant. I am the necessary presence, as the interviewer, by which these narratives have come into being, and so the speech acts presented here are as much a creative product of this research exercise as a representation of the views of the subjects. In collating them into a unifying text I am imposing order and interpretation onto these narratives. But my text is not definitive. Rather, in contextualizing these narratives, I allow the resulting text to offer up interpretive suggestions. Individual narratives thus rest within a larger narrative, a meta-narrative in part constructed from fragments of others' speech, in part a product of my textual engineering.

To complement this more formal data collecting method, the ethnographer is required to make observations in the course of a day, recording conversations, asides, casual remarks, as well as the concrete actions of individuals. Thus some of the narratives presented in the text are unsolicited and were recorded without the speaker's knowledge of my intention. In such cases I have attempted as far as possible to disguise the identity of the individual except where the individual concerned, or surviving friends or family, have requested otherwise. This data collecting method provides valuable supporting, contextualizing information in addition to the more formal methods of, for example, the interview. It is a common device in anthropology and integral to the approach that aims to capture the flavour of a particular lived experience.

A large amount of written material is subject to analysis in the study. Policy documents of various kinds provided useful documentation of the formalized positions held by various organizations on a range of issues. Throughout the course of research Sydney's major newspapers, in particular the daily broadsheet *Sydney Morning Herald*, provided a window onto the wider discursive environment in which homosexuality and AIDS was being constructed. The community gay newspaper, *Sydney Star Observer* (a fortnightly during the period of the study), was regularly monitored for its coverage of AIDS-related issues with a view to the local gay discursive construction of the disease. Some national media, including the two national gay magazines, *Campaign* and *Outrage*, were also reviewed. Throughout the course of this study the literary genre of self-documentation by people with HIV and AIDS underwent an enormous growth in both volume and diversity. This material, in the form of local newsletters, magazines articles, and books by people with the disease represents the progressive systematization of the counter-discourse that is the topic of this study.

A number of short field trips to Europe and the United States informed a wider, global analysis of the phenomena under discussion. No community is isolated. Local gay communities such as that in Sydney are cells of an international gay community whose other parts are located in cities such as San Francisco, New York, Amsterdam, and London. It is worth noting that these are communities centered in Anglo-European (or, in the case of Amsterdam, European) bourgeois traditions. Ideologies, aesthetic styles, forms of political, sexual, and social practice, and forms of community structure are all shaped by the communication between such communities, by the constant flow of people, ideas and images between such sites. AIDS has significantly boosted contact within this international community as gay men conduct study tours of various communities to appreciate different responses to the epidemic, attend international AIDS conferences, coordinate information exchange through electronic media, and generally keep up a high level of day-to-day contact with individuals, groups and organizations working in AIDS in other countries. This is particularly the case for Australian gay men, for whom distance from Europe and North America generates a sense of relative isolation. Herein lies another dialectic shaping the experience of HIV infection and AIDS, in the dialogue between a struggling localized community and international communities.

STRUCTURE OF THE STUDY

The historical formation of strategies for self- and collective definition by people with HIV and AIDS is framed within the hegemonic fields of the state and biomedical science. In Chapter Two, I briefly outline the nature of, and the relations between, these fields and also an important third field, that of community. Together these fields constitute the sociopolitical context within which the drama in this study takes place.

Gay men with HIV and AIDS, and those working within the community sector responding to AIDS see their relation to the state and medicine as one characterized by struggle: for recognition, rights, individual and collective freedoms, protection, and funding; in short, for full citizenship. What I present here is an alternative analysis of the position of gay men with HIV or AIDS. It positions people with HIV or AIDS not as excluded from and marginal to the mainstream of society, but as *included* through the operations of newly specializing discourses of scientific government. The problem is not that gay men with HIV and AIDS are invisible, marginal, and excluded from citizenship. Rather that they are rendered visible in ways that make the experience of the disease a particularly agonizing one. I attempt to demonstrate how this positioning is experienced in the movement from individual tactic to discursive strategy and, given certain conditions, how attempts have been made to overcome their predicament through the development of a transgressive counter-discourse.

Readers familiar with the work of Michele de Certeau will recognize the nomenclature of *tactic* and *strategy*, used to structure the two major sections, Parts Two and Three, of this study. Tactic and strategy refer to two different styles of practice. As framed by de Certeau, tactic is a calculus of action not circumscribed by place, institution, or clearly defined target. It is characteristic of everyday practice: fragmentary, opportunistic, seizing the moment. Its intellectual synthesis is not a discourse but the decision itself. Tactic contrasts with strategy, a calculus of power relations spatially and institutionally localized with identified targets and plans of action (de Certeau 1984). By organizing the material of the study into these two sections, I have sought to reveal a movement from a form of practice that is tactical to one that is strategic. In this movement we detect a shift from opportunistic "ways of operating" to more systematic forms of collective intervention into hegemonic regimes.

Tactical responses to HIV infection are described in Part Two (The Tactics of Health and Illness). Here I guide the reader through the course of the disease, from the moment of diagnosis of infection to death, a kind of sociological life history of a disease. Through the account, the relations between the three fields of government, biomedicine, and community as they are articulated through the tactical practices of people with HIV, begin to reveal themselves. Each chapter in Part Two examines particular issues associated with each stage of the disease with a view to revealing the ways in which people with HIV/AIDS deploy available discourses, such as that of medicine, to their own teleological ends. Chapter Three discusses the technology of HIV-antibody testing, and the ontological implications for those subject to it. Rather than being an unproblematic tool by which an individual is simply identified as being infected with a virus, I argue that testing is the first in a series of surveillance mechanisms whereby new social subjects and social relations are created. Chapter Four explores this argument further, discussing the stigmatizing impact of a diagnosis of HIV infection on an individual's identity and social relationships and the means by which individuals attempt to manage that stigma. Chapter Five begins an exploration of the dialogic relationship between people with HIV and AIDS and medical science. Through narrative accounts of experiences with HIV medicine and medical practitioners we detect the emergence of an HIV "creole," a "street" language through which individuals interpret and understand information and experiences of the disease. Chapter Six looks at attempts by people with HIV/AIDS to explore beyond the hegemonic treatment practices of biomedicine. Experimentation with alternative healing methods represents another way HIV-infected people seek to expand the means by which they speak about, understand, and act upon their bodies. Transgressive at a tactical level during the first years of the epidemic, the ideology and practices of alternative therapies for HIV infection have become increasingly systematic to the point where medicine is beginning to debate the value and challenge of these practices. Chapter Seven illustrates the manner in which individuals with AIDS construct their own deaths. Medical science is seen here as a hegemonic force structuring the death experience. As a counterpoint, examples are given that show how some gay men succeed in reordering death by resisting the imperatives of medical surveillance.

Generally speaking, Part Two illustrates the articulation between the lives and deaths of people with HIV and AIDS and the social and cultural conditions in which they are positioned. By example, it reveals how discourses, for instance that of medicine, shape the experience of having AIDS, while simultaneously exploring the tactical possibilities for innovation or transgression. It is the potential that this transgression raises for the strategic transformation of powerful discursive practices that I then explore in detail in Part Three.

In Part Three (Discursive Strategies of Resistance) the relations between the three fields of power — state, biomedicine and community — begin to harden into strategic struggles. Chapters Eight and Nine document the early moments of the formation of AIDS and HIV identities and organizations from within gay communities. The insertion of this new social personality into public space via the electronic media was a crucial strategy, collapsing the private and public into a new social identity: the "Person Living With AIDS" (PLWA). This PLWA identity, and its group manifestation as "People Living With AIDS" (PLWAs), is shown to be particularly challenging to biomedical definitions of the experience of chronic illness.

Chapter Ten details the relations between PLWAs, community and biomedical research as they re-formed in response to the development of antiviral therapy for HIV infection. In this documentation, biomedical science is revealed as a social practice emergent from these dynamic relations of power. Chapter Eleven then documents a shift in strategic action away from targeting biomedicine to focus on the regulatory apparatus of the state, in the interests of widening citizen access to experimental therapeutic agents. An alliance is seen to form between community and biomedicine in the interests of transforming the state. In the long term, this alliance works to further legitimize certain biomedical practices while ultimately strengthening the relations between community and the state.

Finally, in Chapter Twelve I advance some concluding comments regarding these shifts in relations between community, biomedicine, and the state. I consider the long term effects of these shifts and the implications for the experience of chronic diseases such as HIV infection in a society such as Australia.

TERMINOLOGY

The discourse of AIDS is replete with acronyms. Throughout, I have carefully differentiated between *HIV* (human immunodeficiency virus) and *AIDS* (Acquired Immune Deficiency Syndrome). HIV refers to the virus which is thought by most to be the primary cause of AIDS, a condition defined by a life-threatening depletion of the body's immune system. When referring to *people with HIV* I generally mean those who are infected but for the most part are well or experience little immune system depletion. By contrast, *people with AIDS* (PWA) refers to those diagnosed with one of the many AIDS-defining diseases as listed by the United States Centers for Disease Control.[1] When referring to both those with asymptomatic HIV infection and those with AIDS I use the increasingly common taxonomy of *people with HIV/AIDS*. The term *people living with HIV/AIDS*, reduced to the acronym PLWA, or increasingly PLWHA, is a designation advocated by those who have politicized their predicament. As I document in Chapter Nine, this terminology has become incorporated into the international AIDS discourse of governments, medicine, and community sectors. In this study I also use this term to denote a particular social identity, being those who have deployed the knowledge of their infection as an important feature of their sense of self.

With respect to organizations, I use the terms *community-based AIDS organization* and the more recent term *AIDS service organization* interchangeably. The latter is perhaps slightly more specific in that it refers to those non-government organizations that provide welfare and education services, at times with some (or, in Australia, even a great deal of) government funding. The AIDS Council of NSW (ACON) is an example of a service organization that may also be described as non-government, community-based, and — increasingly so during the period of this study — substantially supported through government grants. Meanwhile, the former term encompasses those remaining non-government organizations that have additional or exclusive political functions. PLWA (NSW) is one such organization. Further acronyms, relating to organizations and in some cases to drug treatments, are explained in the text.

In discussing therapeutic practices I distinguish biomedicine (or medical science, or allopathic medicine) from "alternative" or "complementary" therapies. Biomedicine refers to the currently dominant field of therapeutic scientific medicine, with its ideology of disease and bodily dys/function and accompanying practices organized and supported by a pedagogical, institutional structure, government funding and regulatory apparatuses, and a globalizing pharmaceutical industry. Biomedicine is contrasted specifically with alternative therapeutic practices in Chapter Six. My use of the term alternative therapy encompasses all therapeutic ideologies and practices that stand in opposition to or are outside the hegemonic disciplines of scientific medicine. In my usage, any therapeutic practice that provides an etiological explanation and therapeutic course of action for illness different from that advocated by biomedicine is thus understood as alternative therapy.

* * *

Anthropologists have been slow to appreciate the import of this epidemic. HIV is pandemic, and anthropologists will increasingly face it in their fields of activity. AIDS, like the predicament of illness generally, has a great deal to say about the social and cultural. We can learn from it as much as we can contribute to the effort to live with it. It is with these twin aims in mind that this study was written.

NOTES

1. In the United States from July 1992, AIDS was definable by a CD4 lymphocyte reading of less than 200 per cubic millimetre or, as in conversational parlance, a T-cell count of less than 200. In Australia this is not sufficient for the definition of AIDS, and one needs a diagnosis of at least one AIDS-related opportunistic infection as well.

CHAPTER 2

Governing AIDS:
The State-Medicine-Community Triad

This chapter outlines the broad sociopolitical context in which the experience of HIV infection is shaped and played out. Three key fields and their relation to each other are sketched: the interventionist nature of the Australian state, particularly in the realm of health; the biomedical construction of homosexuality and the counter-discourse of gay movements; and the emergence of community as both a site of population administration and localized resistance.

THE INTERVENTIONIST STATE

Sax, in his history of health care in Australia, has mapped a tradition of political experimentation and reformism in this country going back to the early days of European settlement, experimentation that created a broad public expectation of a "large role of the state in civil life" and the establishment of the broad concept of universal right to health care (Sax 1984:32,28). In Australia's federal system, both national (i.e. federal) and state politics are ordered around a two-party system, consisting of the Labor Party, with roots in socialism and the union movement, and a conservative coalition of the Liberal and National Parties, with its philosophy of individualism, free market capitalism, and small, non-interventionist government. In addition, small, usually one-issue parties vie for positions in local (municipal), state, and federal legislatures. While Labor Party initiatives toward equity of health services have always been resisted by the conservative parties and the emergent medical profession, incremental improvements in the provision of health care have seen a steadily increasing role for government. AIDS is a very recent illustration. When the new epidemic was identified in this country, the federal Labor Government quickly won agreement for a bipartisan approach, and funding to medical, research, and non-government initiatives was quickly forthcoming.

Upon its election to power federally in 1972, the Labor Party injected government funds into "community-based health services," which, together with its national health scheme (Medibank), were aimed at improving the accessibility of health care, though not necessarily the equalization of social and economic disparities (Sax 1984:103). Structures such as Medibank represented the "possible expansion of bureaucratic control of professional services" (Duckett 1984), and have become a point of conflict between government interests in regulation and medical interests in professional autonomy.

While the community health scheme was eclipsed for the period of the returned Liberal/National Coalition Government from 1975, the reelection of Labor in 1983 saw a renewed hope for government-assisted, community-based health efforts. It is Labor's platform to encourage and facilitate public participation in both the political process and in programs as a means to extend the efficacy of its own response to public demands. The emphasis on institutional rather than individual initiative, the alternative doctrine of the conservative parties (Gardner 1989a), allows Labor to support the building of non-governmental infrastructure within identified communities. Since the early 1970s, "community" has become an increasingly important organizing principle in Australian political discourse. The concept of individuals, collectivized through a shared identity under the rubric of a community, has informed both the structure of political relations between peoples and government, and the lived experiences of those individuals who fall under this organizing principle. Women, people from non-English-speaking backgrounds, Australia's Aboriginal peoples, and gay men have all been subject to, and accomplices in, this will to community.

Consider the example of women: The Labor government of the early 1970s provided the political conditions in which it was possible for the feminist movement to make significant gains within the state apparatus, notably in building a health infrastructure suited to the particular needs of women (Yeatman 1990). This period coincided with the rise of a more general consumer health movement that sought to influence government decisions on health-care policy and services. Duckett notes a coincidence of interests between these advocates of "equal health care" and the ascendant corporate rationalists within government (Duckett 1984), a compatibility of interests that has created an environment conducive to the incorporation of such advocates into the structures of the health bureaucracies.

The inclusion of feminists within the bureaucracies of government during this period, a process particularly successful in Australia, stimulated debate among feminists over the effects of the professionalization of the women's movement on the feminist agenda (Aver 1990). Writing at the end of the decade, Yeatman characterizes the 1980s as a period of struggle between the "managerial agenda" of the state and grass-roots efforts to democratize the political process in Australia. The rise of a "femocracy" within the women's movement can be seen as part of this general struggle. Yeatman claims that the managerial agenda has become increasingly dominant, triumphant with its culture of top-down control, "technological promiscuity," fetishism of technique-oriented scientific management, and market-oriented consumer/client approaches to the citizenry. The accommodation of representatives of new social movements has, thus, not necessarily deflected this bureaucratic trajectory, she claims, but only reproduces existing social inequalities by excluding all but those who share a similar class and cultural capital with those already in power (Yeatman 1990).

Aronowitz, in his analysis of politics in the postmodern era, argues against characterizing this kind of process as "cooption." Rather, he sees this trajectory of new social movements as "a process related to the economic and cultural hegemony of late capitalism" (Aronowitz 1987/88:106). In other words, there are no conscious conspiracies on the part of ruling elites to engulf and pacify the troublemaking underclasses. On the contrary, the modern state is inclined to see social movements as a crucial mechanism by which the pluralist democratic model may be realized. Concomitantly, those who participate in such movements are inclined to approach the state and its associated structures not as enemies, but as "important, albeit subordinate, elements of a plural social formation" in which the social movements themselves play a crucial part (Aronowitz 1987/88:110).

Along with this shift from struggle to collaboration comes a change in the targets of action for such movements. Class hegemony is no longer the focus of political analysis and action. What is "new" about the new social movements is that they problematize *power* itself, seeking to realign power relations in the pursuit of democratic ideals. Gamson (1989), in his analysis of the American AIDS activist group ACT UP (AIDS Coalition To Unleash Power), came to a similar conclusion. I will discuss this particular group in more detail in Chapter Eleven.

What is needed now is an assessment of the contribution that the gay movement, through a revised political agenda linked to AIDS, has made to this struggle for democratization. Is Yeatman's accommodation thesis sustainable even after considering the struggles of community-based AIDS organizations and activists to effect change? Is the presence of gay men and people with HIV/AIDS at all levels of government decision-making on AIDS issues really effective in changing a technocratic governmental apparatus? Or are we only accomplices in this juggernaut of power, this trajectory to managerial government?

BIOMEDICINE AND HOMOSEXUALITY

In *Birth of the Clinic*, Foucault describes the emergence, in the eighteenth century, of a medical epistemology that distinguishes disease and patient in a particular configuration. Disease becomes the privileged space, the site of the physician's gaze; the physician becomes a vehicle for its detection; and the patient becomes invisible, or rather is redrawn as "the rediscovered portrait of the disease; he is the disease itself . . . " (Foucault 1973:13).

It might be said that this is precisely what has occurred in the biomedical process of defining "homosexuality" in the late nineteenth century. Since its original inception by a Swiss physician in 1892 (see Weeks 1977), the concept of homosexuality has in turn come to define, through biomedical discourse, a new social "species," in Foucault's term (1978) — the homosexual — characterized by the disease that defines it. Yet biomedicine's construct of homosexuality itself has meanwhile become increasingly problematized. While medical discourse remains hegemonic in that it defines the terms of investigation, evergrowing psychiatric, psychological, social, and welfare disciplines have embraced homosexuality as a valid field of investigation and intervention.

But no force is all-powerful. In addition to biomedical discourse on homosexuality, a homosexual counter-discourse has developed concurrently over the last hundred years, a counter-discourse that at times embraces scientific formulations and at other times defies them. Yet never does this counter-discourse totally escape the hegemonic grip of science. Never does it completely release itself from the suspicion that science must at some time, if not now, be relied upon to describe the reality of homosexuality and, if we are to accept Foucault's thesis, the truth of ourselves.

This counter-discourse is constituted by the voices of individuals embracing the identification of the homosexual and their various forms of collective practice. While not delegitimizing biomedical constructs of homosexuality, it has at least loosened the grip of medical constructs on social-science definitions of homosexuality. The effect has been a reframing of homosexuality in recent decades in less pathological constructs, injecting it with a greater legitimacy by positioning it in relationship to developing concepts of human rights, lifestyle choice, and social (ethnic) identity.

This counter-discourse is positioned within a growing skepticism toward the authority and efficacy of biomedicine. This skepticism comes in the wake of such technological failures as the Thalidomide disaster, the long-term difficulties faced by vaccination programs, and the lack of success in "curing" diseases like cancer. Fueling this erosion of faith is a deteriorating global economic environment that has revealed scientific enterprise often to be highly expensive, of limited benefit, sometimes dangerous, and linked to non-scientific political and economic interests (see for example Klass 1975; Jennett 1984; Latour and Woolgar 1986; Wajcman 1991). Finally, wider processes of democratization have created increasing opportunities for health-care "consumers" to influence the development and implementation of medical technologies and policies (Bates and Lapsley 1985).

Consumer lobby groups have become particularly important in the last twenty years as vehicles for articulating grievances about medical practice. The establishment of patient discourses, in part facilitated by government health bureaucracies, has worked to render the medical subject visible *beyond* the defining pathology of disease. This may be interpreted as a progressive humanizing of health-care systems. Less optimistic analyses have argued that the refocusing of health care on the medical "subject" has served a new, more efficient medical apparatus of human population control (Armstrong 1979; 1984). Whatever the case, groups organized around the experience of disability and of illnesses such as cancer have become established features of health infrastructures. Only the AIDS advocacy groups of the 1980s, however, have achieved any significant transformation in the practices of medical science. On the other hand, we may question to what extent the strategic interventions of the new activist/patient subject have successfully escaped the interests of the discursive practices that created and supports them.

The apparent success of AIDS advocacy and community groups lies in their roots in the gay liberation movement. Gay liberation became an influential force in the 1970s in challenging medical ideologies and technologies that pathologized homosexuality and sought to correct it through various invasive means, including psychiatric programming, electroshock conditioning, and neurosurgery. By the end of the 1970s this gay intervention had achieved a considerable shift in the medical construction and treatment of homosexuality. The American Psychiatric Association had removed homosexuality from its list of mental illnesses, and most forms of correction therapy had been superseded by a psychology that recognised "gay lifestyle" as a viable alternative sexual orientation.

The pathological construct of homosexuality had not, however, been completely eliminated. Debate continued, to the time of the emergence of AIDS, around the relation between a corrective medical science and pathological sexualities. In 1973, for example, during the heyday of gay liberation, the Federal Council of the Australian and New Zealand College of Psychiatrists approved a clinical memorandum that noted:

> Many psychiatrists consider that homosexual feelings and behavior are not necessarily or commonly associated with neurotic symptoms and are compatible with good adjustment and a useful and creative contribution by the individual to society (Barr and Catts 1974:215).

The article from which this memorandum is quoted also, however, reports on a survey of attitudes among psychiatrists in the State of New South Wales suggesting that a prevailing view among professional and trainee psychiatrists was that homosexuality was either "a developmental anomaly" or, slightly less commonly, "a neurotic disorder" (Barr and Catts 1974). Later, in 1978, a debate ensued among mental health therapists regarding the demands of the gay activists. In response to pleas for therapists to consider the social and political dimensions of psychiatric and psychological practice (Davison 1978), Sturgis and Adams reaffirmed the role of corrective psychology in the face of gay liberation, arguing for "an objective and scientific examination of homosexuality and other target behaviors independent of the current social and political pressures exerted by social activist groups" (Sturgis and Adams 1978:165).

The emergence of AIDS as a disease primarily affecting homosexual men, at least in Western countries, revealed the trend toward liberalization of medical opinion on homosexuality to be highly qualified and easily reversible. Some politicians and doctors have deployed AIDS as justification to attack the "gay lobby," claiming AIDS receives an amount of attention that is beyond scientific justification.[1] One recent example from a psychiatrist illustrates the vehemence of this revised discourse against homosexuality:

> If nature created homosexuals for a purpose, we simply have to interfere with that purpose in order to ensure the safety and survival of those outside the risk group. The measures usually taken to contain the spread of infectious disease are not, for some reason, being applied against AIDS. There is no valid reason for not isolating all AIDS sufferers in special units, as was done with tuberculosis. There is no valid reason why every single contact of the victim should not be kept under regular surveillance. There is no reason

why funds should not be made available to research and control homosexuality as a disease (Menon 1989).

Menon's opinion is an extreme one, but its very presence in the widest circulating medical weekly newsletter in Australia is significant. A formal response to this was formulated by Sydney's Gay and Lesbian Rights Lobby and submitted to the journal in which the article appeared, but it was not printed, signaling (among other things) the difficulty gay activists have in penetrating medical discourse.

The beginning of the second decade of the AIDS epidemic has seen a progressive "dehomosexualization" of AIDS within state bureaucracies, a process that allows the state to address the phenomenon without reference to, and therefore avoiding the risk of possible legitimization of, illicit sexualities. This shift has in turn led AIDS activists to return to claims that the gay community (in Australia, at least) bears the greatest burden of the disease, and therefore deserves the largest slice of the funding pie.[2] And in response to this, elements of the medical profession retaliated with another attack on the "gay lobby:"

> This struggle between medical and political and special interest viewpoints in respect of AIDS-related policy still continues, with most successes going to the state-empowered gay lobby rather than the medical profession and the public interest (Browning 1993:80).

This debate represents the most extreme expression of the tensions that structure the relations between homosexuality and biomedicine. Yet while one arm of medical science seeks, in opposition to gay discourse, to sustain the pathological construction of homosexuality, scientific investigation of homosexuality is seen by others as a process that will lead to its enlightened legitimization. Kuhn referred to this view of "science as cumulation" as paradigmatic to the positivist project, yet historically fictional (Kuhn 1962:95,137).

Homosexual-identifying men are not immune to this fiction of the "cumulative acquisition of novelty". Recent examples are found in the revised attempts to demonstrate once again the biological basis of homosexuality in the size of hypothalamus or genetic dispositions (Le Vey 1993). Le Vey's claim that scientific proof of the biological basis of homosexuality will eradicate discrimination against gay men is naive. One need only consider the forms of discrimination leveled against women or blacks to realize that this very connection can legitimize prejudice by naturalizing socially constructed differences. The seemingly irrepressible clamor by AIDS activists for more and more medical research into AIDS and its treatment is another example of this adherence by homosexual men to the enlightenment model of science. The establishment of a vast international research enterprise in AIDS, one which positions homosexuality as a central problematic, should not necessarily be seen as unqualified progress against bigotry or mortality.

Feminists interpret this sustained and pervasive faith in positivist science, despite a multidisciplinary deconstruction at work on scientific practice, as an illustration of the hegemony of a masculine positivist science, a science that sustains gendered power relations (Berman 1989). In this light it is not surprising that such research is conducted by men, albeit even gay ones. One thinks of the many gay men working in AIDS clinical research who fail to question the assumptions and power effects of their discipline.

AIDS has worked to shore up the positivist construction of homosexuality by reinvigorating and endlessly extending the clinical, epidemiological, and psychiatric investigation of homosexual practice and the predicament of the homosexual man with HIV/AIDS. One effect of this has been to undermine the legitimacy of those disciplines, such as anthropology, that once posed an alternative epistemology to positivist science. Worse, such disciplines have increasingly adopted this positivistic framework for their own as they pursue research questions related to AIDS and homosexuality alike.

The entire historical trajectory of research on homosexuality and AIDS can be seen as a symptom of what Foucault described as the incitement to sexuality: the epistemic shift to center sex as the truth of the human condition (Foucault 1978). Scientific research has been instrumental in this "truth game." We are not, as the positivist framework would have us believe, discovering truths about sexuality. Rather, we are investing selected spheres of human activity as loci of truths about ourselves. But it is not the approximation to truth that should capture our attention so much as the social process by which this truth game gains power and effects social life.

COMMUNITY AS ADMINISTERED SOCIAL SPACE (1): FROM GAY LIBERATION TO GAY COMMUNITY

The third player in this truth game of AIDS is "community." In the West, gay community has constituted one important sociocultural terrain that has organized the experience and management of local epidemics. The term is problematic and will be examined in the course of this section.

It is convenient to begin a discussion of a specifically gay history, as opposed to homosexual history, from the time of the emergence of open, politically active groups in the early 1970s. This new sexual politic was international, but largely restricted to the major urban centers of English-speaking, industrialized countries, and to northern Europe. The emergence in Australia of both an identifiable "gay" political and social subject — people who styled themselves as "gay" — was concomitant with the development of a politically left-oriented counter-culture that articulated demands for a broadening of citizen rights.

The origin of the modern gay movement is attributed, in gay discourse, to the "Stonewall" riots in New York in 1969, riots that saw the first public and aggressive resistance by homosexuals and transvestites to police intimidation. The character of homosexual politics took a radical turn following this catalytic event. Homosexuality rapidly shifted from being a secretive, unknown, and highly stigmatized sub-sexuality, toward a more positive, public, and politically radical identity. Within a very short time of this event, literally hundreds of new radical homosexual groups sprang up in the United States (d'Emilio 1983). In other countries, including Australia, events soon followed this example.

A fairly large underground subculture of homosexuals had existed in Sydney since at least the first decades of the twentieth century (Wotherspoon 1991). This clandestine society was organized around private networks, a small number of commercial venues, and brief and anonymous sexual encounters in public "beats:" places such as parks and public toilets where men met for sex.[3] The first homosexual organizations of any significance to form in Sydney were the Knights of the Chameleons (1961) and the Polynesians (1965), both of which continued to exist until recently. These organizations, focused on the provision of social activities and gatherings for members, were also relatively clandestine. Hence, early homosexual organizations failed to challenge the wider heterosexual establishment, effectively sustaining the invisibility of homosexuals in public discourse. Visibility was only rendered by default through events such as prosecution cases and associated media publicity (French 1986). In the absence of an organized homosexual voice, representations of homosexuality were constructed and controlled through medical, legal, religious, and media discourses, often extremely hostile to and judgmental of homosexuality. Prior to the 1970s, homosexuality was constructed as a social problem to be resolved, a notion to which many homosexuals of the time also subscribed (see Wotherspoon 1986).

The social and political unrest of the late 1960s and early 1970s, however, created the conditions for homosexuals to build a new political platform based on the notion of homosexuality as a positive identity. The organization that provided the means for many men and women in Sydney to accomplish a private reidentification of self was also the first, and to date the longest running, public homosexual organization in Australia: Campaign Against Moral Persecution (CAMP). The name mirrors the prevailing self-definition of homosexuals at the time as "camp," a self-definition that was not superseded until later in the decade (Hay 1979) and an identity still to be found among Australian homosexual men with weak ties to gay community. CAMP was established in 1970 in Sydney, and soon similar groups formed in other Australian states. While its agenda was wide, including law reform and political lobbying, as the years progressed it took on an increasingly social and psychological support function for homosexuals: that is, the political agenda was sacrificed for a focus on individual psychological needs. This culminated in its transformation, after securing a grant from the New South Wales State Government to further its support function, into the Gay Counselling Service in 1980 (Thompson 1985).

A small group splintered from CAMP in the early 1970s in order to pursue a radical political agenda. This group, calling itself Gay Liberation, advocated a politics centered around sexual difference, challenging prevailing public representations of homosexuality and the hegemony of the heterosexual establishment. The Gay Liberationists posited a strategy of "coming out" publicly as gay as the first step in a program of sexual revolution. Its members were influenced by, and often members of, the Australian political left, including the nascent Socialist Workers Party and the Australian Communist Party, the women's movement, and the more left-oriented factions of the Labor Party. The adoption by this more radical wing of the movement of the American label "gay" symbolized a challenge to the predominant image of homosexuality as deviant. However, the limitations of the gay movement in its early years, in terms of actual numbers of participants in its activities and its impact on homosexual people generally, may be measured in an observation by one of its activists. Hay noted at the end of the 1970s that the label "gay" was, after a decade of gay liberation, associated in most Australian homosexuals' minds with radical political activism. Most homosexuals, he observed then, continued to prefer to call themselves "camp" (Hay 1979).

The Australian gay movement in the 1970s was indeed small and localized and its impact on the lives of individual men and women may have been very subtle. In terms of public representations and political impact, however, we may gauge a significant degree of success. A precarious alliance with the women's movement in the early 1970s provided homosexuals with a theoretical grammar for an analysis of "sexism" and the hegemonic "patriarchy." It borrowed the political rhetoric of "sexual freedom" and "the personal is political" and added the strategy of "coming out," a public confessional that moved this new homosexuality into the public arena. The basic theoretical premise of gay liberation was the deployment of sexuality as the central issue around which personal identity and political action would emerge. As gay liberation activist, John Lee, then stated, "A person's homosexuality is not a mere appendage to their character . . . but is rather pervasive throughout that character" (Lee 1972).

While gay liberation was a marginal strategy even to many homosexuals, it must be credited with initiating the process that established gay men as a unique identity in the repertoire of social "species." Alongside women, disabled people, and racial or ethnic minorities, gay men began to demand rights on the basis of the legitimacy of that social identity. This is the politics of postmodern societies: social beings organized around shared identities, seeking legitimacy through the extension of citizen rights to those identities. It is the politics of state/identity interface, an interface increasingly organized through community.

The advent of the socialist federal Labor Government in 1972 gave a huge impetus to the demands of the counter-culture in Australia and provided a sympathetic political climate for the development of the gay movement. The new government actively promoted a strategy of political and cultural pluralism that sought to identify and work with specific pressure groups (Simms 1984). Driven by influences from the new social movements, it assisted in the formation of definable groups through which its policies of pluralism and social management could be articulated. Funding became available as a means to this end for those groups that were organized and articulate enough to win government support. Women's groups were particularly successful in this strategy. At this stage, this process did not extend to the gay movement in Sydney, however, as witnessed by the rejection in 1974 of CAMP's first application to the New South Wales Health Commission for state (as opposed to federal) government assistance. In fact State Government recognition and support was not forthcoming until late in the decade and only after a shift in the focus of CAMP's function from a political lobby to a counselling service for homosexuals. This shift brought the organization into closer allegiance with hegemonic constructions that problematized homosexuality as a disorder to be managed through medical/psychological intervention. Thus by 1979, CAMP had restyled itself as "first and foremost a homosexual welfare organization" and become a member of the Mental Health Association and the New South Wales Council of Social Services (CAMP 1979). The transformation of CAMP into the Gay Counselling Service, its rejection of the political left and its registration as a charity effectively secured the organization's incorporation into mainstream cultural and political agendas.

The Gay Liberation cell of the movement, on the other hand, had virtually burnt out by the mid 1970s, "partly because of the dispute . . . between the reformists and the revolutionaries" (Altman 1975), and partly because of the expansion of the commercial gay scene (Altman 1979) that deflected political energies to an emerging social milieu.

By the end of the decade a new radical grouping emerged. This was the Gay Solidarity Group which, taking inspiration from anniversary celebrations of Stonewall in the United States, staged the first gay Mardi Gras in Sydney in June 1978. This event was marked by the Australian gay movement's most violent confrontation with the state to this time. Police intervention in the street march led to fifty-three people being arrested and charged. Subsequent street actions resulted in the charges being dropped and the adoption of new legislation by the New South Wales State Parliament recognizing the rights of groups to public assembly.

What is extraordinary about the subsequent development of Mardi Gras is its rapid transformation from this initial illegal public expression of homosexual dissidence, to a public celebration of a new "gay community." This shift coincided with and was symptomatic of the move, noted by Altman (1979), to a new homosexual sociality. The violence of the first Mardi Gras solidified determination to continue the event in subsequent years. Participants argued to move the event its original winter date (June) to Sydney's summer because, as one gay man explained to me in retrospect, "You could hardly march down Oxford Street in a frock in the middle of winter!" Organizers eventually settled on February. The move broke the connection with Stonewall celebrations in the United States and helped further to establish a unique quality to the Sydney Mardi Gras. Effective lobbying secured street march permits with police protection on future occasions.

Organized resistance to Mardi Gras has now shifted from the state to marginal religious groups such as the extremist Christian sect, the Festival of Light (FOL), which has been singularly unsuccessful in its efforts to have the event banned from Sydney's streets. Rather, some have argued that the publicity generated by the FOL's antics has promoted the event and enhanced its popularity.

The inaugural Mardi Gras clashes were incongruous considering the political climate of the time. For its part, by the late 1970s, a section of the gay movement had shifted its strategy toward a recognition of capitalist interest, state assistance, law reform, parliamentary participation, and a focus of gay life in commercial pubs and clubs. Gay commentators interpreted this shift in strategy as a diffusion of the radical potential of homosexuality through its cooption into capitalist markets (Altman 1979). On the other hand, Altman could comment in the year of the first Mardi Gras that "among many straight Australians there is an increasing readiness to accept homosexuality as in itself something as morally valid as heterosexuality" (Altman 1978:18). This incorporation of homosexuality into Australian society, of which the growing popularity of the annual Mardi Gras parade is but one indicator, was only possible with the emergence of a modified homosexuality, one less threatening to the establishment and compatible with existing consumerist structures and interests. The centering of gay life around a large and influential gay economy — pubs, night clubs, cafes and restaurants, sex-on-premises venues; newspaper, book, video, travel, and holiday enterprises; and, more recently, giant commercial dance parties attracting many thousand paying participants — is the visible evidence of this incorporation of the gay movement into capitalist society. Furthermore, the perceived new acceptability of homosexuality to which Altman alludes is, I would argue, facilitated by the containment of this new gay homosexuality within a perceived, or envisioned, community.

By the end of the 1970s, radical propositions among gay men for social and sexual revolution had given way to the influence of social constructionist theory. A new line of thought demanded the conscious building of a gay "community" as the strategy by which homosexuals could increase their political power.[4] While references to a "gay community" can be found in gay discourses as early as 1973,[5] it was not until the turn of the decade that the notion of community became a central organizing concept in this emerging discursive strategy. As one long-term Sydney gay activist put it to me:

> The role of gay radicals was to create community and the community was the solution for gay people. There are gay people out there in the suburbs and the answer for them is to come in and live in Darlinghurst and develop a minority gay lifestyle.

In many ways, however, this notion of community was very much a contingent one, described by one participant at the time as "a mirage of gay politics in the '80s" yet an ideological basis for a "new politics" (Cozijn 1982). Altman, more positively, acknowledged the potential of community as a "liberated area" of alternative culture that sits in opposition to mainstream society (Altman 1979).

The geographical boundaries of a Sydney gay community are to some extent more measurable than those of sibling communities in such other State capital cities as Melbourne and Brisbane. This is partly a result of an early and conscious political attention directed toward the Darlinghurst area of Sydney's inner city where an evacuating working class left behind low-cost housing, numerous pubs available for renovation, and large commercial spaces offering potential for creating dance clubs. Within a decade of the push for community, a geographic gay heartland had indeed been established there, oriented around the major thoroughfare of Oxford Street.

It is only partly useful to conceptualize this community in geographic terms. Many gay-identifying men have only a periodic and often problematic relation to the gay community of the inner city. While gay identity is only realizable within the supporting cultural environment of such a community, relations to community may take many forms. I will note later in this chapter how a more sophisticated theory of gay community was developed through AIDS research, one which conceptualized community as a matrix of social relations built on forms of attachment between men. I want to note here the discursive nature of community, or community as a concept with political utility for gay men and for those positioned beyond its alleged boundaries.

The utility of this new concept of "community" was potentially far greater than the revolutionary ideology of gay liberation. Gay identity was now socialized via this link to a "community" of like others. "Gay" constituted a quasi-ethnic identity with geographical, social, behavioral, and cultural features shared by its members. By socializing gay identity, political strategies were opened up to include more diverse forms of activities and greater participation in terms of numbers of people involved. The annual Mardi Gras thus carried political meaning, as well as being a good night out. The extraordinary development of the Mardi Gras from a small protest march in 1978, to a festival culminating in a massive public street parade, and a celebratory closing party with 15,000 paying participants in 1990, organized by an incorporated association with a capital turnover of over one million (AUS) dollars, can be seen as a part of this shift to a commercial community identity. As early as 1981, the event's reorientation was recognized by one member of the Mardi Gras Task Force, Paul Young, who wrote: "The primary goal of the event is to be a celebration of coming out with its main political goal being to demonstrate the size of the gay community, its variety of lifestyles, and its right to celebrate in the streets" (Young 1981:13). We will meet Young again in Chapter Eight.

While not all gays participating in Mardi Gras may consciously perceive it as a political event, participation is a very emotionally charged experience, much like a religious ritual. This is particularly so for those coming out into the community for the first time. The ability of Mardi Gras to evoke community simultaneously provides that community with its best self-evidence and self-fulfilment. And the utility of the Mardi Gras has not been lost on the New South Wales State Government, which now acknowledges that the event brings much needed tourist dollars to the local economy. By the beginning of the 1990s, the gay community did indeed appear to have won significant ground in terms of its economic power, and this despite a decade of epidemic.

COMMUNITY AS ADMINISTERED SOCIAL SPACE (2): THE EMERGENCE OF A GAY HEALTH PROFESSIONAL CLASS

The AIDS epidemic was first detected in Australia in March 1983, two years after its detection in the United States. Over 1000 cases of AIDS were already recorded in the U.S. by then. A similar caseload was not recorded in Australia until 1986, and that number of deaths until early 1991.

The immediate response by gay men in Sydney to the experience of what was then an illness of an unknown origin was to provide voluntary, largely untrained care to people with AIDS in their homes. Individual gay men personally affected, either because they were sick themselves, or because lovers and friends were becoming sick and dying, later created the first organizations to deal with the new health problem. In September 1984 a group of people were trained for such home care by gay men with experience in nursing. They soon formally organized into what is now known as the Community Support Network (CSN). The Bobby Goldsmith Foundation (BGF), named after one of the earliest gay-identified men to die from AIDS in Sydney, was formed in July 1984 to provide financial and material assistance to gay men with AIDS, from funds donated by gay men and their friends.

This early response by a loose network of gay men and friends (notably lesbians) to cater to the new health problem prompted one observer to comment that "we are seeing something of a community response to AIDS needs" (Watson 1984:8). By the end of 1984, when forty-nine cases of AIDS were recorded in Australia, the threat of AIDS to the gay community was taken up by a new class of activists as the most pressing cause for gay men. Thus, in February 1985 one activist wrote in a national gay paper:

> We can be certain that if the AIDS epidemic is not stopped, it will destroy us as a community as surely as it destroys us as individuals . . . if we succeed, we will not only assure our survival, we will transform our position in this country, and gain ground that the pioneers of gay liberation never dreamed of . . . we must become a community in fact as well as in name (Carr 1985:21).

To gay community activists, AIDS threatened the decimation of all that had been established in the previous decade. What was necessary to short circuit this disaster was the development of education programs to change men's sexual behavior to "safe sex" practices that would prevent the further spread of HIV infection. Additionally, support was deemed necessary to refine and expand the nascent program of care established for people with AIDS.

Consistent with the political understanding that government plays a significant role in health care, gay activists looked to government as the most important source of funding for shoring up the fight against AIDS. To this end, it was essential to develop "the closest possible cooperation with government" (Carr 1986b:19). If gay health was to become a component of government's responsibility toward its citizens, then relations between gay community and the state would also change. As Carr commented in the national gay press in 1986: "A community which is so thoroughly entwined with government structures can hardly adopt slogans about smashing the patriarchal state with any expectations of being taken seriously" (Carr 1986a:14).

The AIDS Action Committee (NSW) was established in early 1985 as a federation of the then existing service groups, gay (Gay Counselling Service) and AIDS-related (Bobby Goldsmith Foundation, Community Support Network, Ankali). This Committee set out to convince state and federal governments of their roles in the epidemic, and of their responsibility in providing funding for the new gay community-based effort. The argument was consistent with the federal Labor Party's general approach to health: that the state has a responsibility in guaranteeing access to health for all, including in this case gay men and people with AIDS. This construction of health as an issue of right of access is described by Alford as the "equal health solution." Health care is viewed "as a commodity . . . a subject for bargaining over" (Alford in Gardner 1989b:199), and is thereby less of a challenge to the status quo than another transaction within the prevailing capitalist socioeconomic environment. Through this approach, one recognizable to the funding bureaucracies, the sexual identity of the recipients of funding becomes less of an issue than the fact that an identified "community" of citizens must be protected from the risk of disease. The containment of disease to "high risk" communities thereby becomes a means of immunizing those not identified with this group, in this case a putative "general (heterosexual) community." In this way, government support for gay efforts to address AIDS shores up the prevailing gender order (Connell 1990).

The Federal government signalled its acceptance of responsibility by granting AU$74,000 [approximately US$55,000 at the then-current exchange rate] to the AIDS Action Committee in early 1985. With this grant this community-based body became the AIDS Council of New South

Wales (ACON). Gay activist-academic Lex Watson described the establishment of ACON as "the most important and complex political task we have yet achieved within our community, and one which expressed the growing political maturity of the Sydney gay community in the face of AIDS" (Watson 1986:17). ACON's budget was later increased to AU\$200,000 [US\$150,000] in the 1985/86 financial year with funds received from both the federal and New South Wales state (both Labor Party) governments. This second round of funding signaled the acceptance by the state government of its responsibility in combating AIDS and its preparedness to work, within defined parameters, with a gay community. This funding provided for the employment of an Office Coordinator and Receptionist, an Education Officer, and a Community Care Trainer. This three-way division of labour between education, welfare and administration, established what was to be the basic structure of the organization. In conjunction with this new financial relationship to government, ACON also formed working relationships with key ministers and bureaucrats of both state and federal governments.

From its inception then, the operation of ACON — despite its community base — was predicated on state and federal government recognition and financial support. By contrast, non-government funds were a relatively insignificant component of its total budget. This configuration of relations, articulated through funding grants and representation, is consistent with the wider historical trends noted in the beginning of this chapter. Health is one particular area in Australian society where government has traditionally accepted considerable responsibility. The reorganization of the gay political agenda around the issue of health thus gave stimulus for new relationships to be forged between the organized gay community and government. Like the feminist entry into the bureaucracy throughout the 1970s, this interdigitation of government and gay community was, as Connell describes for the development of femocracy, "a necessary response to a historical reality" (Connell 1990:531).

The expansion of ACON's budget and personnel over the following years gives some indication of the increased level of government support and the increased importance with which governments saw the work of the organization. Growth was slow in the first years of operation. In the year ending 1987 ACON's budget had expanded to AU\$288,441 [US\$216,331] most of which was from government sources. These funds supported a staff of twelve (ACON 1987). By the end of the 1989/90 financial year, it had expanded exponentially, with a staff of sixty-six, including eleven located at regional branches, eight from related organizations, and seven from special (not ongoing) projects. Total income was then a little over two million AU dollars [US$1.5 million]. The organization had solidified into a highly specialized and professionalized structure, with target projects for identified groups such as the deaf community, ethnic gay men, men who use beats, people with HIV/AIDS, and women. Two financial years later, ACON had doubled again, with a State-wide staff of 120 and an annual budget of around five million AU dollars [US$3.75 million] (ACON 1992/93). So large and complex had it become by this stage that the organization underwent a complete institutional review in this period and significantly restructured its managerial, administrative, and departmental structure.

With this came a shift in the organization's internal discourse. By 1988 it had, in the words of its president, adopted a "sound administrative and organizational structure" through the adoption of a "comprehensive Management Plan" and a system of issue-based working groups. This structure was clearly intended not only to assist internal functioning, but to present an image of efficiency to funding bodies: "A professionally managed and effective organization also gives confidence to the State and Commonwealth [i.e. federal] Governments" (ACON 1988).

Accompanying the expansion of professional control over the Council was a decline in voluntary participation. Excepting the activity of the Community Support Network (CSN), a pre-existing group later subsumed within ACON while retaining its original structure as a volunteer-based home care service, ACON's unpaid workforce was largely restricted to the twelve-member governing committee of the Council who also supplied much of the unpaid input to a few remaining working groups. These developments precipitated criticism, by 1988, that the Council had lost its community base and effectively become a branch of government health departments (see, for example, Wotherspoon 1988; *Sydney Star Observer* 23 December 1988).

While ACON tried to answer its critics with assertions that "our doors are open for member and volunteer involvement in all aspects of our work" (ACON 1990b), its very structure closed off such possibilities to many. Increasingly rigorous administrative reporting procedures, reliance on complex high-technology equipment and skilled operators, the use of a specialized and acronym-loaded language, the strict division of labour, and a reliance on specialist knowledge and skills all worked to exclude those not familiar with or unskilled in such an office culture. With the elimination, by the end of the decade, of volunteer-based working groups, originally designed to direct units and projects, many interested people were excluded from active involvement in the organization.

This criticism of ACON was most frequently heard from gay men with a particular, rather circumscribed view of gay community as being composed of intimate networks between gay-identifying men living in the inner city. The AIDS councils (ACON and its counterparts in the other state capital cities), on the other hand, were problematizing this notion of community, recognizing its specificity to inner city areas, and developing diverse strategies for reaching men not associated with such networks (see Davis et al. 1991). This tension is symptomatic of Patton's observation of the separation of gay liberationists involved in paid AIDS work from their activists roots (Patton 1990). Whereas gay liberationists sought to "out" a repressed and unproblematic homosexuality, AIDS council workers had come to recognize implicitly, through the rather different program of disseminating health messages to previously unknown populations of men, the complexities of sexual identity and behavior. It was no longer simply a matter of "liberating" the oppressed, though this remained an implicit agenda for gay-identifying men. What was at stake now was the necessity to incorporate within the theory of (homo)sexuality and within health programs a recognition of the fluidity and diversity of sexual identities and behaviors (Ariss et al. 1992; Connell et al. 1991; Dowsett 1990; Kippax et al. 1993).

The work of AIDS education, and to a lesser extent support and care, set those involved apart from other gay men of the inner city. Their newly established links to government and to wider homosexual networks situated these men within a new matrix of social relations. The success of AIDS council educators in transforming the sexual ethics of the gay community only served to highlight the distinctiveness of this limited "gay community" from a much wider, largely unknown network of "men who have sex with men." This realization provided such educators with a cultural capital that set them apart from the narrow sexual culture of gay liberation. Together with their solidifying economic security as a new class of welfare professionals, this put AIDS council workers in a privileged position *vis-à-vis* other gay men.

This organizational trajectory of the community-based AIDS response recalls Goffman's notes on the professionalization of the stigmatic experience. The coming together of individuals defined by a stigmatizing category often leads to the emergence of "speakers" and "representatives" who seek to put the case of the stigmatized to a wider public. Speakers, he notes, are caught in the "catch-22" of at once being positioned in a representative role and of becoming alienated from those they represent because their role necessarily expands the range of persons they must deal with:

> [I]n making a profession of their stigma, native leaders are obliged to have dealings with representatives of other categories, and so find themselves breaking out of the closed circle of their own kind. Instead of leaning on their

crutch, they get to play golf with it, ceasing, in terms of social participation, to be representative of the people they represent (Goffman 1963:39).

The growth of AIDS councils is an illustration of this professionalization process. Young men, often with few skills or previous work experience, are being provided new work opportunities that have a significant influence on their gay identities, their relations to gay community, and to the wider world. In this way, AIDS councils are providing a training ground for gay men, who may later take their skills to other areas of the community and beyond.

Thus while, as Aronowitz has argued, the constructed communities of the counter-cultures of the late twentieth century may constitute sites of a new postmodern politics (Aronowitz 1987/88), an ironic condition of their existence is a power relation with the state that allows the terms of struggle to be set beyond the boundaries of those communities. The gay community has been able to enter into political relations with the Australian state only after undergoing a process of professionalization that draws it into the political culture of a ruling class.

* * *

We are now in a position to bring people with HIV/AIDS into the picture. By the closing years of the 1980s we begin to detect the emergence of a collectivity of HIV-infected people seeking to change the education agendas of still community-based but largely government-funded AIDS councils, such as ACON, away from a focus on education for prevention of HIV infection, toward a greater support and education for the HIV-infected. That shift in agenda was to problematize relations within the "triad," namely between the community-based response on the one hand, and the state and the medical research establishment on the other. I take up these historical developments in Part Three. First, I will examine in detail the complex issues that emerge from a diagnosis of HIV infection.

NOTES

1. See for example conservative politician Wilson Tuckey's address to the Third National Conference on AIDS, August 1988, reproduced in the *National AIDS Bulletin* 2(8):45–47; or Fred Hollows's address to the First Aboriginal Conference on HIV/AIDS, 2 March 1992, and comments in the press: "Hollows Confronts Gay Lobby on AIDS," *The Australian* (3 March 1992).

2. In early 1992, for example, the Australian National Council on AIDS (ANCA), the advisory body to the Federal Minister for Health, adopted a policy which positioned "men who have sex with men" as a research and funding priority above all other interested parties.
3. Known as "cottages" in Britain, and "tearooms" in the United States.
4. Craig Johnston, for example, wrote several commentaries on the changes in Sydney gay life at the beginning of the 1980s. In *Gay Information* 4 he referred to the growth of the Mardi Gras as "a sign that the 'community' (is) taking over and the 'movement' is on the way out" (p. 11). In the following issue he noted, rather inconsistently, that the gay community is more "wishful thinking than thought-out description of concrete reality" (Johnston 1981).
5. "A *real* community would be based not only on a professional commitment to the gay liberation struggle but in a spirit of cooperativeness, compassion, understanding and trust" (Lee 1973).

Part Two

The Tactics of Health and Illness

CHAPTER 3

Identifying the Subject: HIV-Antibody Testing as a Social Process

A SOCIAL TEST

Carl is a professional, middle-aged gay man living in an inner-city neighborhood of Sydney. He has been HIV-infected for five years and has known his status for most of that time. When I spoke with him in 1989 he was living alone after splitting up with his young lover. With some anger he recounted an incident that led to the dissolution of his relationship:

> I have been getting over an affair with a guy I had for about four or five months. It was cheap to get into really. I mean he was only young. He was only nineteen which is full of problems in any case. But we were both positive so we thought we would support each other, be aware of each other's health situation. I mean I've been positive at least eighteen months before that. He'd recently tested positive — I mean full IV drug user and really out on the scene since he was thirteen or fourteen. But subsequent tests were negative so they're assuming his positive was a false positive. So he was given a chance for a clean slate and I guess he didn't want me to dirty it up again. And I can understand that totally, but the end result is that he's gone. It was a painful departure.[1]

Carl's story serves well to illustrate the manner in which HIV-antibody testing takes on multiple and significant meanings for those subject to it. In his rather unusual case the outcome of the test ordered the possibility and expectations of his relationship with another man. In the first instance, his partner's positive test result introduced the possibility of a shared predicament and thus potentially strengthened their relationship. Then, the sudden reversal of his partner's status cancelled these expectations and

39

ended the relationship. The negative result created a predicament of difference: Carl became potentially polluting, his partner at risk.

This is a concise illustration of the kinds of issues raised by HIV-antibody testing discussed in this and the following chapter. This chapter considers the problematic, social nature of HIV testing technology and the two broad uses to which it has been put: epidemiological surveillance and, more recently, health monitoring. Some of the examples discussed within it concern the responses of gay men to the availability of testing, illustrating the complexity of meanings and social implications borne by such a clinical test.

Cindy Patton has pointed out that the commonly named "AIDS test" is "a series of events, not a moment of transcendentally assessing truth." The test is not a means of seeing the virus or the antibodies to it; rather, it is a battery of "chemical reactions that indicate that a particular biochemical process has occurred in the blood of the subject" (Patton 1990:33). The ideological collapsing of the test result within medical and epidemiological discourse into a single function — defining who is and who is not infected with HIV — glosses over the complex cultural processes that collude to produce results, and denies the complex webs of meaning that have settled around the test. Use of the test has been surrounded in controversy since its initial development in 1984, underlining its problematic nature. The inaccurate readings it may produce, in the form of "false positives" or "false negatives," are the most obvious instance of the test's imperfect specificity. Some have argued that such inaccuracies were a result of the technology of the test itself (Imrie et al. 1987), while others believed that procedural methods or statistical effects accounted for different rates of false results among different populations (Schwartz et al. 1988). Either way, the rate of false readings was condemned by gay groups and clinicians as unacceptable (Roy et al. 1987). Thus, by 1988 clinicians and policy makers were arguing for the need to confirm a positive result through a repeated test using a different method, such as Western Blot or immunofluorescence assays, as standard procedure in the identification of HIV-positivity (MDW 1985; Anonymous I 1988).

While such procedures have improved the reliability of the test, the meanings of a positive test result remain fluid. Extensive interventions by counselors, social workers, educators, and activists have sought to stabilize the interpretation of test results culminating, in 1992, in the formulation of National Counselling Guidelines (Laffan 1992). Thus, it is a requirement that the delivery of test results be supervised by professionally trained counselors, or that medical practitioners conducting HIV testing be trained in appropriate methods of informing their patients. News of a positive test result is accompanied by reassurances that HIV infection can be a long-term manageable condition and that measures can be taken to enhance health for as long as possible. If health is already impaired, appropriate clinical interventions are suggested. Advice on the importance of safe sex is considered vital in preventing the individual from infecting others. Thus, in time the use of the HIV test and its interpretations have become systematized and stable under the managerial guidance of an emergent AIDS-dedicated governmental regime.

TECHNOLOGY FOR SURVEILLANCE 1981–1988

Prior to the identification in 1984 of a single etiological agent thought to be responsible for AIDS and the subsequent development of a diagnostic test to detect the presence of antibodies to such a virus in the human body, the only means of "seeing" AIDS was through a diagnosis of an AIDS-related opportunistic infection. The signs of the disease were external, written on the body most clearly by the red or purple raised lesions of Kaposi's sarcoma (KS) or revealed through the presence of swarms of parasites in the lungs: pneumocystis carinii pneumonia (PCP). It was only at this stage of disease, now known to be a later stage of an infection period of up to at least ten years, that one learned of one's condition.

Significantly, the early uncertainty and speculation surrounding the etiology of AIDS did not prevent the urban gay communities in the United States from devising a behavioral response that had potential to reduce the possibility of contracting the disease. In November 1982, little more than a year after the first U.S. diagnosis of AIDS, two gay men with AIDS generated controversy among the gay community of New York by publishing an article in a gay paper condemning promiscuity. As one of the authors later reflected: "With the frenzy of recently reformed whores singing gospel, we were *testifying* about the urgent need to 'avoid the exchange of potentially infectious bodily fluids'" (Callen 1990:7).

The article referred to, entitled "We Know Who We Are: Two Gay Men Declare War on Promiscuity," was followed up with a somewhat more pragmatic booklet by one of the authors, Michael Callen, entitled *How To Have Sex in an Epidemic* (1983). This essay introduced the concept of "safe sex," arming gay men with a behavioral regimen that permitted sexual activity to continue while reducing to a minimum the risk of infection. Today the principle of safe sex — essentially being the use of condoms for penetrative sex — is almost universally accepted as an effective means of avoiding infection with HIV.

The formulation of this regimen *before* the identification of HIV con-tradicts a commonly heard assertion that knowledge of HIV status is pre-requisite for sexual behavior change. At this early stage of the epidemic, the mere assumption of the presence of a transmissable disease-causing agent among gay men, together with the visible presence of the problem in the form of illness and death, was sufficient to mobilize gay communities well before science had identified a biological agent and described its modes of transmission.

There is good evidence, based on subsequent epidemiological and behavioral studies, that this early, pre-test behavior change among gay men was widespread and effective in greatly slowing the spread of HIV infection in the gay communities of countries such as the United States (Stall et al. 1988) and Australia (Tindall et al. 1989). An extensive sur-vey of gay men's AIDS knowledge and sex practices conducted by Macquarie University in Sydney in 1986/87 indicated a majority of gay men had, by that time, adopted safe sex practices as a means of avoid-ing HIV infection (Connell et al. 1989). Even after the introduction of HIV testing, this strategy continued (at least for a number of years) to rest on the principle of universal behavior change: Everyone was as-sumed to be HIV-infected and everyone practiced safe sex. Safe sex became the new cultural norm guiding sex practice among gay men. Rather than embracing the use of the HIV-antibody test gay commun-ity-based AIDS organizations, in a clear break with traditional public-health strategies, quickly adopted an anti-testing position on the ground that knowledge of one's status exposed the individual to the possibility of discrimination.[2]

This community-based approach focusing on civil rights generated an opposing agenda. Politically conservative elements, notably in the medi-cal profession, argued for mandatory HIV testing of particular "risk groups:" immigrants, prisoners, surgery patients, prostitutes, homosexu-als, and intravenous drug users. The consequences of a positive test result for such individuals were rarely considered, though the discourse bears an implicit agenda for the suspension of ordinary civil rights and, in the most extreme case, quarantine of the infected. In one example, the Australian Medical Association (AMA) lobbied to grant health-care workers the right to refuse service to the infected, reinforcing fears among gay men and the infected that the discriminatory potential of testing was genuine. This fear was confirmed in 1989 when a widely publicized legal action against the medical profession by a gay man who had been refused surgery ended in favor of the accused health-care worker.[3] Such events signaled to the HIV-infected that they were somehow excluded from ordinary citizen rights.

In an effort to stabilize the political environment and provide leadership on the national response to AIDS, the federal government undertook to produce a national AIDS policy. Extensive consultations with individuals and groups involved in AIDS, including the various state AIDS councils, people-with-AIDS groups, health-care workers, and bureaucrats culminated in the launch of the National HIV/AIDS Strategy in late 1989. The National Strategy paper described the HIV-infected as a population that cuts across "a wide range of sectors of Australian society." Cooperation was sought "across the three levels of government" (federal, state, and municipal), "between government and non-government sectors and between unions and employers; *and between all these parties and those infected with the virus*" (Commonwealth of Australia 1989:5, emphasis added). The infected represented the unifying thread linking different sectors in society, a gesture not only to homosexuals, but to the broader diversity of the infected populations.

In the consultation process, the AIDS councils advocated informed consent and counseling, but rejected mandatory HIV testing in any circumstances. This position was only partly recognized in the final draft of the national strategy:

> Testing for the presence of HIV, in association with appropriate counselling, peer support and, where necessary, community support has a critical role to play:
> – in clinical diagnosis;
> – in facilitating early intervention in the management of the disease; and
> – in minimizing transmission of HIV.

However, having acknowledged this issue of care in the administration of testing, the strategy then compromises the principle of consent by identifying "risk groups" for mandatory testing, namely blood, tissue, organ, and semen donors; and applicants for permanent residency. Testing of surgery patients was considered appropriate. Compulsory testing was validated for prisoners, persons charged with sexual offenses where the victim requests a test of the offender, where it is necessary to determine medical treatment of another person (for example, after a needle-stick injury), or "testing of a person suspected on reasonable grounds to be HIV-positive, who persistently behaves in such a way as to place other persons at risk of infection" (Commonwealth of Australia 1989:39–41). Thus, while the general policy toward the infected states that "people with HIV are entitled to be regarded with the same rights and dignity afforded to all in the Australian community" (55), the recognition of exceptional situations requiring mandatory testing qualifies the Federal Government's otherwise benign position: applicants for

Australian residency who test positive are universally rejected; prisoners were, for some years, segregated; patients continue to be denied treatment; and those "knowingly infecting others," usually sex workers, are subject to rigorous surveillance and often detention in the name of public health.

TECHNOLOGY FOR HEALTH FROM 1989

Prior to the development of therapies for the prevention of HIV-related diseases, public and political debate largely revolved around the utility of the test for infection prevention. A shift is already apparent by the time of the release of the *National AIDS Strategy*, which positions testing as an important tool in the diagnosis and treatment of infection before any discussion of transmission and prevention. Therapeutic developments that promised earlier and better clinical management of HIV infection were having an impact on the meaning and perceived utility of the HIV-anti-body test.

In March 1989, an American gay activist with AIDS, Vito Russo, published a short critical article in New York's *PWA Coalition Newsline* arguing for gay men to overcome their "denial" and take the HIV-antibody test if they had not already done so. He argued:

> Three years ago there was no good reason to take an HIV test or to monitor T-cells because people who tested positive had no option except to drive themselves crazy with worry. That's not true any more. Every day more and more people ignorant of their health status suddenly and with little warning end up in hospital with the most common and deadly opportunistic infection associated with AIDS, Pneumocystis Carinii. The tragedy of this situation is that it doesn't have to happen. This deadly pneumonia is now largely preventable thanks to prophylaxis treatment with aerosol Pentamadine. Anyone whose T-cells are below 200 should be having regular treatments with this overwhelmingly successful and virtually non-toxic method of using the drug. The bottom line is that we now have weapons against AIDS and if people don't use them, they'll die. It's as simple as that. To sit around in a dream world hoping it won't happen to you is madness (Russo 1989:4).

Russo was echoing the shift by community-based AIDS organizations in the United States toward campaigning to encourage gay men to take the test as a first step in monitoring their health. San Francisco's *Sentinel* newspaper, for example, ran an advertisement: "To all gay and bisexual men who have not taken the HIV-antibody test." The advertisement urged readers to "Think about it" and "seriously consider voluntary, anonymous testing" (*Sentinel* 25 May 1989).

Australians attending the Fifth International Conference on AIDS in Montreal in July 1989 heard these messages about testing and preventive treatment firsthand. Returning to Australia, some of them embarked on a campaign to change the existing testing policies of AIDS service organizations in this country. People Living With AIDS (New South Wales), hereafter PLWA (NSW), a new organization of people infected with the virus, lobbied ACON to reconsider its anti-testing policy. When ACON agreed to this measure, HIV testing was effectively repositioned as a beneficial step for individuals at risk of being infected. A campaign was conducted throughout 1990 in gay newspapers encouraging individuals to take the HIV test. This was followed in late 1991 by yet another campaign, this time sponsored by the manufacturers of the antiviral drug AZT, Burroughs Wellcome. The campaign was similar to those conducted by the company in the United States, using gay magazines as a medium with carefully selected images of men speaking positively about their decision to take the HIV test. In Australia, images of this kind appeared in the gay press and on two occasions in the *Sydney Morning Herald*.

Through this new discourse of monitoring and management, HIV testing was reconstructed as a technology of health rather than one of surveillance, though the latter remained important in monitoring the spread of the epidemic. This reconstruction has been characterized as a shift from public health definitions to a medical construction of the test (Siegal et al. 1989). To know one's HIV status was no longer a threat to one's privacy and rights. It was, rather, a necessary first step in taking control of one's health. The test thus became linked to the emerging project of patient self-empowerment while at the same time offering those pharmaceutical companies with an investment in AIDS the opportunity to expand their potential markets.

RESPONSES TO TESTING

While some research has indicated a majority of Sydney gay men had, by 1987, undergone HIV testing at least once (Kippax et al. 1993), a significant minority remains untested. When I spoke to Andrew in 1989 he rejected the notion of the usefulness of the HIV test, evoking the older construction of the test as a threat to individual rights:

> I don't want to take any of the tests. I refuse to take the tests and I'd be stupid to think I didn't have a damn good chance of being HIV-positive. I've no intention of taking the test 'cause I don't believe at this stage it's a useful thing to do.

Though the pro-testing campaigns were not yet in full swing at this point, this attitude is not a product of simple ignorance of advances in medical treatments. I asked Andrew if he believed the arguments for early medical intervention then beginning put forward by AIDS organizations. His response illustrates an awareness of such arguments, but these alone do not provide him with sufficient reason to change his position:

> The idea of AZT and prolonging your life for an extra period fills me with horror . . . I really would like as little medical intervention as possible. If I become ill I'll be free and dead as soon as possible. I really have no desire to linger on. I've watched it happen in too close quarters to think that there's any merit in prolonging it. You're dead at the end of the day. You've dragged your own life out in considerable discomfort for a longer period and made the lives of other people around you less pleasant than they might have otherwise been. After two-and-a-half years with that, with two people, I've just seen enough to realize that there's nothing there for me.

The potential of the test as a tool for health maintenance is overshadowed by Andrew's own observations of the negative effects of medical intervention. Experience as a caregiver for people with AIDS and his witness to the traumas of dying take on greater significance than any ideological argument for the advantages of early medical intervention.

Those who have, for whatever reason, decided not to undertake testing, only learn of their antibody status when and if illness actually develops and clinical testing is undertaken to identify the cause of the problem. Only an example can adequately illustrate the potential trauma of this sort of situation, trauma that advocates argue can be avoided through early monitoring.

Simon is a professional gay man in his late thirties. His positive status was eventually revealed to him only after he admitted himself to hospital with pains in his chest and breathing difficulties. Up until that point he had been strong and healthy. His sudden illness startled and confused him. He had not taken an HIV test because, as he explains, he had no reason to suspect he was infected. The process of his diagnosis was a prolonged and traumatic one as he was administered an immune function count, a CD4-cell test, and a test for PCP. The waiting period for the results was one of intense anxiety, during which he considered his situation:

> I'm scared. I'd be lying if I said I wasn't scared. It's such a shock, there's nothing else to think except that I'm HIV-positive and probably have AIDS. I should have taken the test earlier but it's one of those things you think it could never happen to me. I was too scared. My lover had the test and it was negative, so we just assumed I would be negative too.

Simon finally received confirmation several days later that he was indeed HIV-positive.

On the basis of these results his doctors prescribed a battery of anti-viral drugs and antibiotics for his condition. On receiving this prescription, Simon telephoned me, as had become his habit during this period of crisis, to explain what had happened and ask advice. "I've just been to see my doctor and he's told me I still have the PCP, I'm going to be on Bactrim (a multipurpose antibiotic) for the rest of my life and he told me I've got two years to live." This final prognosis shocked and angered him. He found it "totally unhelpful" and rejected it, immediately beginning to consider health strategies that would thwart the prediction. He suspected some people who are diagnosed with AIDS outlive their prognosis and sought confirmation of this from me. For the sake of his own peace of mind, I felt obliged to confirm Simon's suspicion and recalled a number of men I had met who had indeed lived well beyond the statistical "two years" survival time with AIDS. He took comfort in this news and assured me he would be joining the ranks of the "long-term survivors."

From this moment of crisis Simon underwent an intense period of adjustment to his newly acquired condition. Simon has a loving partner who helped and supported him through this time, and a number of friends immediately came to his assistance, some traveling a great distance to do so. After four years, Simon has indeed outlived his doctor's predictions and continues to enjoy life. We will meet him again in Chapter Five.

The choice to take the HIV test as an early step toward health care is more likely to occur when the individual in question holds to the principle of personal responsibility for health. Ray, a working-class gay man, interpreted his positive test result as reconfirmation of the need to look after himself:

> If you find out you know where you are. But if you don't check you keep going out, you meet people, every night you have a different person. But if you find out now you can have a cure. But if you go all the way there is no hope, no cure. If you find out now you can help yourself, you can go and see a doctor and he will tell you what to do, but if you don't know you keep going out and then when you find out it's too late.

Interestingly, Ray mirrors a public construction of risk that conflates promiscuity ("going out") with disease. To know one's HIV status impels one to a restraint that provides "hope." Significantly, it is the doctor who provides advice while the individual himself bears ultimate responsibility. This commitment to care for the self is validated for Ray through his witnessing the irresponsibility of others:

> They don't care about themselves — they still do it, and I told them, and
> they say, "We are dying." I said, "Yes, we are going to die." Not because I
> am going to jump off the edge of the building, or go near fire. You have to be
> reserved too. These people who tell me they don't worry about it — but now
> I found out more about my friend and he is very sick and I don't know what
> to say. I just say, "Look we are all going to die, but we have to look after
> ourselves . . . we have to make the most of it."

For Ray, a positive test result confirms his predisposition to care for himself. The fear of illness, the predicament of being potentially ill, is the
motivation for undertaking HIV testing and an intensified regimen of self
care. I will return in greater detail to this form of response in Chapter Six.

While for some a test result provides the grounds on which to build a
new lifestyle, for others a positive result ushers in a crisis period of uncertainty. Bob describes his fear of becoming ill:

> I think the biggest problem that we all have is that we maybe become very
> aware of every little item paid, and I think I've become more aware of
> how I feel. I find that I'm a bit frightened to think that at my age, being
> healthy, that there is a possibility that if I didn't look after myself that I
> could go down, in something that would eventually be the end, because
> normally, or say if it wasn't around, you wouldn't get serious conditions
> until much later in life, you know. And I think that's a bit hard to cope with
> sometimes, is seeing people that are your own age suffering . . . I haven't
> had the neural physical problems. I have had a sort of infection in my nails
> which has gone now. I've had a few swollen ligaments but I mean that's
> part of being sick. I don't know anybody who was totally positive and
> hasn't had something. But you know I was to expect it, certain little things
> would happen and that's why I decided to start, you know, try and improve
> my lifestyle.

For Bob, being positive is a condition of physical fragility, a condition
where "being sick" represents a new normality. On the other hand, one can
seek some sense of mastery through changing "lifestyle."

Because HIV is a long-term condition with an asymptomatic period
of up to ten or fifteen years, individuals cognizant of their status find
themselves living in a protracted state of existential uncertainty.
Walter, a middle-class, professional man in his late forties, has known
of his infection for five years. At the time of our first discussions in
1989, he had not experienced any HIV illnesses. However, the potential for ill-health was for him a major source of anxiety and stress, and
he considered stress itself to be a possible contributor to disease progression. His anxiety is compounded by the fact that his partner is also
HIV-positive:

The most difficult thing still is that both my lover and I are HIV-positive and its the uncertainty as to just what the future holds. I suppose in our modern world no person can go around saying, "Well, I know I'm going to live to sixty or seventy or eighty or whatever." But the majority of people do, they go around with that clear impression that, OK I'm going to live till I'm seventy-five. Whereas with me, I carry around all the time, "OK, I've had the virus for five years now and I'm perfectly well, but what's it going to be like in two years time, four years time, five years time, ten years time and so on?" And what's even harder, is not only what's it going to be like with me but what's it going to be like with my lover? I mean we're both quite well, but he's only had the virus two years, two-and-a-half years. What happens if it affects him before it affects me? I suppose it's a fairly negative sort of approach, but I'd really hate to lose him. 'Cause it's just such a nice warm, really caring relationship, and to go through that loss would be awful. So there's a fear of loss of some sort there.

I asked Walter if he felt if there was any way to resolve this feeling of uncertainty. "No," he replied, " 'cause I don't think you can come to terms with that. I think that's just an everpresent thing." We will hear from Walter again in the next chapter.

Public health policies resting on the principle of widespread, even mandatory testing rarely consider the complex phenomenological and social implications for individuals who receive positive test results. Similarly, programs that encourage individuals "at risk" of HIV infection to undergo the test often fail to take account fully of the fears, disincentives, world views, and complicating life circumstances that may collude to dissuade an individual from taking such action. The failure of certain such programs, conducted by AIDS service organizations since 1989, to attract a large response is testimony to this.[4] The test is more than a simple diagnostic tool for detecting who is infected with HIV and what course of health management they should pursue. The test can have profound impact on the understanding of the self and on one's relations to others. The next chapter pursues these issue in more detail.

NOTES

1. All individuals quoted, except for those with full names, have been given pseudonyms in accordance with confidentiality agreements.
2. No specific material was produced within gay communities in Australia discouraging HIV testing. New York's Gay Men's Health Crisis (GMHC), however, produced a flyer in 1985 entitled "The Test Can Be Almost as Devas-

tating as the Disease". It stated: "The new test for antibodies to the 'AIDS virus' doesn't tell you very much about anything. It only indicates that you have been exposed to the virus. What it can do is frightening. Imagine, if your health insurance company found out that your test came back positive, they might cancel your policy. Even your job and home may be at risk. Names might be reported to the government and find their way onto a master list. In fact, desperately needed research is being hindered because the Federal Government refuses to guarantee confidentiality. So, if you do take the test, make sure you get a guarantee in writing that your name and the results of your test won't ever be released to anyone. Otherwise, our advice is, stay away from the test. It's bad news."

3. "Gay, So No Surgery" (*SSO* 19 May 1989).
4. A campaign conducted by ACON in collaboration with Burroughs Wellcome in 1993, for example, was regarded a failure in that its information hotline only attracted an average of five phone calls a week. By the end of that year, in the wake of negative scientific reports about the efficacy of such therapies, uptake of antiviral treatments had in fact markedly declined (Goddard 1994). I discuss these developments in greater detail in Part Three.

CHAPTER 4

Reconstructing Self and Others: Managing an HIV-Antibody Positive Status

Reading Erving Goffman's seminal work, *Stigma* (1963), one immediately recognizes the predicament of AIDS in the stories of people with other stigmatizing conditions. Despite this one also finds, among the new class of health professionals working in AIDS and among people with HIV/AIDS themselves, a pervasive view that AIDS has generated an historically unique set of circumstances and problems. The youthfulness of many who devote their lives to fighting AIDS and their outrage and disbelief at the horror of the epidemic often produce a feeling of isolation from the rest of humanity, a sense of uniqueness. There is some substance to this, of course. The fact that people with other stigmatizing conditions have not formed an alliance with people with AIDS and their advocates is testimony to the special stigma of AIDS. Yet, reading Goffman one is struck by the applicability of many of his observations to this new problem. Taking Goffman's writings on stigma as a general guide, this chapter illustrates the manner in which HIV/AIDS operates to restructure social relations between the infected and others. The illustrations provide, on the one hand, confirmation of Goffman's general observations regarding stigmatizing conditions. On the other, the specificities of AIDS, namely the collapsing of illness within an already stigmatized sexuality, leads us to some elaborations upon Goffman's theme.

The key insight that Goffman offers to the study of illness is his thesis that illness affects in negative ways the *social* identity of the affected. This hypothesis is central to this study also. "The central feature of the stigmatized individual's situation in life" becomes the question of "acceptance" (Goffman 1963:19). The individual's life project thereby becomes the neutralization of the effects of stigma, and the pursuit of the normalization of life, however that normality may be perceived. Importantly, Goffman's sociological analysis introduces us to a social subject who is not only acted upon, but who also acts. I take his argument one step further and propose that the imposition of stigma excites the subject to types of action toward which he or she would not normally be inclined. In AIDS, this excitation of the stigmatized subject has reached unprecedented limits. The resultant social and political reforms are unparalleled by any other category of stigmatized persons.

Goffman makes an important distinction between the "discredited" and the "discreditable" individual. The first type assumes difference is already known or is immediately evident. The second assumes difference is neither known nor immediately obvious. For the latter the issue of disclosure becomes important: who to tell, how, and when. For the former, disclosure is less an issue than the immediate management problems that arise automatically around interaction with others (Goffman 1963:14). We may conceptualize asymptomatic HIV positivity as a discreditable condition. AIDS is discrediting. The distinction is somewhat crude, as AIDS may not always be evident to the observer. Likewise, AIDS may be presumed, and an individual "discredited" as having it, when it (and, sometimes, HIV infection too) is absent. The suspicion by "normals" that an individual may have AIDS is frequently accompanied or supported by the suspicion of homosexuality. In this case one stigmatic condition is used to signify another and possibly compound it. In this chapter I am concerned largely with the condition of HIV positivity as a discreditable condition. In following chapters I pursue some issues of particular relevance to those with AIDS.

Goffman then characterizes three forms of stigma. "Abominations of the body" represent the physical deformities. "Blemishes of character" are perceived in faults of personality or beliefs, or are inferred from personal history. Goffman lists homosexuality in this type of stigma, together with such things as unemployment and radical political beliefs. Finally, "tribal stigma" is experienced by individuals associated in a social collectivity such as a race, nation, or religion. Tribal stigma is inherited and "contaminates" all members equally (Goffman 1963:14).

The signifying power of AIDS comes from its incorporation of all three of these types of stigma. AIDS produces physical changes ("abominations of the body") such as extreme weight loss or skin lesions, signs now recognizable to society at large through their propagation in the mass media. AIDS "blemishes character" through its association with disapproved sexualities or drug using behavior. Finally, the collectivization of gay men and gay men with HIV into visible and influential "communities" lends an additional "tribal stigma" to the condition. Gay community has been the frequent target of attack by medical, political, and religious factions, as for instance in the case of its perceived "hijacking" of the management of AIDS.

Meanwhile, this collectivization under the rubric of AIDS is a matter of pride for many gay men, and it is the focus of Part Three of this study. But the uniqueness of this achievement is somewhat exaggerated by gay men. As Goffman observes, a stigmatizing category "can function to dispose its members to group formation and relationships" and notes just such a process for the mentally impaired, Jews, ex-cons, the deaf, the blind, and alcoholics (Goffman 1963:36). Categories of stigmatized persons, therefore, are disposed to collectivize. Herein lies the starting point for an important shift that I plot in this study, namely that an imposed stigmatic status, in this case that of the "AIDS victim," can be modified by those who are the subjects of this labelling through the collectivization of experience.

Goffman notes that, to a point, this collectivization occurs through external means, such as through public representations of, or on behalf of, a category of stigmatized person in the media. Thus, most stigmatized people have some access to "an intellectually worked up version of their point of view." Where collectivization of the stigmatized is advanced, this "version" is increasingly modified by the stigmatized themselves (Goffman 1963:38). An isolated young man with AIDS living in rural Australia, who once "knew" the social facts of his condition through media representations of helpless and morally condemned victims, may now recognize himself in the face of the articulate gay man on a national current affairs television program demanding legal protection and access to rare and expensive therapeutic drugs. Such advocates are not, by definition, "representative," says Goffman, though they may claim representative status and be positioned and sanctioned publicly as such. This is a case of the professionalization of a stigmatic condition. The role of representative speaker is unique, setting the speaker apart from those represented. "Representatives are not representative, for representation can hardly come from those who give no attention to their stigma, or who are relatively unlettered" (Goffman 1963:40).

Goffman assumes here that, in ordinary circumstances, the stigmatized work to minimize the fact of their condition. This indeed is what most gay men with HIV and AIDS attempt to do. I explore this style of management in the first sections of this chapter. However, in the narratives of HIV-infected men a new discourse of difference becomes evident, distinct from the more general discourse of gay men. Indeed it is one that often positions the infected as marginal in the gay community. The final section begins to explore the issue of collectivization. This process increasingly occurs through the efforts of professional HIV careerists to gather the infected together. Participating in support groups or AIDS organizations raises the opportunity of recognizing one's experience in others and thus of developing a sense of collective identity. We begin to detect an emerging discourse of "HIV community."

DE-SIGNIFYING A POSITIVE DIAGNOSIS

For some individuals, particularly those who remain well, an HIV-positive diagnosis can be managed by rendering the information as insignificant as possible in the overall context of one's life. Craig is a gay man who has been involved in gay organizations for some years. He has cared for several friends to their deaths and anticipated the deaths of three more friends at the time we spoke. He himself is well, despite the trauma of witnessing his own networks depleted by death. He reflects on his own status:

> I very seldom think about it. In the beginning every time I got a cold it was like this great big drama. Now I don't get a cold any more, I don't stand in the rain. I don't stay out all night. I don't take too many drugs. I don't go out dancing all night. I don't drink too much or I drink less. I'm also older. I also don't, I very seldom think about it. I used to go through this whole thing where I would tell people before I would fuck with them. Now I don't bother. I think unless they bring it up I don't bother because I don't do things, I don't fuck in unsafe ways.

Craig is actively engaged in community-based AIDS groups, holds strong opinions about community politics, and is in regular contact with seriously ill people with AIDS, some of them close friends. Despite this proximity to the epidemic, Craig was able to push to the back of his mind, to de-signify as it were, his own positive status. "So in terms of myself being antibody-positive," he concludes, "I never think about it really."

Walter, whom we met in Chapter Three, is also very involved in community AIDS groups. He greatly values a wide network of friends built up over many years of involvement in both gay community and AIDS organizations. Like Craig, Walter still manages to render his own status of minimal significance, yet identifies a tension between a need not to worry' overly about his health, the necessity to take adequate care of himself, and still maintain his high involvement in gay and AIDS activities:

I don't think it bulks large. I don't think it shadows my every waking minute. But by the same token it is still present there and it comes up at times, it's at times when I'm reflecting, like at the moment, that it comes to the fore.

It's not in the front of my mind, which is fine, but I think one of the things, one of the reasons why I'm looking forward to going back to my previous work is actually just the stepping back from AIDS for a bit. I mean, I think it would be silly to get right out of the area 'cause I've got the expertise and I think I can make a contribution.

Neil, after recently nursing a friend to his death and experiencing an illness himself, has returned to work and managed to some extent to normalize his life once again:

There's just so many other things happening in my life that I've had to get on with. Like my life hasn't actually ended being HIV-positive, which is how I sort of thought at the beginning, like gear up to die sort of thing.

But this process of normalization is, he admits, never complete:

I don't think you ever really get there, so to speak, with HIV. I just find for me to feel comfortable I have to be very realistic about what it really means. Like maybe you never progress, twenty years, you never progress. Who knows? Because I've had one school of thought saying, "Oh, you're antigen-positive, HIV- and hepatitis-positive, a chronic hepatitis carrier, you're in a higher risk of progression." And I've had other people actually say the opposite. Medical people say some things happen with people who are HIV and Hep. But the HIV doesn't seem to be progressing. At least not as fast. So you listen to one, you listen to another, you just have to come to terms with it yourself. I think on realistic terms I've got to expect that I'm able to get on with things without it hanging over me like it used to.

Many issues are raised here that foreshadow discussion to come. Management of HIV infection first involves assessing one's mortality. Interpreting the meaning of being HIV-infected is a continual process of assessing one's health, one's probability of progression, of rendering medical information intelligible. One person with AIDS described to me the situation of being asymptomatic HIV-positive not so much as a stigmatizing condition, as one of "existential crisis." By this he meant, I think, that the problems are internal, not of the kind that the discrediting situation of illness brings: a situation that requires greater anticipation and manipulation of others' responses to self.

Being HIV-positive is a process of self-reconstruction, of becoming, of realizing oneself in a cultural environment of constantly shifting constructions of illness. Even though some may successfully de-signify their status for a period of time, this may not be possible indefinitely.

Events may again bring HIV infection to consciousness. Life again becomes problematic.

STIGMA AND THE DEVELOPMENT OF SPOILED IDENTITY

Changes in one's own physical condition are not by any means the only events that can trigger this return of to consciousness of HIV infection. Other, external circumstances may likewise work to problematize one's condition to the point where it is no longer possible to render an HIV-positive status of small significance.

Jack is, to all appearances, a healthy young man. He has recently retired from his job as a nurse in an AIDS ward in a busy hospital and works instead with cancer patients. The change was necessary, he said, because he was beginning to see friends and acquaintances come into his ward as patients. He has experienced up to four deaths in one week. The stress of the work, together with an attitude of fear and hysteria he perceived among the other workers in the ward, left Jack feeling "burnt out."

Talking to Jack in his cluttered, inner-city house, I sensed that he was relaxed and enjoying the break from AIDS nursing. He puts his improved health down to the fact that he had left the AIDS ward, to the use of AZT together with herbs, relaxation methods, and a positive attitude to life. Yet, when I asked him what he now felt to be the most difficult issue he now faces, he quickly alluded to a spoiled identity:

> The most difficult thing you say? Is not feeling dirty and unclean, in the sense of I'm a poisoned person. Coming to terms with that. I felt unclean like a leper or something, and the sort of prevailing attitude that comes through from different people, particularly who should know better, who don't know better because they haven't the disease yet, and you feel unclean. Whereas when I had hepatitis I didn't feel anywhere near as unclean.

Having HIV does not necessarily generate, in itself, a damaged sense of the self. Self is monitored in the context of social relationships. As a gay man working in a busy AIDS ward, Jack was constantly faced with illnesses among his patients, and the force of condemnatory attitudes of others. In such an environment it is not possible to ignore the significance of one's own status. One is contaminated by association. Jack's resolution was to leave the "AIDS-charged" environment of the ward for one with a different focus.

This feeling of being overwhelmed is common to many gay men who work in AIDS or who otherwise have a high degree of contact with people with the disease. The issue of "grief overload" or "community burnout" is increasingly heard as a problem facing the Sydney community (Crooks 1992).

RELATIONSHIPS AND SEXUALITY

The limited research that has been undertaken on the impact of an HIV status on sociality has suggested that sexuality is the most problematic issue for HIV-positive gay men. It also appears that this is the area in which individuals are least able to manage successfully (Katoff et al. 1991; PLWA (NSW) 1991b). Some of the richest material on this issue comes not from academic research, which remains obsessed with numbers of partners (see, for example, Meyer-Bahlburg et al. 1991) and infectivity (see, for example, Salzman 1991), but from community-based programs and writers (for example, Scott-Hartland 1991; Shernof 1991).

ACON's HIV Support Project, for instance, identified a number of issues linked to sexuality that positive people find most difficult. Loss of a "positive body image and sexual identity" accompanied the physical malformation of AIDS, rendering people shy about having sexual relations with others. The discrediting condition of actual illness negatively affects sexual identity and practice. The issue of whether people with compromised immune systems may be opening themselves to new infections through sexual activity is one on which there is not yet any scientific consensus, and yet many are said to deny themselves physical intimacy because of such fears or for fear of infecting others. This may be an intellectualization of a problem more immediately related to the disruption of sexual identity than to actual fear of infection. Finally, HIV-positive people often feel responsible for explaining safe-sex guidelines to potential partners. Individuals face inconsistencies in the guidelines that may render the processes of negotiating safe practice burdensome and be a disincentive to sex (Morgan 1990).

The decision to tell sexual partners of one's HIV status is problematized in the legal environment in New South Wales where informing a potential sexual partner is mandatory. In reality many people do not do this, particularly when partners are casual and anonymous as they may be for many gay men. Many, like Craig, have the attitude that if sex is safe according to the current guidelines then disclosing one's status is irrelevant. The issue of disclosing to a more regular partner is, however, more problematic and often raises fears of rejection or hurt. ACON's HIV Support Project research found a range of attitudes, from "I always tell my partners," to "I never tell," to "I only have sex with other positive men" (Morgan 1990).

In Chapter Three, Carl spoke about his loss of a lover through the unfortunate and rare situation of a false HIV-test result. This issue of relationships emerged in our discussion as a very problematic one in Carl's life. Of his HIV status he says, "It's the black mark against me in trying to get a relationship going. I think the fact that you are HIV-positive makes it the thing of needing or wanting love looming more largely in your mind than it would normally." I asked Carl why he felt this way, why it has become difficult for him to establish relationships:

> I need to feel love to counter the leper mentality, that I'm still a lovable person despite this. Because of that cut and run mentality of people when they find out, it highlights the fear of rejection, you know. I can go to the gym, I can go swimming, and body looks OK you know. Capable of having pretty good sex with someone. But you know I could win on all of those levels now. I'm an interesting person, good conversation, fun, all that sort of stuff. But there's that little hidden secret, skeleton in the closet sort of thing and not a damn thing you can do about it. It's always going to be there.

Carl does not think of himself as a "leper." It is the "mentality" of prospective partners that he is referring to. This is a spoiling of identity that he experiences through his relationships with others, not one which erupts from his own damaged psychology. Yet, the difficulty it presents reflects back on his own sense of self. He becomes a spoiled identity to himself through his perception of his own inability to counter the discrimination of others.

I met Frank through a community-based AIDS organization. When we spoke the following year, in 1989, his greatest interest was in a new relationship that he had established with another man. Previously he had been unable to find a partner because, he said, he felt undesirable. "I can't be of value because I won't be around that long." Frank described this lack of self-confidence as a product of the intense medical treatment he was having for an illness that was not HIV-related. The new relationship seemed to regenerate his sense of confidence and esteem:

> I've become sexual again! Earlier I said it was really easy to have a one day a week relationship, but he's lovely. But I think one of the reasons I don't want it to become any closer is because I am positive and therefore to allow him to get closer would become threatening. So I think everyday I've got to face the fact that I don't want people to get close to me. Actually I refused to get tested for a huge period of time for the two years prior to being told. I

was absolutely terrified about dragging on and becoming sicker and sicker. That isn't a fear I've got now. My major fear is that I actually stop people from getting close.

Positivity disrupts desire. Intimacy is problematized as the positive individual fears losing control of relationships. Keeping others at a distance is one means of sustaining normality, of preventing a possible stigmatizing situation.

On the other hand, as Frank's experience demonstrates, this fear may be unfounded and others may react in unpredictable ways. The stigmatized always anticipate the worst of possible reactions. Telling his new partner about his status actually cemented Frank's new relationship: "He'd said he'd never met anybody before who actually discussed with him, before they went to bed, that they were antibody-positive. He said that was really amazing. But the really bizarre thing was he said it's almost the reason I went to bed with you!"

This issue of sexuality is of particular importance to gay men because it is through sexuality that they realize their identity as distinct social beings and, by elaboration, realize their community as one cemented by this common issue of sexuality. The gay community, as d'Emilio (1983) referred to it, is essentially a "sexual community." The disruptions to sexual identity and practice that a diagnosis of HIV invokes marginalize many gay men from their gay community. One response is to seek companionship among other infected men through support groups, social events for positive people, and through organizations for the infected (see Hoff et al. 1992). This gradual collectivization of the infected works to strengthen their own sense of difference and thus to separate them further from gay community. Increasingly, as the years pass, positive gay men are heard both extolling and regretting this new division between the infected and the uninfected within the gay community. Most recently one hears of a new collectivity, the "HIV community." It is in such linguistic forms that we begin to detect a new mode of speaking which both reflects and helps to organize the experience of being HIV-positive.

SOCIAL NETWORKS

Unless an individual is already linked into the formal networks of HIV-positive people that have been built up around AIDS organizations, the first networks that will be affected by a diagnosis of HIV, and that an individual will in turn seek support from, are those of friends and family. Because of the stigma attached to homosexuality in Australian society, most

gay men have problematic relationships with their families. Cities, such as
Sydney and to a lesser extent Melbourne, function as centers of migration
for many men seeking to escape judgment and rejection by family, for the
anonymity of modern urban life, and for immersion in gay community.
There they are able to link into networks of other gay men, also often mi-
grants themselves, through entertainment venues such as bars and clubs,
events like Mardi Gras, social and sporting groups, and through personal
matching services provided in gay newspapers and magazines. These networks, rather than kin-based ones, form the main social milieu for gay
men. A diagnosis of HIV positivity can function both to threaten such networks and to strengthen them.

FAMILY

I will consider two examples to illustrate the problematic nature of family
relationships that gay men experience and the implications of HIV for
such relationships.

Ken is a gay man who was living in Melbourne at the time we spoke.
His story evokes the interplay of sexuality and illness that AIDS presents,
creating complex and challenging difficulties for those concerned. Ken
has separated from his wife, who mothered his daughter, and now lives
with his male lover. Diagnosed with HIV in 1985, he reflects on the difficulties he has in revealing his status to his family:

> One of the things is sharing the whole situation with my family, and you
> deal with that. And I'm getting a very positive response lately. One was on
> my birthday just a week or so ago. 'Cause I come from a family of seven
> adopted kids. And I was sort of sharing it with my natural mother who I'd
> met in 1976 and am very close to, and she knew something was wrong
> through my adopted mum. But mum hadn't directly told her, and 'cause she
> kept writing asking me what was going on and I just said its a blood disor-
> der. And she rung me on my birthday and insisted me on telling her what
> was the problem. And she was very determined. She wasn't going to hang
> up or allow me to hang up until I told her. So finally I told her and I think
> that's been the most significant thing to date in relation to the virus. And so
> the next day I sat down and wrote her. I think it was a five page foolscap let-
> ter, in great detail about the virus etcetera, and just said that if she wanted
> me to keep in touch and she wanted literature etcetera.
>
> The other thing that I've confronted is I've got a daughter who will be
> fifteen this year. I don't know if she knows I'm gay. I think she does know.
> She knows there's something wrong but I haven't told her. Her mother's ter-
> rified that she's going to find out that I've got the virus and that's something

that I've got to deal with. The dilemma that I've got there is that if something does go wrong and I get sick, that she may be hurt that I haven't told her before then and there. How do you deal with that situation? It's something I've got to work through.

Basically with my daughter it's fear of rejection in some ways. I don't think she will reject me but the problem is that there's been this ongoing battle since the separation of myself and my ex-wife, of some sort of blame or hatred from her point of view. The sad part about it, in my view, the marriage shouldn't have happened because I was never in love with my wife, and I loved her as a person. We grew up as kids. She's still got a lot of criticism and hatred towards me in her own way 'cause she's still unfortunately or fortunately in love with me, and cannot accept my sexuality.

The management of disclosure is mediated by one's relations to others. Ken's mother sought the information about his status, pressuring him into telling her something he might not otherwise have. By contrast, he is prevented from disclosing his status to his daughter because of pressures from her mother, pressures which, we learn, are related to the issue of Ken's sexuality.

Ken's story illustrates the kind of complexities involved in managing information about the self. In one case his fear of discredit prevented him from disclosing. On the other, his desire to disclose was prevented by the intervention of a third party. The situation precipitates a restructuring of relations between family members. Often the news that a son, partner, or father is HIV-positive may work to distance individuals from each other. Or they may work to bring people closer, as the next example illustrates.

Steven was a young gay man in his early thirties who had recently migrated to Sydney from a smaller city in another state in order live in a gay community. It was here, at this late stage of his life, that he formed a strong sense of gay identity. Prior to living in Sydney he only thought of himself as a homosexual, or "camp," and had no experience with gay organizations or of organized gay political activity.

Soon after arriving in Sydney he established himself within a wide circle of gay friends, joined a gay political group, and occasionally helped out in AIDS organizations. It was at this time, too, that he first tested positive to HIV (although he reasoned that he had probably been infected many years before this). Only twelve months later Steven presented at a hospital with a mild case of PCP and was diagnosed with AIDS. Steven's experience as an infected man has, therefore, been mostly one of managing a discrediting condition.

Because Steven had not led a particularly "promiscuous" life and could count his lovers on two hands, he found his diagnosis perplexing and expressed some resentment about it. "Why did I get it?" he asked himself on one occasion. "I haven't been promiscuous." Gay men themselves sometimes incorporate, in this manner, the public discursive construction of AIDS as a disease of the sexually adventurous. Gay men with much wider sexual experience are often more able to dismiss these moral constructions of AIDS, rejecting the notion of a positive status as something deserved, considering it of little moral significance, or even an inevitable outcome of their past behavior.

On Steven's second admission to hospital later that year, at a time when his health had deteriorated quite significantly, the issue of informing his parents of his condition arose. While in hospital, Steven drafted several letters in which he told them that he was gay, and that he was HIV-positive and experiencing HIV-related ill health. Though neither issue had been raised openly with them before, he reasoned that his parents knew of his homosexuality by default because of his previous long-term relationship with a man.

Steven failed to complete any of these letters to his satisfaction and it remained for friends to telephone his parents and suggest they come to Sydney to visit Steven in hospital. His mother came immediately. On arrival she told me she had considered, having been told that Steven was unwell, the possibility that he had AIDS, but was hoping this was not the case. Before seeing Steven she was counseled by Steven's gay friends and by the social workers at the hospital. She was informed that her son had AIDS, that he would probably recover from this present illness, but would suffer fragile health and need intensive medical treatment for the rest of his life.

She was clearly shocked and distressed by this news and yet spent the next week with her son at his bedside, comforting him, remembering old times with him, and discussing his condition. What I found most extraordinary about this episode was the fact that his mother found the issue of Steven's homosexuality more distressing than the fact of his illness. In conversation she continually returned to this issue, pondering why her son was gay, whether she herself was in any way responsible for it, yet assuring me that she had always known of his homosexuality. "It was just something we never discussed in the family." I found myself constantly reminding her that Steven was not in hospital because of his homosexuality, but because he had AIDS.

This dilemma HIV presents for the families of many gay men is so common that it has been given the appellation "the doublé whammy" by AIDS social workers. Homosexuality and AIDS are inextricably interwoven in the public discourses of AIDS and thus also in many people's minds. In reality, this linkage is experienced in a very immediate sense for the first time by families who learn a son, or brother, or father has AIDS.

Steven, like many young gay men, found it difficult to tell his family that he had AIDS. Supportive friends initiated this disclosure. Yet, to Steven's own surprise and delight, he received renewed strength and support from a family whom he felt had previously been judgmental and rejecting of his sexuality. To the time of his death two years later, Steven's family were frequently with him, providing both emotional and physical comfort through a protracted and difficult illness that ended his life. We will meet Steven again in Chapters Five and Seven.

For some gay men a diagnosis with HIV presents the opportunity to restructure relationships with family. This is a difficult task, given the stigma that homosexuality carries. Many gay men choose not to confront their families with their sexuality and are able to distance themselves from them by moving to gay communities like those in Sydney and Melbourne. This distancing becomes reworked as a result of the new and serious problems that arise from a diagnosis of HIV infection. No matter how much distance gay men may have positioned between themselves and their families, the anticipation or the actual experience of illness forces many to reestablish kinship links. Because of the inextricable connection between homosexuality and AIDS in the public discourse, a disclosure of HIV status invariably raises the question of an individual's homosexuality. In Steven's case, above, this issue was resolved to some extent by the more immediate concerns raised by ill health. In the other, Ken's, homosexuality remained a source of conflict between family members, preventing individuals from dealing with the sometimes more demanding issues that HIV infection raises.

FRIENDS

Walter, as noted earlier, considers his wide circle of friends and colleagues of central importance in his life. At the top of his list of significant people is his lover who is also positive. While the fact that both of them are positive and the possibility that either of them might become sick is a source of anxiety for him, Walter reasons that a positive lover is more sensitive to the issues he faces as an infected man. He actively maintains and widens his networks by inviting old and new acquaintances to his frequent dinner parties, dedicates time to keeping in touch with friends who have moved out of town, and endeavors to meet new people at every opportunity. Walter reflects on the importance of his involvement in gay and AIDS groups:

I think that that involvement also gives me support as well. I mean I've got lots of people I can turn to for support at times when I do get really down. There's people I can talk to. I don't have to worry about that.

Probably the main support would come from the friends that I've developed, mainly personal friends and through the gay organizations I'm involved with. I don't think that I've got a lot of friends who are totally involved in the AIDS industry. OK, I count you as a friend now. And I've got a few people down at ACON, well I mean there's a lot of people that I know, but there's no real closeness. So to that extent most of the people I'm close to, while they're involved in Community Support and things like that, are not really heavily involved in AIDS. I'm not saying I've gone out of my way to avoid it. It's just that at my age I've developed a fairly wide circle of friends and I work to keep those friendships and its a matter of sustaining those.

Walter is very open about his status, frequently speaking in public and to the media about his infection. He is the closest example in the account so far of Goffman's professional, a "native leader" (Goffman 1963:40). This public openness is rare in terms of the overall numbers of people with HIV in Sydney or Australia. Being HIV-positive is, for Walter, now an integral part of his gay identity. His is a privileged position in so far as his wide supportive network, together with a long history of gay activism, has allowed him to deploy the "coming out" strategy, devised in gay politics, for his new condition of HIV infection. His HIV status has restructured his identity as an AIDS activist geared to this public confessional.

For others, the issue of disclosure of status is far more problematic. Oliver is heavily involved in caring for people with AIDS through the gay community HIV/AIDS care organization, Community Support Network (CSN). He described his caution and selectivity in telling others about his own status:

Six, nine months ago I had started to have lots and lots of problems coping with being HIV-positive. And in the ensuing weeks of my lover being here, he came here, there was something that happened between us, in the support we gave and got from each other. Being HIV has allowed me and encouraged me to talk to a lot more people. It made me realize I need the support of people. And I couldn't get the support from people until they knew what they were supporting. And I've been able to talk to them. And it has been a catalyst for that. It's just the way we interact, because the support we give to each other was mind blowing. But it was what I wanted from the relationship.

Jim's the only one I can't talk to. I can talk to all the others, all the others that are significant. I can't talk to Jim. I don't know why. Even people from CSN. People I've known for eighteen years. But I can't talk to Jim. I mean there's other people I won't talk to because it's none of their business, primarily because they don't, won't, can't offer any support anyhow.

When I was in hospital eighteen months ago, I said, "Christ, now I know what its like to be on the receiving end of CSN for ten days." I was flooded in the house with people. I didn't tell anyone then 'cause I didn't want anyone to fuss. I wasn't crook [unwell]. I'm not crook now. But it's just come about that for two years I chose to ignore it, not deny it but ignore it, fine line between the two, I think. I don't need a catalyst any more. The support's still there if I need it.

Selective disclosure restricts the range of possible social networks sensitive to the issue of one's positivity. Because of his privileged position working in a relatively supportive and educated institution, and having a wide circle of friends connected to the issue of AIDS, Walter has been able to inform all his social relationships about his antibody status. Oliver's social support networks are more problematic, less responsive to his particular predicament. Oliver continues to experience discredit because he has been unable to disclose his status fully. This is, in fact, much more the normal experience for people with HIV.

SUPPORT GROUPS

So far I have considered how people with HIV manage information about their situation in relation to those Goffman terms "normals," in this case the uninfected. In this section I begin to consider the issue of collectivization among the HIV-infected. Relations between HIV-positive individuals are qualitatively different from those between positive and negative persons. Goffman recognized these distinct forms of interaction, with normals and with peers, as critical in shaping both the "personal identity" of the stigmatized, the sense of the self, and the "social identity," the self as defined by others. He also situated this sociality within a key sociological theme: "The nature of an individual, as he himself and we impute it to him, is generated by the nature of his group affiliations" (Goffman 1963:138). By beginning to associate with other infected individuals, the HIV-positive gay man learns a new meaning to being HIV infected. As Goffman notes, "in-group" alignments teach the individual to begin to conceptualize his predicament as normal, as shared by others, and to see this alignment as more "natural" than any form of alignment to "normals" (Goffman 1963:137).

For HIV-positive gay men, collectivization became possible through the establishment of support groups, much like those for many other stigmatizing conditions (for discussions of group processes with people with HIV/AIDS see Gambe and Getzel 1989; Getzel and Mahony 1990). Toward the end of the 1980s in Sydney, and to a lesser extent in other major Australian cities, formal support groups for HIV-positive people were beginning to be offered by local AIDS councils. Prior to this, attempts had been made by positive men in Sydney to run groups of various kinds. One, Body Positive, was established by a small group of positive men in the mid-1980s through ACON, and met regularly on the top floor of a gay bar in an inner-city neighborhood. Neil recalls his involvement with that group of men:

> We were involved with the group in the early stages and it really helped to know that we weren't alone. That was the major thing I got from the group, was knowing it's not just happening to me, that there are other people around. The discussion groups and the support and just generally talking, finding out more what was happening, was a great help. And also reading as much as we can, the scientific stuff and all that sort of thing. But the group helped a lot. I don't feel the need for any groups at the moment because I'm not in a position to give much support really to other people who are freaking out at the moment.
>
> It was the antibody positive group which eventually folded because of the usual sort of political hassles, but I think the people living with AIDS group has sort of taken over that role now from what I can gather. And we organized things like dances and things for fundraising. That was really good to be involved with that. But as far as professional help, counseling or anything like that, that just hasn't been needed.

For Neil, the group provided an opportunity to normalize his predicament through association with like others. The stigma associated with having HIV is neutralized in the peer group context as the stigmatic condition immediately becomes the norm. Many positive men lament the fact that they still feel different and stigmatized among other gay men. As positive men collectivize, negative gay men are increasingly constructed as "normals," albeit sympathetic or "wise" ones, to use Goffman's term (1963:41). Interestingly, we may note that Neil felt this form of association was a more effective means of managing his predicament than speaking to professionals. Forms of professional help were available to positive people in Sydney before 1989, typically from social workers or counselors providing only a sympathetic ear or lending advice or referral. Only a collectivity of like others, however, can provide the environment necessary for a long term reconstruction of self necessary for the successful management of spoiled identity.

Body Positive's activities were sporadic and short lived. Alternatively, those seeking support through organized groups initially had to rely on groups run from hospitals and clinics. In mid-1989, however, support groups based on a peer education model began to be offered, again through

ACON: HIV-positive gay men loosely facilitating groups for other HIV-positive gay men. At first, these groups were not widely attended and appeared to service a relatively small number of individuals. Carl, for instance, found the groups were unsuitable for him. He explains why:

> I've joined a few groups who are HIV-positive, discussed things through and all that sort of stuff. But I must admit some of the guys that were in that group — they were working at ACON and, I don't know, seemed to give their life a purpose which they didn't have in their life before. I mean I think they would be lost without their HIV status. They're in sort of clerical jobs with no goals in life and the HIV status has given them something to do. They almost need it to give themselves a goal in life. Well, I have my goals worked out and this has gotten in the way of it. So I feel I didn't have a lot in common with that group.

What Carl recognized in the group was a domination of professionals. It was indeed "career positives" who established and populated the first groups. The distance between their identities as professional positives and Carl's spoiled identity prevented a constructive association between them. For Carl, the group failed to be relevant because he was unwilling to reposition HIV as central in his life, as a reason to restructure his identity in the fashion of others in the group. For him, HIV remained an intrusion, a barrier to the continuation of life in its normal trajectory. Meanwhile, for the others, especially those "working at ACON," HIV provided an opportunity to reconstruct their identity and lives.

More recently the popularity of formal HIV support groups has greatly increased. At the time of writing several hundred individuals had participated in groups, several of which run each week. Two changes are identifiable. First, the nature of group participation has changed. It is less likely, as group participation increases, that groups will be dominated by career positives. A participant is more likely to find others in the group who share his precise predicament. Second, after four years of project activity, the training of up to forty group facilitators, and the participation of many hundreds of men, the collective HIV experience in Sydney is itself changing. The groups have become self-perpetuating, with individuals sustaining relationships beyond the formal group setting, participants getting together outside formal meetings and, more recently, in larger social gatherings of up to several hundred. By the early 1990s, HIV support was beginning to generate a wider presence in the Sydney gay community beyond the networks of positive people themselves. Its very existence as an ongoing project with broadening social functions served to reduce the invisibility of positive gay men and influence attitudes toward the HIV-infected.

Some gay men revealed their thoughts about group activities in a discussion circle organized by the project. From their comments we get a sense of how the group environment provides the context in which specific issues for positive gay men can be recognized, broached, and used to establish a new collective identity. Peter says:

> I wanted to connect more with other positive men to relieve some of the isolation that I think we often feel. I also wanted to regain sexual power and I felt a group where we talked about sexual issues would help me do that.
>
> Our group was diverse too, but even though there were all different backgrounds by the end of it there's a sense that you have a peer identity and that's good. It's great at times when you feel in a degenerate [sic] state and life has no meaning, to have people who can help you get out of that state and into something more meaningful. People can make changes inside themselves (PLWA (NSW) 1991a:9).

For Peter, the groups were an opportunity to meet others who shared his status and to discuss HIV as a critical new feature in his life. But the group process does more than provide a "safe space" for individuals to speak their mind. The space itself generates new social relations and a new language in which to communicate. Peter has become a proficient speaker of this HIV language, with his references to "power," "diversity," and "peer identity". The result is a reconstructed sociality organized around others who are HIV-positive, sometimes extending beyond the formal boundaries of the peer group.

Kim elaborates on the new networks emerging from such groups: "We all formed various friendships with each other. We all feel rather protective of each other now, I think. I certainly do" (PLWA (NSW) 1991a:8). Having found the friendship he was looking for, Kim plans to extend his involvement by becoming a group facilitator, an individual who directs, while himself participating in the discussions within the group. "I'm certainly satisfied for the time being. I'm now doing the facilitators course because I want to be involved and help other people — to give some support back really" (PLWA (NSW) 1991a:9).

It is through the recruitment of group facilitators that the networks emerging from the project perpetuate and expand themselves. Participating individuals are themselves recruited into the peer support system, becoming facilitators in the structure. As facilitators they take on a kind of "healer" role to others. The process thereby transforms an individual's social identity from one of client to, in our cultural terminology, care provider. By restructuring the sociality of participants through relation to a new community of like others, a healing process is actualized. Individuals "healed" by the process are able themselves to take on a role of helper to others who are in the situation they have recently emerged from. Healing is itself a social process realized in the context of social relationships.

HIV support groups thus function in a way reminiscent of therapeutic processes observed by anthropologists in the healing arts of many non-industrial cultures. Finkler, for example, recorded how faith-healing cults in Mexico empowered individuals by transforming their social identities by recruiting the afflicted into the ranks of the healers. "Temple healers and other adherents form a community of individuals who have succeeded in changing the sick role into a publicly acknowledged health providing one" (Finkler 1986:631). She postulates that, phenomenologically, participation in spiritualist healing generates a sense of well-being, in addition to shielding participants from social distinctions extant in class structures, distinctions that have consequences for self image and identity.

This conclusion is compatible with statements by some people with AIDS. "Long-term survivor" Michael Callen, for example, claimed that it was political activism more than anything else that contributed to his surviving AIDS (Callen 1991). It also provides an early hypothesis as to why a number of HIV-positive individuals believe that becoming involved in AIDS support, education, and political action groups is an important step in coming to terms with their own HIV infection. And like Finkler's observation that socioeconomic circumstances render some individuals more disposed to seek out spiritualist healing as a career, collectivization among gay men with HIV is structured by conditions of identity and class (Ariss et al. 1992).

Before pursuing this issue further, however, it is necessary to consider other issues that a arise from a diagnosis of HIV or AIDS. In the next two chapters I will explore the dialogic relationships people with HIV and AIDS develop between medical science and alternative modalities of healing. Through a discussion of these relations I seek to illustrate further the new and developing discursive forms that allow the HIV-infected to reflect upon and render meaningful this new predicament of AIDS.

CHAPTER 5

In Dialogue with Doctors:
Aspects of a Medical "Creole"

T-CELL TALK

Colin was in his early thirties and had been diagnosed with AIDS for several years at the time we spoke about his experiences with medicine and doctors. He had been involved in community AIDS organizations since the epidemic began in Australia, and as a result was regularly exposed to a wide range of information and opinions about medical issues. He spoke of how information about therapeutic developments in AIDS, which he accesses through the gay and mainstream press and his own readings of scientific journals, causes him anxiety:

> There seems to be a lot of negative things coming out from research. Six months ago I felt there's all possibilities of getting over this and surviving it, and now I think it's more, it's really an extension rather than totally resolving the AIDS problem. It seems that that's what's come out of the research lately. It's a bit of a shock really.

Colin sees difficulties arising for him, as well as for AIDS educators, in the rapidly changing views about AIDS treatments. One day news gives him reason to be optimistic; the next conflicting information raises his concern about the efficacy of the treatments he takes and possible future drug developments.

In this environment of rapidly changing and often contradictory information, Colin tries to resolve his fears and uncertainties about his own health and mortality by seeking a better understanding of medical information about AIDS treatment research:

> Some of it took a while for me to wade through. I still can't understand some of it. And then work through the mental effect it's had on me. I mean, I still

read those articles even though I've read them once or twice before, to understand clearly.

I ask him if it is difficult for him to understand the information:

> Oh yeah. But I'm determined to do it. I sit there with an encyclopedia and a medical dictionary and just work my way through it. I might skim through some of it one week and then another attempt to read it again. It's like I remember when I was at school, when you're young you learnt things really slowly, and you learnt paragraph by paragraph, you understand it. It takes a long time to sink in.

Speaking to medical practitioners and researchers is often of little value, says Colin, because they do not speak a language he understands:

> I thought it would be better to go and talk to someone who I knew had studied it, but that didn't help at all because they don't speak the same language. It's probably better to get together with people who have a similar understanding to me and work through it with other people. Or just trying to get it rewritten in another way. I asked people around ACON before to scribble out something in a language I can understand, which helped a bit.

For Colin, the uncertainty accompanying AIDS is in part a product of his reading of scientific literature on therapeutic developments. To be able to read and interpret this discourse, Colin subjects himself to a regimen of self-education in the language of medical science. In reading science, Colin is seeking certainty, the certainty that science promises through the discourse of progress. Rather than finding certainty, however, he only finds uncertainty and anxiety.

Colin's experience introduces the phenomenon to be explored in this chapter: the dialogic relation between patients and medicine. In characterizing this relation as dialogic I am suggesting two things. One, that the relation is essentially a linguistic one. As bearers of a specialized knowledge and practice, physicians must communicate their intention (diagnosis and prescription) to patients who, ordinarily, do not share the language of their science. Patients, on the other hand, must initiate the therapeutic interaction by communicating to the physician their bodily experience of symptoms. The physician offers an interpretation of the symptoms and conveys that interpretation in a form that represents a compromise between technical medical discourse and the language of the patient. But this interaction is not simply one whereby the physician modifies the language of medicine into a lay discourse comprehensible to the ignorant patient. As Colin's story illustrates, in the situation of AIDS at least, patients make some effort to meet their physicians on their own linguistic terms. This is the second intention of the term dialogic:

the interaction between patient and doctor is linguistically dynamic and it provokes a novel, negotiated language in the context of the differentials between the interlocutors. What I want to explore in this chapter, then, are aspects of this medical "creole."

Narratives that explore patient encounters with physicians, clinical scientists, and the apparatus of experimental science reveal an emerging linguistic form which is enabling people with HIV and AIDS to speak about a new predicament in ways that are meaningful, both personally and collectively. This "creole" seeks to render scientific information intelligible at a phenomenological level. Medical anthropologists have observed this process — the teleological reconstruction in the narratives of patients — in a number of settings (Calnan 1984; Charmaz 1983; Comaroff and Maguire 1981; Saillant 1990; Williams 1984). Moving beyond this notion of linguistic self-reconstruction, I detect an emerging social critique in these narratives which, when systematized through collective organizing, enabled gay men with HIV and AIDS to challenge the methods of AIDS clinical science and its supporting bureaucracy.

This brings me to the question of the efficacy of resistance to hegemonic discourses and practices. If medical science is, as Patton (1990) has argued, a master discourse, to what extent is it possible to resist its incursions: its interpretations, prescriptions, and surveillances? The rapid change in medical information about HIV and AIDS, the resultant high level of debate and disagreement within the medical profession, and the relatively limited success of AIDS clinical research to develop effective therapy for HIV infection generate an environment conducive to patient skepticism and dissent. This skepticism rests within a wider environment in which, over recent decades, medical science has lost some of its pervasive prestige (Bates and Lapsley 1985; Jennett 1984). Into this legitimacy crisis comes a patient population of middle-class gay men who have achieved a high medical literacy rate and level of self-organization. When we compare this group with other patient populations (see, for example, Saillant 1990; Balshem 1991), the discrepancy between the language of medicine and that of patients is significantly reduced. This raises interesting questions as to the form and extent of the challenge gay men present to medical science. To what extent are we witnessing the production of a genuine counter-discourse? And to what extent is this discursive closure a symptom of a progressive capturing of the patient by medical science?

From the moment of receiving a diagnosis of HIV infection or AIDS, the individual enters into a discursive relationship with medical science. The HIV-antibody test is couched in a discourse that signifies particular meanings about life and death. The role of the counselor or medical practitioner is important here, as medical discourse is not readily comprehensible to the uninitiated. Such professionals translate technical language into information meaningful to the patient. Thus, in an ideal interaction upon receiving a diagnosis of HIV, a counselor will explain that being HIV-positive means one has the virus, HIV, in one's blood; that this is different from having AIDS, which is a state of serious immune suppression caused by the action of the virus; that the virus may not affect on the immune system for up to ten or fifteen years; that it is necessary for the client to take action not to pass the virus on to others (that is, to practice safe sex and safe needle use).

But this is more than a simple process of translation from specialist to lay language. It involves the active construction of meanings that bear implications for the manner in which one will thereafter understand one's self and one's relations to others. As Mechanic pointed out nearly twenty years ago: "The manner in which symptoms are defined and the meanings attributed to them have a pervasive effect in many instances on the conditions of the patient and the physical, psychological, and social deterioration evident" (Mechanic 1974:119). What Mechanic is alluding to here is the power of medical discourse not only to define a physical condition, to "diagnose," but to set the parameters in which that condition is experienced. This is a hypothesis that medical science rejects, regarding language as a descriptive tool through which physical phenomena are progressively understood in more detail and accuracy. By contrast I am arguing that medical discourse is formative. The power of language lies in its ability to invent the world, not simply in reflecting it.

The sociology of medicine suggests that unequal relations of power are maintained in the doctor/patient interaction through the manipulation of technical scientific language. From this position Waitzkin argued that the medical education of patients could be the first step in the demystification of medical ideology, transforming doctor/patient relations into more equal transactions in which patients may assume greater responsibility for their own health management. Sharing the symbolic system of biomedical language — its technical jargon, labels of therapies, and associated ideologies of treatment — empowers the patient and reduces dependency on and vulnerability to expertise (Waitzkin 1979). This is precisely the strategy gay men with HIV have deployed in negotiating medicine.

Justin provides an example of how a medically literate patient may feel confident to contradict a medical prescription. Justin began AZT treatment shortly after his diagnosis of AIDS. He gained access to the drug through an "open access" trial being conducted at a major research hospital, and was put on a regimen of 800 milligrams per day. He experienced severe headaches one week after beginning this treatment and expressed his concern about these to the hospital researchers. They advised him to "stick with it and persevere." Justin considered reducing his dosage and, after consulting and gaining approval from his personal physician, also a gay man, reduced the dosage to 400 milligrams per day for a few months. He then increased the dose to 600 milligrams after his body "got used to the drug."

He tells of the reaction of the researchers at the hospital to this decision. "They weren't very happy with it. But I'm well educated, I can speak to them in their own language. I'm not easily intimidated. You need to inform yourself as much as possible because they won't tell you." Through the acquisition of some level of medical literacy, Justin felt able to question the advice of the medical staff administering the trial and to choose an alternative course of action.

It is significant that Justin sought confirmation for his action through his own gay medical practitioner. This action reveals a division within the medical profession itself. General medical practitioners, particularly gay doctors with large clienteles of HIV-positive gay men, are structurally situated between patients and hospital-based AIDS researchers. General practitioners feel closer to community-based AIDS efforts and frequently lobby, with activists, for changes to research protocols. For example, in the campaign to gain approval for the early use of AZT, general practitioners formed an alliance with activists because wider access for patients was in their own professional interests. Approval allowed them to prescribe the drug, thereby granting them greater authority over their patients' medical regimens. At the same time, the move released many patients from the hospital drug-trial system.

We may continue to ask, however, to what extent is medical literacy a sound basis for launching a sustainable critique of medical hegemony? I return to Colin's story to illustrate the limitations of this "empowerment" strategy. While Colin may have been in a better position to ask questions of his doctor or even make suggestions of his own about appropriate treatment dosage, the structural limitations of such patient initiatives were clearly illustrated in an incident which Colin interpreted as a clear case of discrimination against him, and which occurred approximately one year after we discussed his efforts to familiarize himself with medical language. At 3.30 pm appointment for surgery was delayed to the end of the day because, he was told, staff did not want to risk contamination of the surgery facilities. Colin wanted to take action against the hospital for this incident but felt constrained because of a fear of future reprisals. He explains:

I really thought, well I should have done something then but I was really annoyed. And you really do get paranoid about, okay if I'm nasty to them and haul them through the courts or haul them through the newspapers, then each time I go in there and my name's getting close to the list for ddI[1], or close to the top for something else, you never know, they could shove it to the bottom.

Colin reported the incident to ACON which had, by that time, begun to keep a list of such occurrences with a view to a future challenge to the hospital in question, and for putting a case for legal protection for people with AIDS to the New South Wales State Anti-Discrimination Board. Meanwhile, because of his fear of being denied future therapy, Colin's grievance was not addressed in the short term.

While there are various forms of legal redress for problems such as Colin's, including lodging complaints with the Complaints Unit of the New South Wales State Department of Health, such avenues are underutilized. One reason is that complainants are frequently unprepared to wait the length of time it takes to receive any form of redress. Some complaints have been known to take years to be addressed, and then sometimes with nothing more than a letter of acknowledgment. Colin discarded this route of redress himself because he felt he had no significant evidence on which to ground a complaint.

Legal redress remains, therefore, of limited use to patients experiencing difficulties and disagreements with the medical system. While it is the state's function to ensure medical practice is efficient and equitable, and while it has sought to achieve some influence over medicine through legal and bureaucratic procedures, available redress remains largely inadequate in influencing medical practice. This is so much so that some patients are more likely to be seek a resolution of their grievances at more immediate, tactical levels of everyday practice through, for example, vocal protest, defiance of prescription, or, if the individual is sufficiently skilled, negotiation. Part Three pursues in detail more strategic forms of protest: patient collectivization and politicization. At this stage it is sufficient to consider the limitations of empowerment through self-education. In the pursuit of knowledge, the patient-subject initiates a program of self-education in the discourse of medicine. The subject has been redefined as a "patient" through diagnosis, and that new subjectivity is then continually renovated via the language of the master discourse of medicine: its symbols, grammar and lexicon, its ideologies and world views.

While Colin's acquisition of medical language gives him a greater sense of mastery over his predicament, it also serves medicine by enhancing the capture of a new "patient" subject. Patient subjects become collaborators in medical surveillance and control, shifting into regimens of self-management. This Foucault-like scenario suggests, in its extreme interpretation, the ultimate futility of patient resistance. The patient cannot escape biomedicine because that clinical subject is defined by the very discourse under question. On the contrary, in seeking to understand it he is more thoroughly encircled, penetrated by it, "managed." The patient can only hope to improve the efficacy of medicine and thereby its very authority. But I want to argue that this does not necessarily negate the possibility of patient creativity and transgression. As de Certeau (1984) notes, we have all become consumers within a socioeconomic order that is outside of ourselves and produced on our behalf. However, from within that order individuals and groups may manipulate given languages for their own interests, deflecting power even if they may never completely escape it.

SYSTEMATIZING A MEDICAL CREOLE

AIDS was not the first medical crisis faced by Sydney's gay community. Gay men living in the inner city had recourse to a medical apparatus in the early 1980s when herpes and other sexually transmitted diseases became prevalent among the sexually active. A team of mostly gay doctors seeking to specialize in venereology established a private clinic within the gay precinct of the city, catering primarily to gay men and sex workers. It was that clinic which saw the first cases of AIDS and HIV infection after several years of operation. It has now become the largest private practice dealing with HIV infection in Australia, its physicians developing considerable skill, expertise, and reputation.

The first news of AIDS reached gay Sydney via the gay media. A fortnightly newspaper distributed in Sydney's gay bars, *The Star* (later *Sydney Star Observer*), published a short article on "a new type of pneumonia . . . found in five young men" in the United States in July 1981. There continued to be sporadic reports of this new disease in the local Sydney gay press until April 1983 when the national gay magazine, *Campaign*, featured a lengthy article on AIDS reporting the first Australian case of the disease (Galbraith 1992). The breadth and complexity of the coverage on AIDS in the local and national gay press increased exponentially in the coming years, providing many gay men with their primary source of information on the disease (Kippax et al. 1993).

Information in the general media, on the other hand, remained extremely sporadic, inconsistent, and sensationalized. In a survey of gay men in Sydney in 1986, most ranked the gay media as far more reliable and accurate than the "straight press" (Kippax et al. 1993). In 1988, shortly after AZT (the first antiviral for AIDS) became available in Australia, this gay media reportage began to become more specialized. To this time, information about transmission and safe-sex practices appeared with far greater frequency than treatment issues. As a result of the activities of a number of people with AIDS in Sydney, attempts began to be made to systematize the further reporting of treatment developments. This was not a simple process of replicating medical information as it became available, however, but constituted a discourse that was interpretive, critical, and bore highly political implications.

Terry Bell, a gay man with AIDS long active in gay politics, established his own treatment information and advocacy newsletter, *AIDS Advocate*, in late 1988. A vocal and active campaigner for people with AIDS, Bell ran his newsletter from his apartment in Darlinghurst, and funded the project himself, despite attempts to gain government assistance. Bell also made a considerable contribution to the *Sydney Star Observer*, sitting on its board of management during this period, and writing many reports on AIDS treatment developments. Assisted by electronic communications links to AIDS-treatment information sources and organizations in the United States, Bell reproduced and wrote articles on AIDS-treatment developments for a local audience. Each issue of *AIDS Advocate* contained an editorial conveying critical interpretations of developments; one, for example, critical of media "magic bullet stories" and drug company profit motives (*AIDS Advocate*, May 1989). In another, Bell spelled out a philosophy for patient participation in medical practice:

> From our medical practitioners, particularly those who are our primary heath care providers, we should expect the best care and advice possible. In this too, we the infected have a role to play. By educating ourselves about the available treatments and options we can help educate our doctors, so that together we can devise the treatment strategy which is best tailored to the needs of each individual (*AIDS Advocate* July 1989:3)

Here Bell was advocating a philosophy of empowerment then being actively promoted by community-based AIDS groups in the United States (see, for example, James 1989). It was quickly to become the standard rhetoric of AIDS activists in Australia also.

At approximately the same time, the newly formed organization People Living with AIDS Incorporated, New South Wales, or PLWA (NSW), established its bimonthly newsletter *Talkabout*. Treatment information was to appear regularly, and the first issue featured a lengthy article from Peter on his eighteen-month experience with AZT. This is one of the first instances in Australia of a printed account of the use of a therapy for AIDS from a personal perspective. Peter describes his experience in a language that oscillates between reference to technical terms: such as T-cells, placebo controlled studies, "pulsed therapy," transfusions, and chemotherapy, and a highly personal account of his feelings and responses to the medical regimen. In this way Peter is able to provide advice to readers based on his personal experience of the drug in a language that seeks legitimacy through the deployment of technical jargon:

> Although AZT has side effects, they are not as bad as dying from the lack of it. Your AIDS specialist will closely monitor your response to the drug. Most people don't have too many troubles with AZT. The earlier you take it after your T4-count falls under 200 the less side effects, and the greater the extension to, and the quality of life.

Peter sums up his experience with the drug:

> The last three years haven't been entirely without anxious moments but I have enjoyed the extra time that AZT has bought me very much. I feel that AZT robs me of some of my previous energy but if I didn't take it I am quite sure I would not be alive today. I have never been brave enough to ask a doctor, "How long do I have to live?" It is a silly question because doctors don't have crystal balls! (PLWA (NSW) 1988).

After considering both side effects and the longevity it has provided him, Peter's assessment of AZT is a positive one.

Developments in treatment science were quickening at this time and there was a concomitant increase in the demand for information that *AIDS Advocate* and *Talkabout* could not adequately meet. In response, the Australian Federation of AIDS Organisations (AFAO), the national umbrella body for the country's community-based state AIDS councils, initiated a new Treatment Information Project aimed to provide updated information on treatment developments in a form and language easily comprehensible to people with HIV/AIDS. Through federal government funding, the project was able to produce treatment information in a more regular and systematic manner for national distribution. The Treatment Information Project's periodical, *HIV Brief*, presented information about new drugs, like ddI and ddC, together with discussion of longer-standing issues, such as pain relief, in a language that, while not replacing medical terminology, used its technical style sparingly and explained the meanings of terms in a discursive, non-technical style.

The first *HIV Brief*, headed "Participating in drug trials" and published in October 1989, raised the need for infected individuals to consider obtaining new treatments through drug trials. It provided introductory information about the kinds of drugs being developed and encouraged individuals to "know your health status," that is, be tested and monitor viral activity, to "inform yourself," "weigh the benefits and risks," and to "consider your own needs/the needs of others." The orientation of the information sheet is thus toward encouraging individuals to take responsibility for treatment decisions. One does this by "actively seeking new information" and "using your initiative to inform yourself" by, for example, talking to doctors and friends, "asking questions," leading finally to "making an informed decision" (AFAO 1989a).

Medical sociologists such as Waitzkin (1979) and Calnan (1984) observed that the medical management of information effectively diffuses resistance to medical authority. In this instance we see the undermining of the monopoly of control over medical information, a transference of information from doctors into the hands of patients via a new class of community-based educators and self-made advocates. The likes of the Treatment Information Project could thus present something of a challenge to the medical management of scientific information. With alternative sources of information available, a patient's dependency on professional advice is reduced. It is not surprising, therefore, that some attempt was made by medical groups representing doctors to wrest government funding away from the Treatment Information Project for their own use. Doctors need educating about AIDS, they argued, more so than patients. This counter-challenge was defeated, however, and federal funding for the project continued.

While *HIV Brief* offered some assessment of new therapeutic developments, the treatment information provided attempted to be as neutral as possible; that is to say, it sought to translate information rather than interpret it. It thereby failed to critique the hegemony of medical knowledge in the way that Peter's narrative attempted. The removal of a phenomenological perspective functioned to align the AFAO project more closely to the discourse of medical science than earlier, more critical efforts. Thus, through the process of information systematization, an emerging critical patient discourse became quickly neutralized through its transformation into a medical "creole." This is a good example of Patton's characterization of the role of AIDS-service organizations as translators and legitimizers of scientific knowledge. She interprets the final effect of this to be the depoliticization of AIDS by rendering it a medical rather than a sociopolitical phenomenon. In so doing, individuals become increasingly dependent on scientific discourses at the expense of experience-based "folk traditions" (Patton 1990).

The development of this medical creole allowed for the more extensive penetration of medical discourse to the patient population. In such a case we would expect patients to express views consistent with the precepts of

science. Rex, who has had AIDS for two years, is a case in point. As a professional social worker, Rex has already been trained to some extent in the
medical paradigm. It is not altogether surprising, then, that he largely
agrees with the conventional practices of AIDS researchers. Since he was
diagnosed HIV-positive three years ago, he has experienced numerous
AIDS research regimens, including the use of AZT, and has participated in
trials for opportunistic infection treatment. In discussing his experiences
of such trials, Rex revealed a qualified adherence to medical precepts. "As
a scientist I agree with the use of placebos," he says. "It's common for
people to make emotional judgments instead of scientific judgments about
these things. For example they experience a side-effect and go around
screaming, 'This drug's killing me'."

However, this adherence had been tempered somewhat by a dramatic
experience. He warned:

> Placebo-based trials have unfortunate side-effects. A friend of mine died a
> few years ago during the AZT trial because he wasn't getting the real drug.
> If someone is sick they should not be on placebo, they should only be used
> with people who arc well. I agree with the use of placebos for people who
> are not sick. Drugs should be studied first on people who are well.

The information provided in relatively formal written discourse, such
as that contained in *HIV Brief*, has a mediating function for people with
HIV/AIDS, becoming a point of discussion, for example, within HIV support groups. It is in these interactive moments that such information is rendered meaningful to individuals; recontextualized through discussions of
the benefits and side-effects of a particular drug as experienced by those
who have taken them. Silverman (1989) has noted that it is just such support groups that provide the key framework in which medical signs and
symptoms are interpreted as practical routines; a "culture of adjustment"
is worked out by people with HIV.

Experience intervenes here and subverts the rational scientific framework of science. People with HIV/AIDS are all too aware of the discrepancy between the effects a drug is supposed to have and experienced
bodily effects. Barry, for example, began taking AZT approximately one
year before our discussions at the close of 1990. He spoke to me about conflicting treatment information he had received:

> You get different stories from people who have been on the drug and from
> the doctors. The doctors say things like, "Well, we don't really know any-
> thing about this yet but I think you should try it." You start to suspect what
> their motivations are for giving the information they do.
>
> I've just gone off AZT again yesterday for the third time. I was only on
> it again for one week but I felt so awful I could hardly walk, couldn't

speak, I was just a zombie. So I missed my dose yesterday afternoon and again last night, and today I feel terrific. Here I am riding around on my push bike!

I was on 500 milligrams a day. That's what they seem to be recommending these days. But even that seems to be too much for me. I just can't tolerate it. And it just doesn't seem to have done me any good anyway. I was on it for six months for a while back, but I had to stop after that 'cause I felt so awful.

I questioned Barry as to whether he had considered the most recent recommendations coming from community treatment groups in the United States that doses of 300 milligrams per day were sufficient (Delaney 1990). "Yes," he commented, "but you don't know what their expertise is, do you? You see, you hear all these different opinions and you get very confused." Here we see a conflict of legitimacy. While the authority of medical science is undermined by physical experiences that contradict theory, the legitimacy of alternative sources of information, such as those from community groups, is also questioned. The result is an informational environment of uncertainty and crisis. The fact that the recommendation for low doses of AZT was, in fact, later challenged by clinicians, on the grounds that such a low dose was insufficient to prevent dementia, only aggravated the legitimacy crisis.

The factors that influence an individual's decision making in such an information environment are complex and interrelated. They may include class background, and, related to this, strength of gay identity and attachment to gay community and its alternative sources of information. And related to these factors is the form of understanding of medical information one may construct and the extent of one's ability to contradict the authority of medical experts (see Ariss et al. 1992 for further discussion of this issue).

Exposure to others with experiences of AIDS treatments influences how individuals perceive their own health and the appropriateness of medical intervention. Kerry discusses the time when he began on the "open" (non-placebo-blinded) AZT trial for those with over 200 T-cells:

They kept pushing me to take the full dose of 1200 milligrams a day but I spun out on that dose after two weeks. To wake up to an alarm to take drugs is just fucked. Three or four nights of that just fucks you up. So you just drop taking the night dose. I gave my spare drugs to other people who needed it.

You ask around and hear what most people try. People prefer taking it with their food. Also you get informed from doing reading. You have to get them [drugs] to fit into your routine, not the other way round. We can learn from diabetics about that. The best way to live with HIV is to take things on board. Don't organize it around this new clock doctors are giving us. That totally fucks people up.

Despite Kerry's relatively high level of medical literacy, we hear a discontinuity between the formulations of medical science and patient interpretations and resultant practices. In this instance it is not a question of accuracy of medical knowledge so much as a misfit between clinical practice and the life routine of the patient.

In the context of a new or little-understood disease, medical regimens are often structured to answer scientific questions with little consideration for the ability of patients to realize them. The AZT trial, a regimen calling for a dose of the drug to be taken every four hours, demanded trial subjects wake up in the middle of the night to take the drug on schedule. This was unachievable for Kerry and many others. His solution was to rework the regimen into his pre-existing daily routine. In this way we see how medical information and practice is rendered meaningful and realizable only through its incorporation into a pre-existing life routine. Medicine must be an integral part of, not a graft onto, life's structured patterns of behavior and meaning.

This last example illustrates the movement of HIV patient discourse beyond teleological reconstructions toward a more critical, politically informed practice. In turn, the practice of medicine is under transformation through patient negotiation of therapeutic regimen. As a result of patient pressure and researcher awareness of these transgressions, AZT regimens were simplified allowing patients to take the drug two or three times a day, making its self-administration far easier. It was no longer necessary to transgress prescription.

Let us reconsider the concept of "empowerment" here. Kerry sees himself as an empowered patient, one who is sensitive to the manipulations of medical science and who sees himself as presenting something of a challenge to doctors. "I don't know if it's because I'm an empowered person," he says, "but this doctor found me a bit intimidating." Kerry is unusual for a patient generally, but for AIDS activists he represents an ideal. More common are patients like Steven, who ordinarily will not contest the authority of medical science. "I've trusted the people around me who've given me these drugs," he says. "Surely they're not going to give me a drug that's going to screw me up are they?" Because of his willingness to follow medical prescription Steven, unlike Kerry, had little difficulty in incorporating a high dose of AZT into his daily routine. "It got automatic," he said. "I started waking up before the alarm went off."

An interesting and significant transformation of Steven's position occurred, however, as he became increasingly ill with AIDS. After eighteen months on AZT, he became chronically anemic and was unable to continue the treatment. It was only at this point, when the drug was failing him, that he was moved to question the advice of his doctors:

Sometimes I wonder if we're told as much as we should be, about anything really. Like my doctor had me on one thousand milligrams of AZT right up to the time they took me off it. And sometimes I wonder: if I was taking a smaller dose it wouldn't have fucked my blood up so much? I never thought to cut down on my dose because I thought it was doing me good. It was only towards the end that I thought it wasn't.

Steven's doubts about his doctor's wisdom were in part inspired by information he had read in a national gay magazine which suggested lower doses of AZT were safer, and as effective:

I asked my doctor today why he kept me on one thousand [mg] and he said, "Because it was doing exactly what it was supposed to be doing." I mentioned to him the story in the gay paper about low doses of AZT being just as effective and he just said, "Yeah, I've heard about that." I don't know, sometimes he's really chatty and explains everything and sometimes he seems very distant and thinking about lots of things. He's usually pretty good, he's just like that sometimes.

It is through mediums such as gay newspapers and magazines, then, that many gay men receive information complementary to that provided by their doctors. Indeed, new developments often reach the gay papers before patients hear about such issues from more formal sources such as health-care providers. In extreme circumstances, the best informed patients know about a new treatment development even before their doctor. This fast rate of information change is the necessary discursive environment in which the authority of medical researchers and doctors becomes diminished. Those patients with greater access to such sources of information are far more likely to question the decisions and opinions of their health-care providers.

Steven was ordinarily not an avid reader of gay magazines or alternative treatment information sources such as *HIV Brief*. This was not, it should be noted, because he was not aware of them, or could not obtain them. Steven was close to individuals who worked in community AIDS organizations and could easily have gotten such information. His was a conscious choice *not* to pursue actively the self-responsibility program as represented in the first *HIV Brief*. For the period that his medical regimen was effective, Steven had little reason to doubt the authority of his medical care providers.

It was the failure of treatment that threw Steven into temporary doubt, doubt then reinforced by information and opinion read in the gay press. Delays to begin a new treatment regimen of the newly available trial drug, ddI, increased his anger and anxiety and further undermined his willingness to leave his medical care in the hands of others. And yet, while these problems were occurring, he maintained a relationship with his doctor that was, on occasion, highly personal and warm. He commented to me after one visit to his clinic:

> I had a good laugh with my doctor today. I said, "What's my T-cells like? Last time there was one." He said, "Now there's none." I just burst out laughing and said, "Oh, well," and he had a giggle. I spent half an hour with him today. That's the longest I've had with him. He said, "I've got no other appointments today, if there's anything you'd like to discuss?" We talked a bit about my legs. I get these shots of pain down them every so often. He said I should just get more walking done.

Steven invested a great deal in this personal relationship with his health-care provider. For Steven, it was in this interpersonal context that medical information and practice was realized and rendered meaningful to him. Rather than turning to printed sources of information, Steven relied on professional opinion relayed in the context of a clinical relationship. For him, the detail of treatment science was less important than a rounded, warm relationship with his medical practitioner.

This is a rather different approach to therapy than that advocated by activists. "Knowledge = Power" says a slogan of the Sydney chapter of ACT UP.[2] Taking Foucault's lead, I would argue rather that power is the condition for the arrangements of knowledge and particular forms of knowledge are deployed in support and confirmation of power. In seeking medical knowledge one does little to subvert it. One can only hope to refine its positive effects.

"Empowerment" is a concept premised on a high evaluation of information for its own sake and on individual autonomy. For Steven, neither knowledge nor power are of interest. The sociality of the therapeutic relationship is itself the key to a satisfactory health care regimen. Knowledge in his case worked to undermine his confidence in his medical practitioner's competence and yet, ultimately, the centrality of the therapeutic relationship was sustained.

EARLY TREATMENT: "RESISTANCE"

Initially, AZT was only available to those with AIDS (that is, with T4-cell counts under 200, plus defining opportunistic infections). Peter, cited above, was one of the first people in Australia to use this form of therapy. More recently, access to the drug has been approved for people at earlier stages of the disease, for those whose T4-cell count is under 500. The initiation of antiviral therapy at this stage of the disease raises a new issue: medical intervention for those who are relatively well. For medicine, the health of the HIV-infected person is measured through the signs traced in a range of blood tests: CD4- and CD8-cell counts, antigen readings, platelet counts, beta-microglobulin counts, liver function tests, and so on. For the positive individual health is read through the body: in the experience of wellness or illness. The two epistemologies frequently come into conflict, raising dilemmas particularly for people who now have the choice of taking a drug at an early stage of HIV disease.

Tony is a gay man in his mid-twenties. Originally diagnosed HIV-positive some years ago, he is now being encouraged by his doctor to take up AZT therapy as an early intervention. When Tony discussed his predicament with me he confessed to a confusion about the medical information on the effectiveness of AZT. His doctor's strong recommendations to begin treatment conflicted with his reluctance to avoid taking treatments while he was still feeling well:

> My doctor is trying to get me onto AZT but I'm putting off the decision, because you think while you're well why should you take things like that? And the thought of going into the hospital every time for it is horrible.

Individuals are faced with a choice of following a course of action based on their own perceptions of their health — an "if it's not broken don't fix it" approaching; and one based on an external authority that claims to be able to detect a decline in health before the individual may perceive any change, a science that now advocates early medical intervention.

Tony's resolution of the issue began when he reconsidered his own ability to sustain his health. "I've been on a health kick for nearly two years now," he says, "but I still get sick with diarrhea sometimes." Upon getting a T-cell count of 350, his friend advised him to begin taking the drug. "My friend who's got 150 T-cells says that you should do what you can to keep them while you've still got them." This is a reflection of the medical assertion that AZT only sustains the immune system for a period at the level at which therapy is initiated. At the same time, Tony's fear and anxiety about the possibility of his own health deteriorating was reinforced when another friend with HIV developed a severe illness. These events collectively led him to agree to begin treatment.

As with Steven, Tony's decision to begin treatment was not significantly influenced by a concerted reading of medical information. Rather, information was filtered through both medical personnel and friends. Of far greater significance was the experience of witnessing illness developing in others. Tony's experience again suggests that, for many, informal sources of information are more important than the written word in determining responses to medical advice.

ALTRUISM VERSUS ACCESS

Here I introduce Tom, whose narrative continues in following chapters. Tom is a gay man in his late twenties who had become involved in community AIDS organizations after being diagnosed with HIV infection several years before we met in 1988. In that time he had become an active care provider for people with AIDS, an educator about safe sex, and then, at the time of our meeting, a lobbyist for people with HIV/AIDS. He succinctly summarizes the issue I wish to pursue in this section: the discrepancies between the requirements demanded of patients by clinical science and the needs and expectations of clinical trial participants themselves:

> There needs to be more creative ways of making it more appealing to be involved in drug trials. The altruist stuff's not enough because those participating in trials are already doing a lot for the gay community. The altruistic expectation is unrealistic. They should offer you party tickets or vouchers or something. People either participate for one of two reasons — altruism, or for selfish reasons — to get access to a drug they otherwise wouldn't have.

When I spoke to Vern, he had known he was HIV-positive for two years. He was diagnosed at a point where his immune system was already showing signs of impairment and immediately entered a "high risk" trial for AZT, a double-blind study for individuals with fewer than 400 T-cells. The study was designed to investigate whether AZT was an effective treatment at earlier stages of HIV disease. After two years, at the time we spoke, Vern was told the trial was being discontinued because results were indicating that the drug was of some benefit to those in his situation. He was told that he had been on the placebo for all of this time, and that only now was he to receive the active drug. He initially responded with anger to this news:

> I felt upset when I heard about it, especially when I did have side effects. I did feel genuinely quite bad but it must have been the virus and not the tablets.
> Since I've gone onto AZT I had a lot of nausea initially but I got better. The first weeks were terrible. I had constipation, night sweats, headaches, sleeplessness, minor effects. I'm now better after one month.
> I feel better mentally knowing I'm on the active drug and knowing I'm able to tolerate it. My symptoms are few and far between, nothing serious.

I asked Vern how he felt about having been on the placebo all that time:

> Because AZT is now more widely available the trial was a bit pointless, but
> I guess it did help to show that it does work. But it was trialled in the US.
> Those trials did prove that it did work. A lot of the trials we had in Australia
> weren't really necessary. I was prepàred to take the risk when I started. I had
> a fifty percent chance of getting the real drug, it didn't cost me anything.
> After two years I was a bit pissed off, because I did go about the trial seri-
> ously. I did everything by the book but that was all pointless. It didn't do me
> any good. It wasn't stopping the virus anyway. ·

Les is a gay man in his early thirties who works in a government office.
His health was good but his depleted T4-cell count qualified him for entry
to the high-risk AZT trial. Les made the decision to begin early treatment,
through this clinical trial, out of a faith in the scientific project and a desire
to reap the benefits of medical monitoring:

> If there was going to be some beneficial effect then so much the better. It's
> better to be in there if it did turn out to be useful. Also it's going to help
> prove if it does work. I do have faith in the scientific system.

Participation in early intervention trials, however, presents a dilemma for
him:

> Being basically healthy you find yourself caught in the medical world, but
> that's unavoidable. There's still something funny about being healthy and
> popping pills every day, I don't feel like getting involved in the medical es-
> tablishment any more than I have to.

Les had an interest in the activities of community groups like PLWA
(NSW) and aspired to the role of the empowered patient. But Les is inex-
perienced in this role. He says making decisions about your own treatment
is a good ideal but, nonetheless, a difficult one to live up to because "the
medical model is one that doesn't like you having power:"

> There's the problem about who to go to about what to do. You end up being your
> own expert. While we are saying we should be consulted, on the other hand we
> don't have a medical background. You're suddenly faced with the situation of
> having to be expert about something that no one's expert about. Also there's the
> problem about deciding how much poison to put into your body.

This difficulty is illustrated by the predicament he found himself in
when he began to suspect he was taking the placebo substitute and not the
real drug. Failing to note any effects after three months of taking the pills,
he decided to substitute his assumed placebo for real AZT provided by a
friend who had reduced his own dosage. "When I could be sure of getting
the real drug," he said, "it seemed silly to not do something about it." But

this decision to flaunt the trial requirements meant that he had to lie to his physician. "It's not a problem now," he reflected, "because I'm not experiencing any side effects. But if I start having problems or something goes wrong the game will be up." And should this happen, he was concerned about losing the respect of his physician.

The decision to circumvent the placebo-controlled trial to gain access to physician monitoring illustrates the conflict. On the one hand Les enrolled in the trial through a willingness to participate for the sake of furthering the progress of science. "Basically you're doing the medical profession a favor." On the other hand, this altruism was short-circuited by a desire to be taking a genuine therapy:

> I respect the use of trials in testing the efficacy of drugs. There is a place for placebos but trials need to be more humane and sensible by not replicating trials elsewhere. If people are sick then give them the fucking drug!

By the time he decided to replace his placebo pills with the active drug, it would seem that Les had accepted the diagnosis of "sick" for himself.

Doug is also enrolled in an early AZT/placebo-controlled trial. He discovered that he was taking the placebo after his personal medical practitioner tested his blood and found no evidence of the drug in his system. Unlike Les however, Doug felt content for the time being to stay on the trial:

> If I really wanted to go on the drug I could have gone round till I found a doctor to give it to me. My health is OK and I've still got a few doubts about AZT. I'm still taking the placebo on the belief that I don't need it at this stage. Until there's indications through blood tests I don't think I'd go onto AZT. I've been stable for three years and I hope I'd go on like that. The only benefit to staying on the trial is monitoring my health. I'm being fairly closely watched and so if anything does change they will be able to tell me.

While he conceded that this free monitoring was the real advantage to being enrolled in the trial, Doug perceived that within this system:

> Basically you're a guinea pig. They're only interested in your health in relation to AZT. There's not much assistance given to coping with problems that arise such as skin rashes. Anything like that they refer you back to your own doctor. Their main interest is in AZT.

In contrast to his own doctor's care then, Doug found the trial system alienating and impersonal. In this instance the motivation for staying on the trial is for medical attention and monitoring, and not any altruistic desire to assist medical research. While this participant thought he, too, was doing the doctors a favor, the integrity of a double-blind placebo trial was wholly undermined by the fact that he knows he is taking the active drug.

It was patient practices of this exactly kind that medical researchers feared would undermine the validity of their studies. The success of such studies rests on the collaboration of patients to uphold trial conditions (Arras 1990). With AIDS it became increasingly obvious, once activists started to lobby for trial protocols to attend to real treatment needs, that trial designs needed to be modified in order to sustain their scientific integrity.

This nonconformist behavior of trial participants was, in some contexts, a powerful argument in the hands of activists when lobbying for changes to trial designs. Later, when this lobby campaign had matured to the stage where the federal government was looking for ways to encourage international drug companies and trial-program participation in Australia, the relatively high compliance rate of local trial participants by international standards was stressed. Activist discourse shifted over this period, therefore, according to its intent. The medical research establishment, needless to say, only stood to benefit by this reversal of argument.

With the widening of use of AZT for people with over 200 T-cells in late 1990, licensed medical practitioners could prescribe the drug to a much greater percentage of their HIV-positive patients. One year after this approval was granted, an approval accelerated by the demands of activists, the widespread uptake of AZT as an early therapy for people with early stages of HIV infection was still not yet common. Of the maximum estimate of 12,000 people eligible for AZT therapy in Australia at this time, less than 1,500 were taking advantage of its availability and less than half of these were asymptomatic (NCHECR 1992). Activists had realized their goal of expanding the availability of this choice of treatment for people with HIV. However, in an information environment where the efficacy of a drug for early treatment is still not conclusive, and where treatment regimens are intrusive and threatening to an individual's sense of well-being, scientists should not be too surprised that the option of submitting to a medical regimen is not unconditionally taken up.

This "resistance" to the use of the drug suggests a discrepancy between the views and experiences of many people with HIV on the one hand, and doctors and AIDS activists on the other. It also supports further the hypothesis of a discontinuity between formal scientific views, more-or-less shared by activists, and the phenomenological understandings of those who are themselves the subjects of medical intervention. We detect here a widening gap between people with HIV and AIDS, the great majority of whom are not a part of the collectivity that is strategically interfacing with the medical research establishment, and this second, much smaller group who are consciously constructing themselves as the vanguard of self-help and community development. The former are tactically manipulating and transforming dominant practices to their own requirements. The latter are beginning to elaborate a systematic strategy of interface with the dominant medical order.

GUINEA PIGS AND MEN

Les's and Doug's comments reflect widely held concerns emerging in the late 1980s about the ethical use of placebos in trial-testing drugs for life-threatening conditions such as HIV infection. The use of placebos is a more controversial practice for people with AIDS than for those at earlier stages of HIV disease because their health is more precarious. Such experimental practices have now become rare, especially when involving people with AIDS, due to the lobbying of AIDS activists. The placebo arms of the original trials testing AZT for people with AIDS were terminated, for example, when interim data attested to the drug's efficacy in slowing progress to death. The drug ddI became available in 1990 in Sydney through a trial that included only an optional placebo arm. Not surprisingly, few chose this option.

Yet, still, this issue of being a "guinea pig" to science is salient for people considering therapy at all stages. Having a disease that is little understood opens the body to the exploratory gaze of medical science. The primary objective of medical science at this stage is research, the accumulation of knowledge. The individual is rendered an experimental subject first, a patient second. For the person with the disease, participation in research becomes the only avenue to therapy in the absence of approved treatments.

Further comments from people with HIV will illustrate this predicament, and serve to introduce the reader to the political issues to be discussed in Part Three.

Vern, in summing up his experience with the early AZT trial, reaches this conclusion: "I can't help feeling like I was a guinea pig. I know they have to do trials to try these things out but they should have had it where everyone got the active treatment."

Les, after his experience on the early AZT trial, began to formulate a political opinion about research methodology. When discussing the limited options available for himself and his friends, he makes the following suggestions:

I feel very angry about it all but I don't know enough about it and that's part of the problem. We should go the way of Canada and New Zealand who have opted out of trialing drugs because their population is too small, and they have difficulty attracting drug companies to do trials there. There's just no market for them. Why are we duplicating things here? Should we even be trying to do trials in Australia except as part of international trials? International trial participation should be independent of Australian government regulations. When a trial stops overseas then Australia should pick up the results and not block access for our people. Like Terry Bell used to say, people would rather die fighting. If people die of a drug, they at least died fighting rather than waiting for it to become available. Then it's too late.

Recalling experiences of the AZT trial, Kerry angrily describes hours of waiting time in hospital:

> You're being used as a guinea pig. You know you're not going to get anything back. There's no assistance, not even like with taxi fares or even a sandwich after waiting hours in the waiting room. It ends up being one hundred percent give. I work for a private company and any time off is a loss to me.

By now Kerry had developed strong opinions about how the system could change. His extensive experience with trials and hospital clinics, together with his avid attention to overseas information developments and activist interventions, led him to consider alternative strategies:

> I can't see why Australia can't be considered the fifty-first state, or a province of France or something like that. All we need is a dedicated computer here. It's no different. I can understand the size of our population means maybe trials are difficult to run. But why do we have to run our own trials? If we join overseas trials then we in Sydney can do the same for Perth and Lismore. The drug companies should be pushing for that. We can do more too because of PLWA and ACT UP and ACON. Maybe if we all approached the drug companies at the same time. But because of the hens up in the rooster's house we won't be able to use their facilities because they want to control trials. If PLWA and user groups were involved in trials at an earlier stage, like being on panels, we could monitor the conduct of these things and stop things happening like drug users being taken off trials when they're found out to be taking drugs.

Simon, whom we met in Chapter Three, quickly developed a critique of AIDS-trial systems soon after his diagnosis of AIDS. Over a period of several months Simon familiarized himself with HIV clinics, doctors, and treatment regimens. He threw himself into studying all the information he could find on treatments against AIDS. Through his home computer system, he regularly consulted an international AIDS information bulletin, and had subscribed to a number of local and North American AIDS treatment bulletins. Almost immediately, he began questioning his doctors about the drugs he was being prescribed and those that he had heard were available elsewhere, but not in Australia.

As a result of these studies and experiences, it was not long before he developed a critical position toward his doctors:

> Those doctors know just a little bit more about AIDS than what I do. Just a little, not very much. 'Cause it's new. Nobody knows anything about it. What is it? Five years we've had it?
>
> I think I'm not going to do as they tell me. You have to tell them that we are not going to treat them like supermen any more. If their medicine is going to work, then we will treat them like supermen. But the only treatment they have doesn't work. So they shouldn't expect us to treat them like supermen. They have to work with us to find a cure for this, not tell us what to do and expect us to accept everything they say. People with the disease know as much about this as they do.
>
> The researchers want to behave like physicists, they want to control everything. But testing something on humans is not the same as testing something on animals. If you are going to test something on us you have to change the rules.

I challenged him: "What if the doctors say, as they do, that, in the long term, placebo testing gives the fastest and most reliable results?"

> What, if after a thousand deaths, they know for sure a drug works? Can they then say this is the best way to find out? If they want people to volunteer for their tests, then they need our respect. If they won't work with us then they will lose people's respect and they won't have any results at all.

In time, Simon settled down into a regimen of treatments that stabilized his condition. His improved health tempered his critique somewhat, yet he retained a skeptical view of medicine and explored a number of alternative and unapproved treatments out of a desire to maximize his chances of staying well. For example, he sought out a gay doctor whom he found easy to talk with and who was willing to provide him with an unapproved experimental drug. I take up Simon's story again in the following chapter.

* * *

To recap the points made in this chapter: Medical science can only continue to pursue its research agenda through human experimentation if research participants incorporate the biomedical paradigm within their world view; research subjects will only collaborate if they believe to some extent in the paradigms of science. However, experiencing medical research and treatment practices as a subject positions many people with HIV and AIDS in a conflictual relationship with medicine. For patients and physicians are in a relationship of inequality. The latter deploy a specialized, technical language with which they reinterpret the patient's bodily experience. This language progressively repositions the patient within a web of surveillance technologies. Patients respond to this regime by way of tactical operations that appropriate the language of medicine for their own perceived ends. These "procedures of consumption" (de Certeau 1984) work to define a patient-space within medical science, transforming technological medical regimens into practices meaningful at an individual level. With the gradual systematization of these practices into institutionally localized strategies, we begin to detect the emergence of an anti-discipline with wide-reaching implications.

NOTES

1. Dideoxyinosine, a second generation antiviral used for the treatment of HIV infection. At the time of this interview, ddI was not yet approved in Australia for general use.
2. ACT UP (AIDS Coalition to Unleash Power). See Chapter Eleven for discussion of the establishment of this important advocacy group in Australia.

CHAPTER 6

Beyond Medicine:
Alternative Therapies for HIV

In the heart of Sydney's busy Chinatown one can find a number of herb dispensaries, businesses which import many different kinds of herbs from China ordinarily unavailable in Australia, substances now referred to in the West as the ingredients of traditional Chinese medicine (TCM). One business is much like another. The store will sell a range of herbal teas, dried fruits, soup mixes, and sweets. In addition, there will be a wall of drawers. Roots, bark, berries, flowers, dried fruits, and many other substances unidentifiable to the Western eye are stored in these drawers as well as in a myriad of jars and bottles scattered around.

Attached to the enterprise one will find a consulting herbalist who will prescribe a unique mix of herbs suited to your particular complaint. One such herbalist, Mr. Lee, had, in 1989, a large and regular clientele that included forty HIV-infected individuals. One awaits Mr. Lee's consultation, with Chinese- and European-Australian clients alike, on a long wooden bench at the rear of the store. Dressed in a plain white coat, Mr. Lee delivers his consultation in a tiny room partitioned off from the shop by a swinging half door. Mr. Lee sits behind his cluttered desk and asks why you have come to see him. You tell him you are HIV-positive. Perhaps you are taking AZT. You have heard from friends that he can prescribe herbs to help. He nods. His English is poor and difficult to understand, but he seems familiar with your predicament. He is curious for any additional information of the sort available to a conventional doctor. "What's your T-cell count? Any symptoms? What other medications or treatments have you taken? How long do you think you've been infected?" He takes brief notes on a client record card. Without referring to a timer of any sort, he intently feels your pulse on each hand and quickly checks your tongue. Mr. Lee then writes, in flourishing Chinese script, a prescription for a herbal mix. "This will help you with the AZT," he says, clearly disapproving of the use of such a substance, and suggests the herbs will help the body process the toxins from the drug. "We'll try to build your immune system up." Boil one bag of the mix leaving one cup of tea, he advises. Drink one cup each day while the broth is still warm. Use each package twice and then discard the herbs. For your ten-minute consultancy he asks for ten dollars [US$7.50] and suggests you come back for a second visit when the prescription is all used up.

On presenting your prescription to one of the young men at the counter, the herbs will be gathered from the drawers and bottles, divided into several piles and wrapped in paper. The cost may vary from AU twenty dollars [US$15] to forty dollars depending on the quantity Mr. Lee has prescribed. One must also buy a five-dollar ceramic pot in which to cook the mix: the herbs must not come into contact with artificial materials such as plastic or metals. The cost for such a visit may, therefore, amount to around AU $35–$55 [US$26–41].

Simon, though initially skeptical of any form of non-allopathic medicine, was encouraged by his lover to consult Mr. Lee. For several months he regularly drank a large cup of the thick, pungent liquid brewed from the herbal mix Lee had prescribed for him. Initially, Simon was reluctant to ascribe any effect to the herbs but in time noted his level of energy and sense of well-being improving. "I can't say for sure if it's the herbs," he said cautiously:

> I'm taking so many other things now, AZT, ddC, vitamin supplements, and now these herbs, that it's difficult to say what's doing what. All I can say is that in the last month or so I've been feeling really great, full of energy. Much better than before. I believe it could be the herbs. So I'm going to keep taking them.

"They taste disgusting!" he adds with a laugh, "but I've found a way of making it taste better by putting sugar or honey in it. It makes it bearable."

Simon's use of Chinese herbs is part of a tactical exploration of therapeutic options that aims to secure some sense of control over his own body. The extension of the tactics of consumption to non-allopathic medicine is what I explore in this chapter. More specifically, I want to canvas further ideas from the preceding chapter regarding the tactics and strategies deployed by people with HIV and AIDS to insert themselves into, and creatively modify, available therapeutic disciplines for their own purposes. This time I will focus on that rather amorphous collage of practices known as "alternative therapies." This fragmentary phenomenon is largely ignored in the literature despite widespread interest and use among this population. The discussion has a theoretical dimension. By shifting the gaze beyond biomedical practices, we may expand our appreciation of the multiple tactics by which individuals seek control over their own degenerating bodies. We have seen, in the previous chapter, the emerging conflict between a new patient class and an emerging AIDS clinical science. Here, I document practices that contribute to another form of critique of allopathic medicine, a critique implicit in the tactical use of alternative therapies, but one more systematically formulated in recent years in Sydney.

THE STRUCTURE OF A TACTICAL ALTERNATIVE (1): CLASS

The medical profession is generally reluctant to acknowledge, and frequently displays alarm at, the use of non-allopathic health-care modalities. Operating under a very different health/illness philosophy, the two modalities have, by and large, offered mutually exclusive options. There are recent signs, however, of a shift in this exclusiveness and a growing willingness for each to acknowledge, if not approve of, the other.

The Australian Medical Acupuncture Society, for example, has a membership of six hundred, all of them doctors who include acupuncture in their practice. More broadly, about 2,000 general medical practitioners are interested in alternative therapies, many of them members of the Australian College of Nutritional and Environmental Medicine. One of Australia's greatest enthusiasts for alternative medicines, Dr. Gisselle Cooke claims that 16 million visits are made to alternative practitioners annually (*The Independent Monthly*, April 1994). With respect to AIDS, in Sydney in 1989 there were six successful alternative health practitioners with large HIV-positive clienteles. Five of these practitioners were gay men and one a woman. Several of the men shared premises in an inner-city area just a short walk from Oxford Street. They offered "lifestyle and diet consultation," naturopathy, herbal medicine, homoeopathy, intravenous vitamin treatment, and Ozone therapy. The remaining practitioners, scattered throughout the inner suburbs, offered herb treatment, iridology, Bach flower remedy, tissue salt therapy, meditation and visualization, hypnotherapy, massage, acupuncture, traditional Chinese medicine, and Reikei (an alternative therapy focusing mainly on the transfer of healing energy through the systematic laying-on of hands).

These modalities are not recognized by the federal health system, Medicare, leaving the client to pay the full cost of consultations and prescriptions. The federal government's refusal to legitimize such therapies through its welfare system signals the state's allegiance to allopathic medicine and the marginality of the practices themselves. This political economy renders alternative therapies accessible only to those who can afford additional health expenses not covered by Medicare. One would expect, therefore, that alternative therapies would be more accessible to middle-class gay men than to those with lower incomes. Many HIV-positive gay men experience a significant decline in income once they become too ill to work, and a sickness pension may often be the only income source. Professionals may be more fortunate and "retire" with a superannuation payout. A consultation with an alternative practitioner may cost around AU \$50 [US \$38], or \$25 [US \$19] for a client on a sickness pension (that is, approximately one-fifth of his weekly pension). While many practitioners offer further discounts for those on pensions, these individuals face far greater restrictions in their options than those who are well and still working, or those with reserves of funds.

THE STRUCTURE OF A TACTICAL ALTERNATIVE (2): GENDER

A number of North American studies have demonstrated a greater proclivity among gay men with HIV and AIDS to explore such alternative therapy options than individuals experiencing other terminal illnesses. Abrams for example, cites studies suggesting that between 21 percent and 36 percent of patients at a Chicago AIDS clinic used such treatments, compared with 6 percent of cancer patients, and less than 5 percent of general patients. Abrams observes that, of all patient groups inclined to explore nonmedical therapies, "perhaps the most vocal and critical individuals have been representatives from the male homosexual community" (Abrams 1990:1179), a community that is informed, organized, and well resourced.[1]

Other studies in Philadelphia also suggested that Anglo-American gay men are more inclined than any other group of patients with HIV to explore alternative therapy options (O'Connor et al. 1991). Anderson and colleagues recorded that up to 40 percent of HIV-positive patients at a conventional medical clinic explored such therapeutic alternatives. They note that while age, race, income, religion, or severity of symptoms were not significantly related to the decision to try such therapies, gay men with higher levels of education were more likely to explore a wider range of options. They hypothesize that "affiliation to gay community" and AIDS-therapy groups promoting alternative and conventional medicines are the most important factors stimulating these practices (Anderson 1991). Some have argued, however, that attachment to gay community is itself a function of class (Kippax et al. 1993). Considering a great number of people who have contracted HIV or developed AIDS in Sydney have been middleclass, the epidemic provides an environment in which alternative therapeutic practices may flourish.

Gay men, on the one hand, and women, on the other, have come to constitute an alliance among alternative health practitioners in AIDS. As noted, five of the six alternative therapists working with HIV-infected people in Sydney in the late 1980s were gay men. Several women in Australia and the United States have been the most significant alternative-therapy practitioners for HIV and AIDS. In Australia, Petria King inspired a large following of HIV-positive individuals and has rereleased her book, *Quest for Life*, targeted at people with cancer or HIV infection (King 1992). In the United States, Louise Hay came from a background of treating people with cancer and moved into the area of AIDS with the rise of the epidemic. Like King, her methods combined positive thinking, meditation, group work, and a range of practical activities such as dietary modification and avoidance of toxins like drugs and alcohol (Hay 1988). Hay enjoys a large following in both the United States and Australia. Of note also is Joan Priestley, who runs the Center for 21st Century Medicine in Los Angeles. Priestley's practice for HIV-positive clients included prescriptions of concentrated vitamins B and C, diet modification, aloe vera extract juice, Hypericin (St John's Wort extract), "nutrient therapy," and SST, a treatment regimen of "an ancient combination formula of very powerful herbs used in traditional Chinese medicine to treat various immune system dysfunctions" (Priestley 1991).

Gay men, and women, have thus come together to provide an opportunity for individuals to explore health care practices beyond medicine. Positioned outside and in opposition to allopathic medicine, this gendered anti-discipline constitutes a challenge to the heterosexual male-dominated regime of biomedicine.

THE STRUCTURE OF A TACTICAL ALTERNATIVE (3): IDEOLOGY

San Francisco, home of one of the world's largest and best organized gay communities, a community profoundly affected by the AIDS epidemic, is also a leading center for alternative therapeutic practice. The October 1989 issue of the *San Francisco Bay Times* profiled two health practitioners, themselves HIV-positive. Based on their own experience of hospital care, Jay and Jim provide a critique of allopathic medicine:

> You have to realize that you were not in a health care system; you were in a medical system. There's a big difference. A medical system is set up for the convenience of the medical staff and is not patient oriented. It is not a holistic spa. Our country has the fifteenth highest infant/adult mortality rate in the world, yet we spend the most on health care. The only industrialized nations that don't have national health care are the USA and South Africa. As long as medicine is for profit, you're going to have this rift between profit making synthetic medicines and non-patentable natural substances.

And on the scientific world view:

> The medical system clings to the belief that if it can't be proven scientifically, then it is not proven a fact. Intuitive knowledge is not acceptable. When people self-heal from serious disease, their recovery is noted as "anecdotal" or sometimes explained away in terms of misdiagnosis.

Through such media as newsletters, newspapers, videos, books, and public speaking, alternative practitioners are progressively systematizing their critique of biomedicine. This discourse posits the drive behind allopathic medicine to be the pursuit of profit. Scientific paradigms of disease causation and cure are considered a veneer behind which capitalist interests are pursued. Biomedical practice is "unnatural," disruptive to human life through its chemical substances and technologies and in its insistence on separating the biological being from the spiritual. Because they are unnatural, the therapeutic practices of biomedicine are thus inferior. It is through this ideological construction that the discourse of alternative therapy links itself to western Romantic tradition, juxtaposing the artificial and the natural, the profane with the spiritual, the corrupt and the pure.

Central to Joan Priestley's therapeutic ideology is the principle of "healing through empowerment," that is, the adoption by the client of "many simple alterations in his/her lifestyle, eating habits, and attitudes to lessen the effects of . . . AIDS co-factors" (Priestley 1991). The individual pursues health through a regimen of self-discipline, not through technological medical interventions. Ironically, Priestley's Center has attempted to legitimize its practices through the conduct of a number of clinical-type trials involving people with HIV, in an attempt to document scientifically the effects of the therapies. This seeking after legitimacy through the appropriation of scientific method suggests the continuing hegemony of scientific logic. While alternative modalities challenge allopathic medicine, they are simultaneously captured by and replicate medicine's own logic.

In Australia, as in the United States, one may find a great variety of alternative therapeutic practices. Some, like Mr. Lee's Chinese herbal practice, rely on a therapeutic relationship similar to that of allopathic medicine: the client defers to an authority for diagnosis and prescription. Others more closely resemble the "self-empowerment" philosophy of American practices such as that of Priestley. Peter Todd, for example, is a gay man who has run a successful private practice for the HIV-infected in Sydney for some years. In the late 1980s, Todd was a frequent contributor to gay newspapers, promoting his theories of alternative health care in regular columns. His writing represents the local discursive variant of an international counter-discourse:

> Perhaps AIDS could be an opportunity for growth and transformation on a mass scale. For it faces us with the challenge of healing ourselves, through achieving "wholeness," that truly miraculous harmony of body, mind and spirit, in which we become fully human, capable of being loving and being loved; and instruments of compassion and constructive change . . . The "how" of the inner journey is firstly the admission of our "dis-ease," of our lack of harmony between body, mind and spirit; of our alienation or separateness from our Selves and Others. The second step is to do something. Get involved in meditation classes, counselling or groups, focusing upon the prevention of illness, in HIV-antibody positive persons. Such groups aim to promote "wholeness," full aliveness, well-being and a spiritual awakening. We may not be responsible for our exposure to HIV, but we certainly can be responsible for our healing and recovery! Why choose to self-destruct if another option exists (*Village Voice*, 3 June 1988).

The source of illness lies in the discord between self and environment. The possibility that one's own environment may not itself be harmonious is not a factor in this argument, though, as we will see later, individuals may incorporate this into etiological explanations of bodily disorder. Health is harmony, illness discord. Therapy rests in the restoration of harmony. So far this is not altogether different to the mechanistic models of health offered by allopathic medicine. The difference lies in the method. If discord comes from within, then healing must also emanate from the self. And this is precisely where many people with AIDS have expressed dissent with alternative therapists. If taken literally, illness is a product of one's wrong thinking and doing (thinking negatively, eating inadequately), and not, as science will have it, the inevitable erosion of the body through the action of a virus. In the first model, illness is owned by the self, is self relinquishing self. In the second, illness is the product of the invasion of the self by a foreign agent.

Where alternative therapy and allopathic medicine frequently disagree is on the issue of the role of HIV in disease progression. Alternative practitioners recognize to varying degrees the role of the virus in disease progression. Some completely reject HIV as having any role, though this position is an increasingly marginal one. In its place such advocates identify promiscuity, sexual guilt, and social- or self-oppression as causes of the high mortality among gay men since the early 1980s. It is increasingly common, however, as evidence and opinion mounts in its favor, for HIV to be acknowledged within the discourse of alternative therapy. The resolution, in keeping with the ideology of body/environment harmony, is for one to learn to live in harmony with the virus in one's body. When illness impedes, contortions of logic become necessary in order to accept, indeed "love," one's illness in order to sustain harmony, certainly a powerful reversal of the scientific discourse of "the body at war" (see Dwyer 1993).

The development and progressive refinement of the use of AZT as chemotherapy for HIV infection has become a focal point in the dialogue between alternative and medical practitioners. AZT represents confirmation of the allopathic hypothesis that HIV causes AIDS, and that technological intervention can be efficacious in combating the disease. Initial responses by alternative therapists to AZT were to reject the drug as an appropriate method for combating the disease. When AZT first became approved for people with AIDS in 1988, at a time when activists were celebrating a brief victory over a slow-moving research establishment and a seemingly indifferent state bureaucracy, it was alternative therapists and their followers in the gay community who were condemning AZT as poison, even genocidal in its implications.

Controversy has always surrounded the drug, with scientists, activists, and people with AIDS alike questioning its efficacy, toxicity, and exploitative relations of production. In time this critique has waned, however, as more is known about the drug and how to administer it to maximum effect and with least harm. Yet there is still a staunch critique of the drug, developed in the United States by 1988, particularly due to the efforts of Dr. Peter Duesberg and writers of the New York weekly, the *Village Voice* (Duesberg 1989; Lauritsen 1990). Their campaign was also joined by some highly public people with AIDS who had taken the drug, among them Michael Callen. Callen maintained, for example, that long-term survivors of AIDS are more critical of AZT and explore a wider range of therapy options. Commenting in 1990 on the recent approval of the wider use of the drug, he said:

> The idea that individuals should take chemotherapy every day for the rest of their lives is completely unprecedented . . . I predict that the approval of

AZT will prove to be a scandal of the magnitude of thalidomide (Callen 1990:213,216).

Of course, AIDS has generated many unprecedented developments, not least of which are in the field of therapeutics. Nonetheless, Callen's protest reflects a caution and skepticism against allopathic medicine that is but one expression of a pervasive critical discourse.

In Australia, this extreme position has not been a significant feature of AIDS-treatment discourse. Indeed, the anti-AZT critique has been systematically rejected by AIDS activists in Australia as irresponsible quackery.[2] Thus, not only are Australian community organizations critically supportive of scientific medicine, many have adopted a hostile approach to alternative therapies. One may note, first of all, the relative infrequency with which alternative therapies are discussed in the gay press, though there has been slightly more coverage in recent years, particularly with the establishment of a second regular gay newspaper in Sydney. Articles discussing the possible benefits of "lifestyle issues", modifications such as diet, regular exercise, meditation, or oriental therapies such as Chinese medicine appear periodically in national gay magazines. AIDS information projects infrequently produce health information pamphlets and booklets aimed at people with HIV or with a specific focus on "lifestyle" issues.[3] Significantly, this issue attracts far less attention than do scientific developments. Discussions of the value of such interventions are usually prefaced by a reference to the absence of any "scientific evidence" of their value, qualifying the legitimacy of the information.[4]

This general disapproval on the part of community-based organizations is passively expressed in a lack of support for efforts to promote alternative therapies. More active forms of disapproval have also been recorded. In 1988, for example, ACON called upon alternative practitioners to record and evaluate their practices in line with established scientific principles. Its representatives have also been critical of gay media which advertise trials of alternative substances.

People with HIV and AIDS may also be critical of alternative practitioners. At a conference for people with AIDS in 1989,[5] for example, several practitioners came under intense scrutiny, both for the fees they charge for services and for a therapeutic philosophy that many viewed as rather too esoteric. In another instance, a popular alternative therapist, who described AZT as a toxic and false "magic bullet", was criticized by activist Paul Young. Young described the call to "take responsibility for your own health" as "reinforcing doom and gloom theories about HIV that run contrary to growing orthodox medical opinion that it is an infection which is chronic and manageable just as diabetes is a chronic and manageable condition" (Young 1990). To Young, the emerging scientific construction of HIV infection as a chronic manageable illness is more appealing than the rigors of self-care demanded by alternative therapies. Despite the less than perfect record of medical science, we still live in a therapeutic culture of magic bullets, of quick-and-easy cures. The alternative course, the reconstruction of lifestyle, demands often rigorous dietary regimes or time-consuming healing methods, practices many individuals are unable to accommodate within their life routines.

The dominance of the issue of AZT in the therapeutic discourse of AIDS and the relative weak position of non-medical interventions together speak of the hegemony of science and the failure of alternative therapy discourse to provide a serious challenge to the ideology and practices of biomedicine. Instead, what we have witnessed since the introduction of AZT is a debate between the scientific establishment and urban gay communities that challenges not the value of the scientific enterprise itself, but the form of its undertakings and the ethical principles that organize its practices.

On the other hand, people with AIDS and HIV themselves have widely sought therapeutic alternatives, despite this sustained critique from both the medical establishment and AIDS organizations (see, for example, Carr 1989c). In this hostile environment, the discourse of alternative therapy becomes fragmentary and defensive, and the exploration of such modalities far more tactical in nature than the institutionalized consumption of allopathic AIDS therapies. To illustrate further the precarious status of alternative modalities, I present the case of a practitioner and, in the final section, the narratives of several people with HIV with experience as consumers of alternative therapies.

AN ALTERNATIVE PRACTITIONER

Faced with critical wariness from gay community-based AIDS organizations and outright hostility from the medical establishment, alternative therapists stand very much alone in promoting their practices. Their ability to do so is constrained by their marginal position within the total field of medical power. The two therapies are not entirely separate and independent, however. For example, one of Sydney's leading AIDS clinics agreed to accommodate a number of alternative therapists within its walls.

Michael, an HIV-positive gay man in his early forties, ran his practice, targeting people with HIV/AIDS specifically, from this clinic. He offered dietary advice, massage, acupuncture, and Chinese herbal remedies to a steady clientele. Yet running such a practice from a medical center ge-nerated conflicts with the clinic staff and its scientific ethos. Michael reflected on his relationship to the clinic in our discussion in 1989:

> I do this work at the AIDS clinic and I really have my hands tied behind my back. Of course, my opinions usually don't reflect favorably on drug trials at the AIDS clinic office so I have to keep mum about what I think. Which is maybe a good thing because then what the people get are choices. Which is pretty wonderful. . . . The orthodox medical role is set up and established to provide these kind of services. 'Cause I don't agree with them, I'm not in a place to go into that establishment and sort of say, "You're doing the wrong thing." So if I want to be there I've actu-ally got to play their ballgame. So it is difficult for my own personal philosophy.

I asked Michael what he thought he could do to resolve this conflict:

> The way I resolve it is to offer the two sides of the stories. This is what I know about AZT. This is what the doctors are saying it does. And this is the bad side of AZT, it does this and this, without saying I prefer you to go one way or the other. And I actually offer them a third choice, to do acu-puncture, Chinese herbs, massage, visualization, meditation, positive thinking, exercise, instead of doing anything orthodox. . . . It's the only solution without risking my removal from the clinic and if I'm removed then I don't reach anybody. So in one way I think I have a positive influ-ence by being there. 'Cause people do get to see a different side of the story.

Thus, while alternative practices are available to individuals who seek them, their authenticity is constantly in question through this conflict with scientific orthodoxy. Michael's place in the clinic gives him access to cli-ents while silencing his critique of conventional medicine. His resolution is to present his therapies as neutral alternatives. This neutrality is dis-turbed, however, by Michael's willingness to present himself to clients as an example of his therapies' efficacy:

> People say, "You look well and you're doing well. What are you doing?" And I say, "Well, I'm doing this." I don't say, "I'm not doing AZT." But I say, "I'm doing this."

Michael embodies his ideology and practice. He has no empirical clinical language with which to state his case. He alone is the proof of the philo-sophy he advocates.

The growing popularity of alternative therapeutic practices has pro-duced small shifts in the power relations with biomedicine. In the time of

AIDS, both science and alternative practices have achieved a precarious coexistence. We may even be witnessing transformations in clinical theory and practice as a result. Some would go so far as to suggest that science is becoming less scientific in the process. I would argue, rather, that due to its flexibility and curiosity, science may accommodate concepts from alternative therapies, modifying its discursive forms somewhat. To consider a recent case, the U. S. National Institute of Health established, in 1992, an Office of Alternative Medicine, on which it bestowed the task of generating research to demonstrate, by conventional scientific means, the efficacy or otherwise of non-conventional therapies. In another example, a discussion appeared in 1989 in the *Medical Journal of Australia* regarding the credibility of "New Age" approaches to cancer. Professor Michael Baum warned of the loss of superior scientific positivism in the face of the "absurd" dictums of "alternative medicines," claiming that "the cultural dominance of empirical science in this century is in danger of being eclipsed by the 'New Age' counter-culture of irrationalism." He refuted the accusation that modern medicine is limited by a "Descartian" mechanistic theory of the body. "In modern scientific medicine," he wrote, "our concepts of holism are based on well defined neuroendocrinal pathways which are known to link the psyche and soma" (Baum 1989:607–8). Thus, modern medicine can be as holistic as the "irrational" alternatives, or even more so because it is a holism built on established scientific principles.

Further to this debate, Lowenthal demanded that popular alternative cancer therapists, such as Ian Gawler, submit evidence of their treatments as a means of protection against "the potentially harmful effects of accepting such unproved ideas about cancer:"

> Gawler's success clearly is telling us that we have not been meeting many patients' needs. Perhaps in embracing the empiricist Zeitgeist we have overlooked the importance of the transcendental, to the detriment of our patients. . . . To ignore the Gawler phenomenon is not in the best interests of patients or doctors; rather we should learn from it. We always must instill hope, and ensure that patients are able to receive care for physiological and spiritual needs as well as their physical needs. We must reaffirm the medical profession's historic role as friend and advocate of the sick. In this way each patient will achieve the best result for his or her individual cancer — cure for some, comfort for all (Lowenthal 1989:714).

Unlike Baum, Lowenthal then went on to admit the failings of modern medicine in the face of patient practices. Because of this discrepancy between theory and practice, medical science must pay attention to the non-biological needs of patients or continue to risk a loss of influence in the face of challenges from non-medical therapists.

In the above debate, medical practice seems to be addressing a crisis of legitimacy arising from its perceived inability to solve the problem of cancer. The proposed solution is to appropriate alternative therapy paradigms, or rejuvenate "holism" within medical practice, in order to retain science's legitimacy in the eyes of patients. This crisis is continued in AIDS clinical science, but on a new level of complexity. Thus we see therapeutic practices such as Michael's thriving within a medical clinic. Abrams argues for physicians to "question patients with regard to their use of alternative regimens in a non-judgmental and informed manner" in order to rescue the doctor-patient relationship and the accuracy of clinical trials (Abrams 1990:1186).

While patient interest in and practice of alternative modes of health care is being increasingly acknowledged by medical science, alternative practitioners are changing their views of conventional medicine. By 1991, for example, Michael was more willing to accept that AZT therapy held some benefit for people with HIV and AIDS, now that prescribed dosages of the drug were being reduced, minimalizing its toxic effects. Joan Priestley, mentioned earlier, acknowledged a "minor role" for AZT in limited circumstances; nevertheless, she remains highly critical of the motives of allopathic doctors and pharmaceutical drug companies (*San Francisco Bay Times* 1990). In Sydney, toward the end of the 1980s, holistic health clinics were being established with services offered by a wide range of alternative practitioners such as dietitians, masseurs, acupuncturists, homoeopaths, naturopaths, Reikei specialists, osteopaths, hypnotherapists, and herbalists together with conventional medical practitioners. Holistic health care can now consist of consulting any or all of these practitioners, often within the same building. This accommodation has been reflected in a taxonomic shift that replaces "alternative therapy" with the appellation "complementary therapy." Rather than competing, science and the New Age now join hands for the benefit of each other and of patients.

ALTERNATIVE MEDICINE AS A HEALTH TACTIC

This last section illustrates the tactical maneuvres of people with HIV/ AIDS as they explore beyond the therapeutic limits of allopathic medicine. These practices generate meanings well beyond the issue of health, contributing to patients' reconstruction of their world views.

Ken returned to experimenting with alternative therapies and lifestyle changes after a period of illness led him to face his mortality:

When is your five years up? You don't know. Was it up two months ago? Whatever. One of the most significant things for me was last year, when my T-cell count dropped to just thirty-one and I was pretty sick and I thought, "This is it!" But within four weeks, six weeks I got back into transcendental meditation, looked at a number of things with diet and a whole heap of things and within six weeks pushed my T-cells up to 460 odd and that speaks for itself. The doctors couldn't believe it. And they didn't know what I was doing. And from then on it was just a matter of keeping a tab on what was going on.

For Ken, illness was a signal to undertake a more intensive regimen of self-care. The technological means to monitor one's health is provided by the T4-cell count together with other blood tests. Despite the declining significance of T4-cell counts in the diagnosis of individual conditions, many HIV-positive individuals still regard it as the key to reading their own health. With the test, Ken was able to "keep a tab on things" while returning to practices such as meditation and diets that he was already familiar with.

Frank's HIV infection was complicated by a non-HIV-related illness that required him to undergo intensive chemotherapy and surgery:

I've been taking vitamin C twice a week as injections and having acupuncture once a week. And I don't know whether it's that, or whatever it is, but I just feel better within myself. Like I just have more energy from what I had this time last year anyway. And like I should be a little bit slowed down, really, because I had chemo. I had major surgery. And like now I feel better. I have more energy. And not only that, my T-cell results appear to be going through the ceiling. So all that's really healthy. So, I'm not quite sure at the moment. I think I'm possibly really healthy. Not only that, I feel really healthy.

The expectation of a negative side-effects from his medical therapy, together with a surprising feeling of well-being after the treatment, a feeling he hypothesizes might be a result of the use of alternative therapies, led Frank to begin constructing a critique of HIV medicine:

I think that maybe not always people should go onto AZT, things like that, but I'm slowly more and more opposed to the fact that automatically saying AZT's an answer.

Frank's experience of recovery without the aid of AZT, a recovery that concluded with his use of a range of alternative therapies, reinforced his belief in the efficacy of such alternative modalities.

Through this combination of technical and experiential body readings people with HIV and AIDS construct their belief systems regarding therapeutic interventions and health. Tentative causal relations are hypo-thesized, tested out, and confirmed or rejected through observations of the self. O'Connor has also noted this systematic approach among HIV-positive consumers of alternative therapies in the United States. One of her informants described the tactic as the "cafeteria approach," which she summarizes thus: "Treatment options are pursued for as long as they ap-pear to be fruitful, discarded, or replaced as they appear to fail or as more promising options become available" (O'Connor 1990:208). She records how individuals combine readings of bodily responses with empirical methods of measurement, such as conventional blood tests, together with information and opinions offered by other users, to build up an evaluation of various kinds of therapies (O'Connor 1991). This tactic of hypothesis generation, observation, and hypothesis modification is quite consistent with the cultural logic of science. Thus, while the material explanations that science offers for AIDS may not be epistemologically adequate for the individual with the disease, the search for meaning, a search that does not necessarily require logical consistency, does proceed by way of this pre-vailing cultural logic.

I want to complete this chapter with a more detailed case study to illus-trate the point further.

Phillip was a vigorous, youthful-looking gay man in his mid-forties. He owned a small terrace-house close to the inner-city which he shared with his lover of eight years, until the latter's death from AIDS. It had been sev-eral years since Phillip had been diagnosed with AIDS at the time of our discussions. He remembered that, when diagnosed, he had responded by attempting to reduce his stress levels:

> When I first confronted HIV, I was working in the advertising industry —
> high stress. And so I gave up my job right away and went on the dole and
> started working in restaurants for extra money and so on, and reducing that
> stress level.

For Phillip, a diagnosis of HIV provided an opportunity to reevaluate what was important in his life. He made contact with a number of alterna-tive practitioners who were to have significant impact on his self care. His first experience was a very positive one. His health "bounced back," he said, while on a strict, two-year macrobiotic diet, strengthening his faith in alternative modalities. Yet despite this, Phillip is reluctant to accept the claims of alternative medicine dogmatically:

> After two years I slowly went back to a more regular diet. I mean I still eat
> macrobiotic food, particularly when I prepare it myself, but I'm certainly
> not dogmatic about it. I eat meat when it's given to me. I've come to a point

where I find there are some things I enjoy therefore I will enjoy them, regardless of whether they are in the long term not very good for you, like
cigarettes for example.

Thus, pleasures not necessarily consistent with the philosophy of natural
health care can be accommodated into a healthy lifestyle by rejecting in-
flexible dogma for a more pragmatic regimen. It is this pragmatic orientation to health that informs Phillip's approach to medical science. He is
prepared to consider when conventional therapy would be useful and when
it would not:

> I will use drugs that have been proven to be successful or efficient. Like I'm
> taking two drugs for prophylaxis for PCP now. I know those things work
> and I will not neglect to take them.

In this case, Phillip displays some degree of trust in medical science. I
asked him how he assesses the effectiveness of such treatments:

> Research seems to indicate that those are pretty efficient in keeping PCP at
> bay, and yeah I don't experience any side effects from them. I take them
> three times a week. Just when you started talking then I thought I'll mention
> that. And I haven't really looked into the long-term side effects of that. But
> I'm not particularly concerned about long-term effects because I'm very
> much living for the moment. So while my orientation is towards the natural
> therapies I don't exclude the medical drugs if they are shown to work really
> efficiently. AZT is far too tricky for me. I mean for example it causes side
> effects, it causes anemia which I can't seem to get rid of, and yeah people
> suffer side effects like nausea, and I just don't want to go through that.

Phillip approached medical science pragmatically, taking from it whatever,
in his view, would help him. The real test, however, is the response of his
body to particular drugs. If a drug appeared to be effective and did not cause
unpleasant side effects, he would accept medical intervention as necessary
and effective. If, however, a drug had unpleasant side effects, he deemed it
damaging and undesirable. Phillip prioritized bodily comfort and self-con-
trol of his body over the intangible or hypothetical benefits of a drug:

> I want to remain absolutely in control of my own health. If I take a herbal
> mixture, if it doesn't do any good at least it doesn't do any bad. I feel more
> in control of that.

This ongoing effort to maintain control of the body is, in part, mediated
and informed by the doctor/patient dialogue. Phillip consulted both a
medical practitioner and an alternative therapist. His alternative therapist
monitored his health, Phillip said, through the technology provided by his
doctor. "He gets copies of my test results to immediately adjust the herbal

formula that he gives me." And his doctor was aware of the alternative therapist. About him, Phillip said:

> I go in there and tell them how I am. And say I would like their advice. And in the end of their advice I say, "Thank you very much for that, I will consider it, I will think about it, and I will decide what I will do." And if one gives me advice I immediately go to the other and talk that advice through with him. I do it both ways and I've had no problems with that with either of them.

"How do you make a decision?" I asked him.

"The decision is essentially in terms of my orientation, which is towards natural therapies," he replied.

If the situation was a "crisis," Phillip turned to medical treatment. "I have no reservations at that point to use medical drugs to deal with a crisis. And I use them for as short a period as possible, high dosage antibiotics, intravenous, and get rid of that infection. And then I go back to my usual regime." For less pressing problems, or if the available treatment was of uncertain efficacy, he would favor alternative treatments, sure in the knowledge that these at least will not have negative side effects. Phillips's position was one of intellectual flexibility: available options are considered and judgment based on a prevailing world view yet with an eye to the best outcome.

We can recall here observations by medical anthropologists regarding the epistemological inadequacy of the scientific world view. Phillip only allows science to intervene into his life when he anticipated direct benefits. With AIDS this desire for results is often unrealized, frequently fueling anger and distrust. Yet desperation would be a grossly inaccurate description of this predicament. I have attempted to show, by way of example, how individuals measure the use of science and alternative therapies through a system of scientific-like experimentation based on a complex information loop centered on the reading of the body.

This is the realm of bodily function and intervention. But another realm is approached in this investigation, one that I pursue further in the following chapter. For now, Phillip's narrative will serve to reveal the link between the experience of illness and eschatological beliefs. Scientific intervention rests on the will to preserve life. Herein lies a more profound inadequacy. Science provides neither a total explanation for AIDS, nor an eschatology. Phillip must move beyond science if he is to find meaning in the death that science promises him through its prognosis:

> I see AIDS very much a symptom of the times we live in and is only one of the symptoms. I find it really easy to deal with AIDS. It's just part of me. Just part of life, part of the times that we live in. And hence reduced life expectancy I see as a perfectly natural thing. This is what we are at the

moment. And with that orientation it seems to me much easier to have fun and go out and enjoy yourself rather than fret about some infection you've picked up somewhere.

In this way Phillip interpreted his predicament as a metaphor of a wider human condition. And through this metaphor-making he remains very much a part of humanity. He described himself as:

a very spiritual person, believing very much in a continuation of my spirit being after this life. I do not buy into any of the established religions as they are defined because it seems to me restrictive. They all are dogmatic. They all are exclusive of other opinions and they are all living out of ivory towers.

Thus the resistance to dogmatism in health care extends to broader spiritual systems. Phillip has developed a highly personalized world view by taking from available discourses that which appeals to him as an individual and reconstructing it in an individualized manner, custom made as it were. Some have cynically described this as "shopping for a religion," the ultimate consumerist irony. The great success of Phillip's world view, nonetheless, is a profound ability to accommodate the potentially shattering condition of a life-threatening illness within a natural order of things. Beyond this, his condition bears lessons about life. It provides, in his words, "opportunities:"

It comes back to that concept of balance, that the whole world or universe is in balance. And so it creates for me, and again I can't emphasis enough that this is my own perceptions, a very strong consciousness of reality, a really strong sense of the good life. Everything is good. AIDS is good. It's given me so many opportunities, in a short period of time, to learn so much about myself and about living and about enjoying myself.

Even death is something that has its place. It is not something to be denied, through medical drugs or other artificial means, but a future event to be embraced. "I think its quite an experience ahead to die, and so in a sense I'm almost looking forward to that."

Phillip's narrative provides us with a detailed case study of, in de Certeau's terms, a contemporary "way of using" (de Certeau 1984). As de Certeau argues, the "practice of everyday life" is characterized by a tactical negotiation through given social conditions, in this case the disciplinary technologies of medicine and the range of somewhat less systematized alternative therapies. Through this negotiation process social space is appropriated, disciplines transformed, and meaning and practice constructed. The tactical negotiation of therapeutic options, which is so much a feature of the lives of people with HIV and AIDS, can be viewed as a creative play within available structures. This creative movement results in a web of practices which, while never escaping power, is never totally submissive and, in many and minute ways, transgresses and transforms the dominant social order. Phillips's narrative rescues the subject from disciplinary submission.

Phillip's condition declined very rapidly shortly after our conversations. After several hospitalizations for treatment, he reentered hospital for the last time. A week before his death we enjoyed a Sunday afternoon together there, discussing his condition, sharing some jokes, enjoying the brilliant sunshine of Sydney's summer. "I feel very good," he told me. "My body's giving me a little discomfort, but otherwise I feel fabulous. My head is clear." When I left, he hugged me with an intensity that told me that he knew our friendship was coming to an end.

Phillip died surrounded by family and friends. His liver had ceased to function and his mind, flushed with toxins, became confused. By that time, neither Phillip nor I recognized each other. It was as if he had begun his journey already, impatient with his imperfect body.

NOTES

1. Abrams (1990) includes in the genre of alternative practices those therapies which were developed through conventional scientific clinical trials. I discuss some of these liminal substances in Chapter Nine, substances such as AL721 and GLQ223 which, because of their mode of discovery or deployment, cut across both conventional scientific medicine and alternative therapy.
2. See, for example, "Bald AZT Claim 'Irresponsible'", *Sydney Star Observer* 153.
3. See, for example, the pamphlets: "Good Eating and You" (New South Wales State Department of Health's AIDS Bureau 1988); "Healthy Lifestyles" (ACON 1987).
4. Over the last few years, the visibility of interest in alternative therapy has significantly increased. An important development came in December 1991, when an individual gay man initiated an occasional newsletter, *with Complements*, covering issues such as visualization, Chinese medicine, meditation, and the latest therapies such as bitter melon treatment. The exercise receives little institutional support and relies entirely on volunteer contributions. ACON began expanding its vitamin and food supplement services, and lends out a room on a weekly basis to a meditation group. It has occasionally included alternative therapy on its HIV-information nights.
5. Living Well II, organised by PLWA (NSW), and funded by the New South Wales State Department of Health AIDS Bureau, was staged in February 1989 on the campus of the University of Sydney. Over 200 people with HIV and AIDS participated, including some from other states.

CHAPTER 7

Reinventing Death

> The certain prospect of death could sweeten every life with a precious and fragrant drop of levity — and now you strange apothecary souls have turned it into an ill-tasting drop of poison that makes the whole of life repulsive.
>
> – Nietzsche, *Beyond Good and Evil*

Not long after Phillip's death, a small brown envelope was delivered to my mailbox. It contained a black and white photograph of Phillip as he was some weeks before he died. Phillip had commissioned a photographer to take a series of portraits of himself as his illness progressed. This was one of the last photographs taken of him. It showed his smiling half-profile, his eyes turned to the camera. His face was gaunt, though not without its familiar, friendly warmth. On the reverse of the photograph Phillip had prepared a message. It read:

I discarded this body as it is now too worn for the times we live in.

At the beginning of a new day, without ceremony or ritual, my ashes will be thrown over a cliff into a valley of serene beauty and eternal peace.

I leave full of love and excitement, for at last I will have complete wisdom.

The correspondence was a poignant and haunting one, not least because my friend had engineered a means of informing me of his own death. And yet, knowing him, it seemed a familiar gesture, for the key issue in the last years of his life had always been control: of his health, his therapeutic modalities, and finally his own death. To Phillip, having control meant doing things for himself, at his own discretion, with an almost deliberate, self-conscious idiosyncrasy. Part of the impact of this final gesture lay in its sheer novelty, and the wit inherent in the celebration of one's own death while allowing one's survivors the indulgence of a photographic trace of a life "discarded."

The novelty of my friend's final communication raised for me a question: in what ways are the untimely deaths of so many young men influencing the contemporary organization of life's end? How do such novel practices developing around death by AIDS speak about our wider cultural predicament? What is novel about these acts of sentiment? And what is enduring?

THE MODERN WAY TO GO

Ariès, in a short exegesis of death in western society, described shifts from the Middle Ages, where death was considered a familiar part of the natural order, to a present attitude he describes as "an anxiety of sufficiently being." Death has become anxiety-generating, and through the medicalization of death since the 1930s, a threat to the modern (American) goal of the pursuit of happiness. He notes, in his final observations, the emergence of an interdiction on death, a kind of cultural denial of the inevitable, which has stripped death of its public functions, where "solitary and shameful mourning is the only recourse, like a sort of masturbation" (Ariès 1974:90).

The social response to this interdiction has been to remove death from the mundane realms of everyday living. Death is rendered a special problem to be managed in discrete social spaces such as hospitals, hospices, and crematoriums. Death thereby offers a career for a new professional:

> Death in the hospital is no longer the occasion of a ritual ceremony, over which the dying person presides amidst his assembled relatives and friends. Death is a technical phenomenon obtained by a cessation of care (Ariès 1974:88).

Family and friends have no role in the technical management of death. Indeed, Elias has noted how the presence of family and friends actually obstructs professional routines (Elias 1985).

A shift away from this predicament is evident in a range of new phenomena, however. "Death is once more becoming something one can talk about," Ariès claims, gesturing toward the emerging critique of medicalized death (Ariès 1974:103). Kübler-Ross, for example, has retrieved death from the hands of medical professionals, reconstructing the discourse of death from the perspective of the dying, beautifying it, rendering it a challenging and positive experience (Kübler-Ross 1969, 1989). Anthropology has joined the chorus of complainants against the medicalization of illness and death (see, for example, Comaroff 1978, 1982; Connor 1982; Scheper-Hughes 1990; Singer 1990; Singer, Baer and Lazarus 1990; Taussig 1980; Finkler 1991). Farmer and Kleinman, in a moving account of two experiences of AIDS, compare a death in a modern United States hospital to a death in rural Haiti. In the former case, a young man died surrounded by perplexed and inquiring medical specialists. Between probing tests and inquiries Robert, with bitterness in his eyes, pleads in shaky handwriting: "I just want to be kept clean." By contrast, the latter person dies in the poverty-stricken surroundings of a Haitian village, without modern medical care, but peacefully nonetheless, surrounded by family and friends (Farmer and Kleinman 1990). The contrast is a powerful one, raising fundamental questions regarding the technological management of death. Farmer and Kleinman's message is that there are other, possibly better, ways in which death can be organized, understood, and experienced.

This chapter illustrates experiences of death in the time of AIDS. Three case studies document the struggle for release from life-sustaining technology and the meanings generated for the individuals engaged in this struggle.

Considering these examples, one begins to suspect a shift away from the construction of "death as a technical error" (Freeman et al. 1970). The return of plague may well provide an answer in the negative to Ariès's pleading question regarding the contemporary organization of death: "Must we take for granted that it is impossible for our technological culture ever to regain the naive confidence in Destiny which had for so long been shown by simple men when dying?" (Ariès 1974:107).

DURING STORMY WEATHER

Tom and I came to know and respect each other well over the period of my involvement in the Sydney gay community and its AIDS organizations, and it was with great pain that I observed his progressive decline of health. Tom was bright, educated, and active in AIDS organizations. In the early stages of his illness he quickly discovered how to deploy his predicament to make political points about health-care services in Sydney. I discuss some of his activities further in Chapter Nine. Here I want to present some of his observations, made to me over the two-and-a-half years of his illness, regarding medical treatment, his own body, and his death.

In an early interview Tom conveyed to me the difficulties he experienced being HIV-positive. At this time he was for the most part healthy, having experienced only passing illnesses which had hospitalized him for short periods of fairly routine treatment:

> The most difficult thing is seeing a number of friends who are antibody positive getting sick. It's that constant thought of, "Is this going to happen

to me," and I don't want to have to go through that process. That's the hardest thing, is looking at people going through that all the time and wondering, "Am I next?"

Tom's difficulty, at this time, was the heightened anticipation of death which came from living in close proximity to the epidemic. His active engagement in the gay community had linked him with many other people with HIV, many of whom had already died, many who were by now becoming ill:

It's a fear of death . . . the problem is a fear of the process, and that fear of how am I going to cope with so many people going through this process around me, and dying. That process. As well as not becoming shell shocked or totally whacko.

To help explain to me his feelings, Tom ventured a metaphor I heard him use on a number of occasions:

During stormy weather there'd be these huge waves getting washed up on the shore. It's like you can play the game. You can see the waves coming and you know when one's going to be really enormous. There's been a series of other waves in the last four years. That's how I've felt many times. When I felt totally overwhelmed. But I always manage to float to the top. And I can see all those waves coming in the distance. It'll be some time this year when I'll be totally surrounded by death and all those feelings of grief and I'll be really submerged. There's nothing I can do to change that. There's no option for getting out of it. I know that's coming. It's a little bit like deliberately being dumped in those games when you were kids. We let ourselves be dumped even though the water shot up your nose and tossed you around in the wave and you'd come up gasping for breath. It's a bit like that. And you know you're about to be dumped and its going to dump the shit out of you and there's nothing you can do about it.

Some time after this, Tom was again hospitalized. Initially, he found the experience a fairly positive one, and commented on his relationship with the hospital staff:

I expect lots more information, I have no problems getting answers. They tend to theorize a lot and make unsupportive answers, but the staff are good and the doctors are approachable. I would be left in the dark if I didn't ask questions. As far as I'm concerned the treatment I've got has been first class. Because I'm informed, and people know I'm informed, they're a little more careful to give me answers, I'm treated as a quasi-professional.

His remarks about the behavior of health-care providers suggest a belief that technical information and education is the key to empowerment in the doctor/patient relationship. But to what extent does this empowerment translate into real determination over the healing process? Over the following months, it became evident that Tom's negotiating power was increasingly reduced the more ill he became. We see a growing dependency on medicine for physical care, and an erosion of his critical will.

Tom then underwent a period of aggressive chemotherapy. At first he was optimistic about the therapy because, he explained, it provided him with a better prognosis than if he had no therapy at all. "They would have given me eight months anyway," he said. "That's the usual diagnosis, so it's either that or put up with this for a while and hopefully have it in remission."

When his treatment was complete, several weeks later, I visited Tom in his home where he was now spending most of his time. He had lost much of his vitality and was deeply depressed:

> I'm feeling really awful. The treatment has really fucked me over. I feel worse than I did when I was doing treatment. I'm feeling more depressed than I ever have in my life. Like nothing about my life seems worthwhile and nothing I try to do seems worthwhile. After all I've said about taking control, there's still something about being in that situation that makes it very hard to make your own decisions. You wonder whether you have all the information, whether you're able to make decisions.

The combined effect of intensifying bodily experience of illness, together with the intensified management of the body in a hospital setting, had the net result of completely alienating Tom from the healing process. This alienation had precipitated such a degree of hopelessness and depression that Tom now considered suicide:

> I came home and went to bed and laid there for two hours and fantasized about how I was going to end it all. I'm just really fed up with it all. I thought of putting myself into hospital and stopping all my treatments.

This fantasy was "not very imaginative," he conceded, yet it is significant that Tom's imagined suicide was associated with medical treatment manipulation. To imagine one's death through a removal of medical treatment, a kind of reverse therapy, suggests Tom's existence had, by this time, become framed wholly in medical terms. The total medicalization of illness leads to the point where even death can only be conceptualized within the context of the medical apparatus.

Suicide was not a novel consideration for Tom. Some time earlier, Tom had engaged in conversations with Brian McGahen, a gay man with a high profile in Sydney known for his gay and socialist political agenda. McGahen was at the time strongly advocating the right of terminally ill people to take their own lives. Tom described these conversations as having opened new doors for him. "That gave me new options," he said, options he had then not considered before, and that now, through the experience of debilitating health, he was considering again.

By now, Tom had lost his vigor and enthusiasm for his political work. I met him at the Mardi Gras Fair Day. He had lost a great deal of weight and his hair had failed to grow back after the treatment. He made a damning indictment against his peers:

> Being sick is the most disempowering thing that has ever happened to me. I'm starting to hate positive people that are still healthy. You get messages like, "It's your fault that it's happened to you." And it usually comes from the people who are always talking about sickness being empowering, even if they don't realize it.

In the context of a celebratory fair surrounded by thousands of gay men and lesbians, Tom's comments could not have more clearly stated his sense of alienation from the community he once felt so much a part of.

Within a few months, Tom had resigned himself to the fact that he was not going to get any better. He had given up all possibility of returning to work, and was planning to spend his time catching up with friends and looking after himself. He moved into a family member's home and made several trips to see distant friends. His condition deteriorated quite rapidly thereafter. He began to lose motor control: his walk became precarious and unbalanced, his speech slurred and confused, he was unable to eat without vomiting. Tom's condition deteriorated further to a point where he was bedridden and totally dependant on others for even the most rudimentary human needs such as moving his body into a comfortable position in bed, or going to the toilet. His doctors considered his condition manageable, nonetheless, and hospitalized him for intensive care. Under intensive monitoring in hospital, Tom was then shocked and angered when his doctors delivered a new diagnosis of toxoplasmosis in the brain. They admitted they may have been wrong in their original diagnosis of lymphoma, but this new diagnosis brought hope, they assured him, because treatment was more advanced. In response to questioning from friends and family, however, they conceded that treatment could not guarantee his illness would become manageable, or that his quality of life would improve.

With this admission of uncertainty, Tom's faith in his medical management appeared finally to break. He immediately decided not to accept further treatment. "They won't trick me again," he said, and thereafter refused all treatment except that which relieved pain. Even then, he only permitted a close family member to administer the drugs. Despite his refusal, his medical team insisted on maintaining treatment. Tom stubbornly maintained his resistance, however, even to the point of holding pills under his tongue and then spitting them out after his nurse had left the room.

At this point, Tom made it clear to his family and friends that he was then ready to take his own life. In order to carry out Tom's final wish, negotiations were necessary in order to secure his release from the hospital and put him under palliative care at home. His deliverance could not proceed under the eye of the hospital medical staff. Staff were suspicious of Tom's intentions and refused to sign his release because, they insisted, treatment still offered some hope of improvement. He was not sick enough to have treatment withdrawn and receive only palliative home care. The negotiations took over a week before a physician was found who was willing to sign his release. In the time it took to secure his release, Tom frequently became impatient and angry. The relief he felt upon finally being told he was free to go home was evident to all.

In the comfort and familiar surroundings of his home, Tom spent a final twenty-four hours with family and friends, exchanging expressions of love, and saying goodbye. A preparation of pure heroin was injected into his veins and he quietly and painlessly achieved death.

MANDATORY LIFE

The practices of euthanasia, increasingly common because of AIDS, are at odds with both legal proscription against aiding suicide, and prevailing Christian discourses about the preeminence of life over death. In the state of New South Wales, for example, suicide is no longer a criminal act, having been secularized and distinguished from religious sanctions against the taking of life. It remains, however, illegal to assist others in taking their own lives, and those who do so may be charged with murder, manslaughter, or the offense of assisting suicide and be liable to ten years imprisonment. To be found guilty of administering a poison amounts to murder and is liable to twenty-five years imprisonment (Godwin et al. 1991).

The illegality of euthanasia does not prevent its occurrence. Several men I came to know in the course of this study undertook action similar to Tom's. On April 2, 1990, Brian McGahen, the gay activist mentioned above who had spoken to Tom about this very issue, concluded two years of advocacy for euthanasia by making a personal example of his beliefs. After careful consideration and planning he took his own life in his apartment surrounded by friends. Unlike others, McGahen fully politicized his act by publicizing the circumstances of his death. The *Sydney Star Observer* published his final statement, written only hours before his death: "Brian McGahen was an advocate of voluntary euthanasia and wanted the right of people with terminal illness to end their own lives with control and dignity at a time that they want to. Brian did this" (*Sydney Star Observer* 6 April 1990).

Euthanasia is a relatively common practice within terminal hospital wards and hospices. Nurses remove life-sustaining mechanisms — "passive euthanasia" — at the request of friends, family, or patients. Additionally, it is not unknown for health workers to engage in "active" euthanasia, that is, the administering of a drug or drugs intended to arrest the life of a patient. In a study conducted in the state of South Australia, for example, Hassan revealed that 19 percent of surveyed health workers had "taken active steps to bring about a patient's death, whether by assisting suicide or administering a lethal procedure" (AFAO 1993). In the United States, Slome and Moulton (1991) conducted a study of attitudes to euthanasia among Californian physicians and found a greater percentage of those working in AIDS clinical research were willing to prescribe lethal doses of drugs for "self delivery." The experience of AIDS appears to have generated a greater willingness among health-care workers to consider and conduct euthanasia on patients.

Several organizations in Australia have attempted to deal strategically with the issue of euthanasia, notably the New South Wales Euthanasia Society, and People Living with AIDS (NSW). The former keeps a library of literature, some of which is "banned" in Australia, and counsels individuals seeking information. It has proposed a "living will" as a means whereby a person specifies in advance, when still sound of mind, and circumscribes with legal constraints, the procedure for their "self-deliverance." PLWA (NSW) advocates the legalization of euthanasia and supports the "living will" concept as a guarantee of safe, legal, and consensual practice.

The outcomes of the actions of individuals such as McGahen and of collectivities such as PLWA (NSW) are still uncertain. Some shifts in the formal status of euthanasia appeared to be underway in 1990 when the New South Wales State Government began debating proposed legislation to allow doctors the right not to resuscitate very old or terminally ill patients.[1] No changes have yet been made, however, to the legal status of either "passive" or "active" euthanasia in the State.

Because of its illegal and invisible nature, it is impossible to assess just how frequent the practice of euthanasia is. However, the facts that euthanasia *is* practiced, that its status remains politically sensitive, and that there is a cost in this status to the terminally ill, can all be noted. In this last respect, it is significant that the duty of a medical practitioner to do everything possible to sustain a person's life, even to the point of overriding an individual's own wishes, remains encoded in criminal law. However, the practice of euthanasia, despite the law, challenges the stability of that medico-legal power.

RENOUNCING LIFE-SUSTAINING TECHNOLOGY

Steven, whom we met in Chapter Five, became for me an intimate friend in the course of this study. It was as a friend as well as an observer that I became involved in the complex issues and events that emerged as this young man developed AIDS and progressed to death. It was this intimate experience with his illness, more than any other, that familiarized me with the predicament of AIDS among gay men in Sydney. It was thus with some difficulty that I maintained a journal during the period of his decline, recording his progress, our conversations, his comments and observations. In the following account I draw heavily from that journal, reproducing slabs of it where I feel the mood of the moment has been well captured.

Steven's story dramatically illustrates the medicalization of death. The last few months of Steven's life were shaped by a difficult process of negotiation with medical practitioners, health-care providers, friends, and family, as well as his own deteriorating body. As his illness progressed and the integrity of his body was more threatened, his dependence on medical support increased. Disengagement from this technological support system became for Steven a traumatic process, requiring his acceptance of his imminent death, and a renunciation of his extraordinary faith in medicine.

The account begins only a few months before Steven's death. Steven had been diagnosed with cytomegalovirus (CMV), a viral infection that threatened his eyesight. He had begun treatment; the regimen was demanding, requiring a visit to the hospital outpatient clinic once a week for an hour at a time for intravenous therapy. The hospital visits consumed time and energy and Steven needed transport to and from the hospital in the community bus provided by the local government health service.

Steven signaled something was amiss with this course of therapy during a conversation late one night:

> I woke up this morning and as I was rubbing my left eye I realized my right eye was completely black — couldn't see a thing. So one of the doctors looked at it this morning at the hospital and said, "We'll have a proper look at it tomorrow, I don't want to talk about blindness yet", and I thought, "Well no, neither do I, love!" I just freaked this morning.

"So what's the use of the treatment if it hasn't worked?" I asked.

"Exactly!" he exclaimed. "Why not just stop taking it? But you can't do that. That's giving up."

The following day, on returning to the hospital, Steven was diagnosed with complete blindness in his right eye. He was advised to continue the treatment in order to prevent further spread of the infection. The eye specialist mentioned the possibility of an operation on his retina to restore sight, but delayed a decision on this in order to monitor Steven's progress.

The following week I met Steven at the hospital after another appointment with the eye specialist. He had been counseled not to undergo an operation due to his weakened state. He himself agreed he would not be able to withstand another operation, especially so soon after a recent operation to insert an "Infuse-A-Port" [implanted catheter allowing easy access to a vein] into his chest. Yet Steven was extremely upset at this news and cried a little. He took comfort in my assertion that many people go through life with one eye, and was soon heading to the treatment room for his regular treatment.

It was at this time that Steven began considering his own death, making inquiries with various professionals at the hospital, and discussing the issue with friends. "I was wondering if it would be better if I died in hospital or at home," he mused one day:

> I just wanted to know when I should start organizing it, and when I asked my social worker she listened and went away and came back with an information brochure about funeral directors and stuff. I haven't looked at it yet, but the last time I mentioned it to Mum and Dad they said, "Leave it to us, we'll take care of it."
>
> I'm being cremated, I don't want to be buried. I just wanted to know the best place to die, apparently its more complicated to die at home. My sister says you have to have the doctor practically there, and the funeral director arranged.

I counseled that those issues should not interfere with his decision:

> No. If I last another year I want to die right there in that bed. I love that little bed and whoever happens to be there at the time is fine. I mean the social worker wanted to know who I want to be there, who'll hold my hand at the time. I mean really! If I've got the energy to get home from the hospital I will. I'll come home and just lie down, maybe talk a little with whoever's there, maybe not talk, and just pass away.

Despite his extremely debilitated state, Steven showed some enthusiasm for attending an out-of-town conference for people with HIV and AIDS. He did attend, aided by a timely blood transfusion that boosted his energy levels. Immediately after returning to Sydney his condition deteriorated to the stage where he was permanently bedridden. At his sister's suggestion, Steven's parents arrived to stay and care for him earlier than they had planned. His father projected optimism, despite the seriousness of Steven's condition. "I still like to think it might just be a remission," he commented. His mother asked me on the first night of their arrival, "Do you think he's got very much longer?" I simply replied, "I don't think so." She said, "Neither do I. I guess all we can do is be here and make him as comfortable as possible."

Family and close friends quickly settled into a stable and calm routine of providing Steven with intensive care in the home. He received his infusion treatment at his bedside, thanks to portable infusion equipment, and the training of a friend to administer the treatment. This relieved Steven of his, by then, daily hospital visits, visits which had become far too strenuous for him. Steven became increasingly reluctant to make the trip upstairs to the bathroom to wash. Allowing someone to assist was an admission of his weakening condition. He was soon being cleaned in bed to avoid the difficulty of the ascent. Twice a week, Community Support Network volunteers came to relieve Steven's parents who appreciated the opportunity to get out of the house.

Steven's appetite was now very limited. After eating some food his mother had prepared one night, she asked Steven, "Are you feeling better now?" To which he replied, "Nothing will ever make me feel better ever again." After this his mother confessed to me that, while she had to this point harbored secret hopes of his recovery, she now accepted Steven would die soon.

By now, Steven was virtually skeletal in build, without energy, and totally dependant on others. Shaving had become too arduous. He was unable to get out of bed by himself and a commode was positioned nearby so that he did not have to make the trip to the bathroom. He had virtually ceased to eat, though he continued to ask for food. The ritual of taking meals, if not eating them, remained important to him. Some days he would not eat at all. On others he ate a morning and evening meal.

Finally, Steven lost the sight in his other eye. I asked the doctor how long he thought Steven would live. He replied, "He shouldn't be alive now." Lying in bed, blind, Steven asked unexpectedly and without further comment, "How many days to Christmas?" His doctor later said to me in passing, "Sometimes people hang on for special days."

Several days before Steven's death, the doctor gave him a brief examination and told him there was nothing else he could do for him. At this information Steven cried. The nurse then asked Steven if he wanted his treatment and he said, "I thought I said I didn't want it today." The doctor asked how he felt, if he was in pain. He said no he wasn't. The doctor asked Steven if he was aware that the treatment was not going to do him any good and if he still wanted to continue with it. He then replied, "Why not?" Like the ritual of eating, regular treatment had taken on an extra-clinical significance for Steven. Continuing treatment represented a continuation of life's routine, of life itself. Clearly by now he was struggling with the issue of his release from this clinical technology.

Several days later he no longer requested treatment. Three days after Christmas Steven died peacefully, in his bed, surrounded by family and friends.

The deaths of Tom and Steven were unique in many ways. Yet each may be taken to represent a cultural predicament broader than these individual lives and deaths. For one, the question of medical intervention was a paramount issue in each case. Tom and Steven embodied contemporary faith in technology that was tempered only by its ultimate failure.

Steven never conceptualized his condition in political terms, as Tom was wont to do at most opportunities. Yet, toward the end of his life, Tom was less able to see the political dimension of his condition, and less able to act politically. The fact that he was becoming disempowered disturbed Tom. To lose control over his destiny was anathema to his very existence. Toward the end, Tom found it necessary to invest friends and family with the right to carry out his will. The return of death to the home environment is significant here, for without medical sanction, it is only in the secrecy of the home that an illegal act of euthanasia can be enacted.

True to gay liberation ideology, Tom saw his personal situation as a political one. Illness had come to replace sexuality as the personal issue through which he built his self identity and enacted his politics. To take his own life before technology had itself defined the time of his death was, for Tom, a final resuscitation of self-determination. Death itself becomes a political act and euthanasia at home the tactic by which this is realized.

For Steven, a man with considerable faith in the ability of medical technology to sustain his life, his decision to die at home was the first step in renouncing clinical management. Admittedly, this decision was made possible only by a mobile technology that allowed an intensive treatment regimen to be continued outside of the hospital setting. This home technology is only serviceable with the backup of a community nursing system, providing regular home visits by nurses who oversee the administration of treatments and the monitor the patient's condition. The surveillance and management powers of the hospital were thereby insinuated into the private space of the home.

A BEAUTIFUL SUNSET

Charley and Paul, young professional men in their late twenties had been together as a couple for eight years. Unlike Tom, Paul does not consider himself a gay activist. He positions his sexuality, not in political terms, but in the discourse of an "alternative lifestyle." Paul is a practicing Catholic. He attends church, prays, and holds conventional eschatological beliefs.

When I visited Paul in his small but comfortable city apartment, shortly after his lover's death, he was physically tired yet in a state of emotional excitement. The events leading up to Charley's death were dramatic and exhausting for him. Now he appeared more relaxed, reflective, and somewhat relieved. With his partner's death fresh in his mind, Paul narrated to me their final moments together with great enthusiasm, investing incidents with enormous personal significance, exercising his rhetorical skills with some audacity.

Paul's story captivated me. It had all the elements of a rounded narrative, with a plot development, conflicts, sub-plots, climax, humor, and pathos. For Paul, the telling of the story was emotionally cathartic, allowing him to explore the meaning of his lover's death. I asked him if he would be willing to retell his account for me, this time on tape. He was very enthusiastic to do so, and one month later I returned to his apartment.

In the interim Paul had time to reflect further on the experience. I was surprised, therefore, to hear that the second account reproduced almost identically the form and tone of the first, except for the addition of a few details. He spoke with great emotion, at times failing to hold back tears. And yet he pressed on to complete the story, as if only in its telling could the pain be fully exorcised and its meaning realized. His account represents a moment of meaning production within the context of our researcher/subject relationship. We will see how his Catholic beliefs guide his interpretation of events, the account culminating in an elaborate theological rendering of this death experience.

Charley's illness was painful and debilitating but, compared with Tom's, relatively short. Charley died of tuberculosis made fatal by his depleted immune status caused by HIV infection. Paul is also HIV-infected and experienced ill health while Charley was approaching death, complicating Paul's ability to provide care and support for him. Paul's story begins when he and Charley were both very ill, Charley critically so. Returning to Sydney from a work-related trip in extreme pain caused by a viral infection, Paul immediately admitted himself to hospital. Charley was left at home in the care of volunteer carers and a friend. Paul emotionally recalls the trauma of the separation: "I was very worried about him.

And he was very worried about me. He couldn't get to me and I couldn't get to him. And neither one of us did very well without the other."

The separation was too stressful for Paul and he left the hospital before his treatment was completed, intending to return at the first opportunity. Back at home, Paul realized that Charley needed hospitalization and persuaded him to go to the hospital overnight for a blood transfusion. But the plan for just a short stay was thwarted when Charley tested positive for active tuberculosis and was required to remain in hospital. This detention presented Charley with an ultimate challenge:

> When they get him to the hospital they decide his TB is active. And because he had active TB he wasn't going to be able to get out for fourteen days in what was, in effect, a quarantine situation, where he was told by the Health Department that he had to stay in the hospital for fourteen days whether he liked it or not. He had to receive these treatments whether he liked it or not, for the welfare of the rest of society. Now Charley had never been controlled by anything in his life. No institutions. And I knew as soon as it had started that he would die before he would stay fourteen days under a court order. And he did.

Paul was probably not that sure of this outcome at the time. Later, he states that he was not anticipating Charley's death for some months. The point here, however, is that the nexus between Charley's serious state of illness and the social conditions that structured his experience of it facilitated his approach to death and the manner in which it was to be played out.

Charley was in a great deal of pain at this stage and Paul related to me, with some emotional pain to himself, how, with the help of friends, he came to an acceptance of Charley's imminent death:

> There was no joy in life for him. His medications were intense, twenty-five or thirty pills a day, which nauseated him, made him totally unable to eat, gave him great discomfort. He was taking 100 milligrams of morphine four to five hours apart. So having already made the decision that enough was enough, he had a hard time telling me. But other people starting telling me that it was time to let him proceed with that sort of path.
>
> Right, so 8.30 or so I tell him, I say, "Look Charley, I love you and I will always love you. And I wish we could live forever as we are but we can't. If what you need and want now is to die I'll bless that choice. I'll understand and I support your needs to determine your own fate. And I know that we'll be with each other again. And I believe that the world is bigger than it seems. And in many ways there could be more peace for you in another realm."

Paul's acceptance of Charley's imminent death had an immediate and dramatic affect on Charley:

When I told him that his eyes just looked really grateful. And then with a ferocity that I had never seen in him, he ripped everything out of his body, food tubes out of his nose. I had to physically hold his arms to keep him from ripping the catheter out of his arm, for fear that he was going to really tear a hole in his arm. And trying to calm him down, "Look, I'll have it removed! Stop this! Stop it!" He was in a frantic ferocious pace. He was so anxious to leave.

Charley's will to die was facilitated by a release from both his lover and the medical technology that was sustaining him. But a compromise was negotiated by the medical staff at this point. Maintaining a fluid tube was suggested as a means of keeping Charley comfortable in his final moments. Paul continues:

So I went back in and said, "I know that you trust me. And I'm not going to have them do something which is going to keep you alive now. Only the things which will keep you comfortable and maintain your dignity." And I'm holding his hand and he's holding mine. And I suggested that this is the case with the fluids. And he agreed to have them connect him and gave him the fluids. And he became extremely relieved at this decision.

Paul's account reveals a tension between Charley's desire to escape the hospital for the familiar environment of home and the physical comfort which the hospital environment could provide him:

The week that he'd been there he was really horrified. He wanted to escape. He wanted me to get a taxi and just get him away. He would cry, "Please get me out of here!" It was really terrible. There was just nothing I could do about it unless we did escape and have the Health Department searching for us. It was very sad for me that he wanted something different and that there was nothing I could do by law. They had control of his death to be like this, and not for us to be in our bed at home. It was very sad yet, I'm going to be frank, the oxygen, the fluids, there were a whole lot of things that made the hospital a better place to die.

And so it was here that Charley died. Having negotiated a withdrawal of his life-sustaining treatments the couple, in the company of two close friends, had their last moments together:

We saw the sunrise together. He had collapsed in my arms at that point, a little bit like the statue of Christ in Mary's arms.

We had been just sitting with him and I was sitting with him, holding his hand. And the three of us had been quite normal, talking and laughing and smiling and making little jokes with him. We weren't being somber. We just acted like normal life right to the moment when he died.

And I noticed his breathing had moved to a stilted, erratic, manic sort of breathing pattern. And that's what made me decide to get in bed with him.

'Cause he'd been in a fine sleep till this started. Well not quite asleep. He'd open his eyes and smile and laugh a little bit. When I climbed into bed with him and put my arm across his chest his breathing completely changed. What he needed was the security and warmth. He was getting scared I suspect. And just before I got into bed with him he said with his last breaths: "I love you." Only that wasn't said with one breath. He needed a separate breath with every word, and he repeated it seven, eight, nine times: "I . . . love . . . you . . . I . . . love . . . you." So earnest! So heartfelt that it was one of the most beautiful moments of my life.

So I was in the bed and I just held him. And his breathing was like a piano concerto, each passage became slower and more subtle. Until finally in his last moment he stopped breathing and at that point quite a clever thing happened. Julie said, "He's gone, he's gone." And we stood there and gasped. And then he took this huge breath and we all burst out laughing in this really hearty laugher that was just totally contagious. And in a moment he really did stop breathing. Gave a little spew of black goo from his lungs and his body jolted as though you could feel something leaving. 'Cause he was in my arms and I could feel as though something had quickly left and his body had been tossed.

Paul found profundity in his lover's death through the guiding eschatology of Catholicism, his narrative framed in Catholic imagery. Witness Paul's final comment on Charley's moment of death as he lay in Paul's arms:

This expression came upon his face, his last expression, it was an Old Testament-type value of scorn to an earth which had humiliated itself with its abuse to humanity.

Refracted through Christian theology, Paul's interpretation of Charley's death was as an enactment of Judeo-Christian suffering, Charley himself at one point standing in for the persecuted Christ — "collapsed in my arms, like the statue of Christ in Mary's arms", with Paul himself transformed into the nurturing mother. There is little room in this scenario for clinical interference. Only with medicine repositioned in a non-interventionist role can this morality tale take its course.

*   *   *

Taken together these death stories illustrate the tactical maneuvres people with AIDS and those close to them may undertake in order to retain control of their predicament. Imminent death presents acute difficulties in this respect, in that the serious loss of bodily, and sometimes cognitive, integrity greatly impedes the will to control. These examples show how, despite these extraordinary odds, people with AIDS are yet able to deflect authoritative regimes through innovative tactical practices.

As Tom's, Steven's and Charley's stories illustrate, death in the home has become a desirable, and increasingly frequent phenomenon since the advent of AIDS. What was once, in the first half of this century, a practice viewed as primitive and unhygienic, now appears to be undergoing some renewal among gay men. This return to death at home suggests a reconsideration of the value of clinical care. It is a symptom of a wider reassessment of medicine and the trend to critique the progressive medicalization of life.

Each man struggled against technological interventions during the last stages of life. Release was facilitated in each case with the assistance of friends and family. Death was not a solitary effort, but a collective enterprise.

The moment of death focuses those present on the meaning of life. It is here, at this final moment, that the cosmologies of a people become most visible. I have attempted to illustrate here the active, creative processes involved in generating meaning out of the death experience.

His lover's death helped Paul prepare for his own. Paul has never, in the systematic sense of being a member of a gay organization, considered himself a gay activist. His sexuality and lifestyle are not conceptualized in political terms. Rather, coming from a strong Catholic family background, his understanding of his life with Charley and of his lover's death from AIDS is framed in Christian imagery. Charley's suffering and death provided Paul with the opportunity to reenact, as it were, the philosophy of Christian suffering and redemption. In Charley's death the suffering of Christ is echoed and confirmed:

> He made that statement with his last expression. But we've taken to inhumanity — decrepit, decadent, disgusting, mortal. And to have four billion people living in such ineptitude and mortality in contradiction to the things we believed in was too much for him. He didn't want to any more. He suffered a lot because he couldn't just ignore it every night of his life.

For those gay men whose sexual identity is a political telos, the Roman Catholic Church is frequently identified with the repression of homosexuality. The relative detachment, even hostility of such men to the Christian church leaves many without eschatological beliefs of any kind or struggling with eclectic and unstructured belief systems patched together from the available pool of orthodoxies.

Tom for example, never expressed any thoughts of afterlife to me. His illness and death were secular, political events. In the absence of a firm eschatology the imminence of death suffers a lack of significance. It is this absence of belief that has produced Nietzsche's poisoned death. Medicine is the new faith for men like Tom, but it is one which is capable of only looking back at life, not forward to death. Psychologists recognize this effect as "denial." But it is not an incapacity within the individual to face up to the inevitable, for this denial has been learned. Only our history makes such an astonishing rejection of the inevitable possible. And it is our technology that supports this denial, to the point where bodies can be kept alive indefinitely, long after life abandons them. This medicalization of death empties death of its significance as the final rite of passage, for in death the struggle is lost, finality realized. There is nowhere else to go.

The new contradiction to be resolved lies in the failed promise of science. Death becomes, not a passage into afterlife, but a struggle for the release of the body from medical management and a relegitimation of sociality at the time of death.

NOTES

1. "Protection For Doctors Who Say No", *Sydney Morning Herald* 20 September 1990.

Part Three

Discursive Strategies of Resistance

CHAPTER 8

People Living With AIDS Inc.:
The Genealogy of a New Identity

In this chapter I focus on the strategic practices of a small collectivity of gay men with HIV/AIDS that marked the emergence of a new social identity organized around the predicament of being HIV-infected. These practices progressively constituted a discursive systematization of the experience of HIV positivity into a strategic "anti-discipline." This new identity, frail because built on the anticipation of death, drew on the established formations of gay identity and the "empowered" patient, the latter formulated within women's groups and groups for the disabled. The effect of their conflation is the formation of a new social subject centered on being HIV-infected and articulated through confrontational relations with medicine and the state. This new subject-centered anti-discipline has transformed both the phenomenological experience of this illness, notably in its public representations, and patient relations to medicine and the state generally.

The first section of this chapter traces the beginnings of a distinct PWA (people with AIDS) patient discourse in the United States and its infiltration into Australia. This discourse emerged from and was strongly influenced by gay political strategies, and yet it demonstrates characteristics distinctly its own. I then trace the pathway of a number of individual illness "careers," taking the concept as framed by Goffman (1963) and illustrating the forms and directions such a career may take with this new illness. I document some formative activities of a new organization seeking to represent people with AIDS, illustrating the first moments when the tactics of living with HIV/AIDS were strategically ordered into a potentially powerful anti-discipline. Two regimes became the focus of protest in, and counterpoints to, identity formation: namely medical research, and the state.

THE PROJECT OF EMPOWERMENT: FOUNDATIONS

The idea struck like a bolt of lightning. Until then, it simply hadn't occurred to those of us in New York who were diagnosed that we couldn't be anything more than the passive recipients of the genuine care and concern of those who hadn't (yet) been diagnosed. As soon as the concept of PWAs representing themselves was proposed, the idea caught on like wildfire (with small pockets of resistance coming from factions at GMHC).[1] Part of the widespread acceptance of the notion of self-empowerment must be attributed to lessons learned from the feminist and civil rights struggles. Many of the earliest and most vocal supporters of the right to self-empowerment were the lesbians and feminists among the AIDS Network attendees (Callen and Turner 1988:290).

So wrote Michael Callen and Dan Turner in 1988 when retelling the history of the "PWA self-empowerment movement." People with AIDS, until that time labelled as AIDS "patients," "sufferers," or "victims" had indeed been collectivizing, largely within support groups, ever since the disease was first identified in 1981 in San Francisco. As their statement suggests, however, it was not until 1983 that the concepts of self-empowerment and self-organization were considered. A manifesto known as the "Denver Principles" represents the earliest discursive fixation of this concept of "self-empowerment" for those with the disease. It presented a new strategy for the reorganization of the identity and collective social representation of people with AIDS:

THE DENVER PRINCIPLES
STATEMENT FROM THE ADVISORY COMMITTEE
OF PEOPLE WITH AIDS

We condemn attempts to label us as "victims", a term which implies defeat, and we are only occasionally "patients", a term which implies passivity, helplessness, and dependence upon the care of others. We are "People with AIDS".

Recommendations for Health Care Professionals

1. Come out, especially to their patients who have AIDS.
2. Always clearly identify and discuss the theory they favor as to the cause of AIDS, since this bias affects the treatments and advice they give.
3. Get in touch with their feelings (e.g. fears, anxieties, hopes, etc.) about AIDS and not simply deal with AIDS intellectually.

4. Take a thorough personal inventory and identify and examine their own agendas around AIDS.
5. Treat People with AIDS as whole people, and address psychological issues as well as biophysical ones.
6. Address the question of sexuality in people with AIDS specifically, sensitively and with information about gay male sexuality in general, and the sexuality of people with AIDS in particular.

Recommendations for all People

1. Support us in our struggle against those who would fire us from our jobs, evict us from our homes, refuse to touch us or separate us from our loved ones, our community or our peers, since available evidence does not support the view that AIDS can be spread by casual, social contact.
2. Not scapegoat people with AIDS, blame us for the epidemic or generalize about our lifestyles.

Recommendations for People with AIDS

1. Form caucuses to choose their own representatives, to deal with the media, to choose their own agenda and to plan their own strategies.
2. Be involved at every level of decision-making and specifically serve on the boards of directors of provider organizations.
3. Be included in all AIDS forums with equal credibility as other participants, to share their own experiences and knowledge.
4. Substitute low risk sexual behaviors for those which could endanger themselves or their partners; we feel that people with AIDS have an ethical responsibility to inform their potential sexual partners of their health status.

Rights of People with AIDS

1. To as full and satisfying and emotional lives as anyone else.
2. To quality medical treatment and quality social service provision without discrimination of any form including sexual orientation, gender, diagnosis, economic status or race.
3. To full explanations of all medical procedures and risks, to choose or refuse their treatment modalities, to refuse to participate in research without jeopardizing their treatment and to make informed decisions about their lives.
4. To privacy, to confidentiality of medical records, to human respect and to choose who their significant others are.
5. To die — and to LIVE — in dignity.

(Callen and Turner 1988:294–95)

The rhetoric of "coming out" signals a commitment to an established gay liberation agenda. It was assumed that the political and phenomenological benefits demonstrated in coming out as gay would transfer unproblematically to the situation of being diagnosed with AIDS. Sensitivity of professionals to welfare clients' sexuality is demanded. The rendering of a previously medically defined identity as a social one is a strategy borrowed directly from gay and women's liberation. The concepts of "patient rights" emerges in demands for control over medical treatment regimens, to freedom from discrimination, to representation on decision-making bodies, and the recognition of non-biomedical forces ("psychosocial issues," personal "agendas," "feelings") within the healing/illness complex.

The catalytic event for Australians with HIV/AIDS was a visit by Michael Callen to the Third National AIDS Conference in Hobart in August 1988. The previous National AIDS Conference in 1987 had seen a public address by three people with AIDS, but with little consequence for a self-organization movement. In 1988, however, Callen spoke of a movement of "self-empowerment" among "people with AIDS" in the United States. He advocated that people with HIV and AIDS come out about their status, speak openly about their experiences, and challenge the stigmatized stereotype of the AIDS "victim." "In a survey of long-term survivors of AIDS in the U.S.A.," he said, "the only common factors to their survival was their will to live and their political activism" (ACON 1988). In this way, Callen attempted to link coming out with actual physical survival, as it were, raising the political and moral stakes. Previous forms of local resistance by gay men rested on the demand for rights to freedom from discrimination or sexual self-determination. The agenda was now being reorganized around the continuity of life itself.

The strategy of visibility advocated by Callen was rehearsed at the closing plenary of the conference when people with HIV and AIDS stepped onto the stage. This novel ceremony of disclosure resulted in the coming out of many conference participants, some of whom were in key positions in AIDS organizations but previously secretive about their infection. This was a coming out within a particular and limited context, however. It was not a public media disclosure, but a declaration to those who work in AIDS: researchers, government bureaucrats, health professionals, and community organization workers. Yet the pervasive invisibility of people with HIV/AIDS to this point in Australia, even within this select milieu, is striking. Community-based AIDS organizations themselves sustained this absence. For example, prior to the conference, workers and volunteers at the AIDS Council of NSW (ACON) were still disclosing their status only selectively, even within the organization. As one person who worked for an AIDS organization wrote in response to the conference:

Even though I work in an AIDS organization, I rarely come into contact with PWAs, people infected with HIV, their carers, or their families. I have read a lot of material written by such people, but to hear them actually talk to a room full of people really does have quite a unique effect (Andrews 1988:38).

This first public statement about "living with AIDS" in this country was to have dramatic effects far beyond the limited milieu of the AIDS sector.

Only two weeks after the 1988 Third National Conference on AIDS, another conference was held in Melbourne, this one specifically for people with HIV and AIDS. The event, "Living Well," was organized by a small collective of people with AIDS and funded by the federal government and the various state AIDS councils. Reflecting this governmental support, the conference received the blessings, in the form of telegrams, from the health ministers of both the Victorian state and federal governments. The aim of the conference was to provide opportunity for the infected to share their experiences.

While gay men, in conjunction with the state AIDS councils, were the driving force behind the organization of the conference, the issue of sexuality and sexual identity was played down. Rather, the emphasis was on the uniting bond of HIV infection: a condition that cuts across boundaries of sexuality, gender, and ethnicity. One speaker, Bill, identified as an injecting drug user, expressed it in this way: "It's not whether you're white or black or a woman or a male or gay or straight. We're here because of the virus."[2] Thus, through a negation of the social, all human differences are neutralized and unity reorganized under the umbrella of an invisible biological enemy.

Yet, even at this stage, cracks were appearing in this new HIV collectivity. Listen to a positive woman, Bernice, for example:

Up until now the correct focus of support has been targeted to those most seriously affected: gay men and IV users. However, women have not been catered for by the groups in terms of our specific needs as women. We're isolated by our roles . . . traditionally, whores, mothers, sisters and wives, caregivers, rather than care receivers. We see the need for an independent mutual support group as urgent and have formed Positive Women to deal with the gaps. Our main objective is mutual support: getting together, exchanging information, linking with others, outreaching people who are isolated. I now believe we no longer have to suffer the powerlessness of isolation common to women and have achieved a voice in the AIDS dialogue. We exist.

Bernice not only came out positive, but as a positive woman. This gesture asserts a separate identity from the gay man and the IV user, identities perceived as hegemonic within AIDS discourses (the "AIDS dialogue"). A cohesion among the infected emerges on the issue of empowerment. Yet on closer inspection the individual narratives coming out suggest rather different ideas of what empowerment means. Infected gay men stress "taking control of myself," being a "survivor," and express interests in organization building. In contrast, the women emphasize "support," reproduction, and relationship issues. Despite the ideal of unity, therefore, gender appears to be a force working to fracture the unifying signifier of HIV.

But let's consider this notion of empowerment further. What does it mean to these people to be "empowered?" How is power realized for the self? Bruce, using Michael Callen's terminology, tells us he is a "long-term survivor." He was first diagnosed seven years ago with "an AIDS-related condition." By the end of 1984 he was told he had AIDS:

> The question of claiming to be a long-term survivor would never have occurred to me until Michael Callen from America came here and talked about this. He urged me to try and use it because, he said, one of the things people don't learn is that people are often living for quite a long time after being diagnosed.

Empowerment begins, therefore, in redefining one's status from that of a dying patient to that of a person living with AIDS. He continues:

> I had made the decision that what was killing me wasn't so much the virus but the fact that everybody was saying, "Look, you've met these criteria, you're going to die." I decided to consider myself only as ARC [AIDS-related condition]. I think that decision certainly helped to keep me alive a lot longer. Since then I think there isn't a point where people should consider themselves one category or another, but really we're all living with the virus. . . . I was also very much struck at first with a feeling of powerlessness, because the medical profession, although they didn't know what to do about AIDS, kept telling you to do what they told you. I still find this difficult to overcome being dependant on the great "god" the doctor. I know I've got a lot to learn about being more in control of myself and my life but I feel much better when I know that I can take control.

This narrative contains all the elements of a commonly felt disempowerment in the hands of a medical profession that defines one's health in terms of stages of inevitable progression to death. As I documented in Part Two, many infected people resist the demand to organize their sense of self around such medically defined categories. Such categorizations may be far too complex and difficult to understand, and therefore irrelevant at a personal level of meaning, may frequently change according to scientific developments, or simply do not match lived experience. Many find such systems destructive in that they contain implications incompatible with a will to live. It is significant to note in this context that it is another gay man who has realized Callen's concept of empowerment, successfully reorganizing his identity from "victim" to "long-term survivor," to a person *living* with AIDS. The ontological focus has shifted from the threat of death implicit in the medical meanings of AIDS to the promise of life implicit in the philosophy of empowerment.

This is the essential intention of this new discourse: to disengage from a negative medical identity and reconstruct the self in life-affirming terms.

ILLNESS CAREERS (1): SYDNEY, OCTOBER 1988

The Melbourne "Living Well" Conference generated no fewer than sixty recommendations, aimed at both the "AIDS industry" and people with HIV/AIDS themselves, on issues of funding, welfare organization agendas and structures, self-organization guidelines, therapy and information needs, and political representation (Carter 1988).

It was shortly after these conferences, at the ACON Annual General Meeting on the night of September 6, 1988, that Paul Young spoke about the empowerment of people with AIDS to a Sydney audience. Tall, thin, and having a propensity for flamboyant dress, Paul delivered his "Surviving and Thriving" speech to the meeting of 150 ACON members. The title of his speech was taken from Michael Callen's book and article of the same name (Callen 1988) and closely reflected Callen's philosophy. Paul Young spoke with engaging humor about his three years as a person living with AIDS, of the need for the terms "victim" and "sufferer" to be discarded for the preferred label "person with AIDS," and the need to establish a People-With-AIDS (PWA) coalition in New South Wales. "We need new education approaches also," he stated, "which drop the beautiful-young-men image, for positive and realistic images of people with AIDS. We need a 'KS is Beautiful' campaign." The audience registered its agreement with short applause.

Paul had been strongly motivated by his encounter with Callen in Hobart and referred to it on many occasions. Paul's subsequent attendance at the Living Well conference in Melbourne further stimulated him to work toward building a movement for people with HIV and AIDS in this country. In Melbourne, a small group of individuals from each Australian State and Territory had come together with the idea of establishing a National PLWA Coalition (NPLWAC). On returning to Sydney, Paul directly approached his local AIDS Council, ACON, for support in setting up a local branch of this national coalition. His suggestion was welcomed by the

Council, and some infrastructure, such as office space and a small budget for a newsletter, was quickly forthcoming.

It should be noted that issues of importance for the infected were not entirely absent from ACON's agenda at this time. Various individuals were already advocating increased attention to treatment issues, both medical and alternative, and a proposal was being prepared for the establishment of a support-group program for infected people. This agenda was peripheral, however, to programs of prevention education, and home-care services. The establishment of a formal PWA presence within the Council, however, was to provide additional impetus for these other issues to be more aggressively pursued. A great deal of energy was invested, in these formative days of PWA collectivity, in lobbying ACON to modify its constitution so as to guarantee formal representation of the infected on its managing committee. The ACON committee had, in fact, five HIV-infected people serving on it. However, what was being demanded was a constitutional guarantee for PWA representation.

Outside ACON, the path toward the formation of the new PWA organization progressed. At the first public meeting on September 28, 1988 of what called itself the "PLWA Coalition NSW," a flyer prepared by Paul Young and others proclaimed:

> The Coalition of People Living with AIDS refers to people with AIDS, ARC, and HIV infection and the lovers, partners, family and close friends, and primary carers. This is meant to also include all HIV support, advocacy, and charity groups.

In effect, this early vision of a coalition included every conceivable individual that had any involvement with AIDS at all. The discourse of unity was sustained, although we may note this vision is already a significant departure from the original recommendations of the Denver Principles. Speakers at this meeting were deliberately selected, largely through Paul Young's personal networks, to represent a diversity of affected people: Vince, whose wife had died of AIDS and whose young son was infected; a woman known to many as a compassionate care provider; John, a gay man with AIDS; and finally a federal government bureaucrat, Liz, whose husband had died of AIDS. John echoed the familiar coming out strategy of gay liberation. "There is a new breed of person," he proclaimed, "the PLWA is one who goes public, there is a need to come out of that closet." In contrast to this ostensibly gay strategy, Vince called for the "dehomosexualization" of AIDS, a point reiterated by Liz who spoke of the need for a coalition that recognizes the diversity of those people affected by AIDS. About the new organization she said, "It needs to be a coalition of people living with AIDS, not just a coalition of those infected with HIV or people with AIDS."

This sentiment was echoed by Paul Young, in his new capacity as interim convener of PLWA, in a rather contradictory statement to the *Sydney Star Observer* shortly after that inaugural meeting: "If we attempt to hang onto AIDS as the 'gay plague,' the vital contributions of the gay community (including ACON, BGF, and CSN) will be lost and will put us back five years."

At this point, when the discourse of unity had established public status through the Sydney gay newspaper, an alternative position was quickly forthcoming. Terry Bell composed a response to the meeting that sought to restrict the new organization to those who were infected with the virus. In the following issue of the *Sydney Star Observer* he reasserted an agenda of gay community-building and identity reminiscent of the discourse of the late 1970s and early 1980s:

> They (Vince and Liz) both seem to be suggesting that communality of interest and purpose is something that comes naturally, by having the same virus in our bloodstreams, rather than something that has to be worked for, and which gay politics has been striving to build for years. . . . Those who are indirectly (i.e. uninfected) affected by AIDS already have places where they can interact collectively. For carers, it is the organizations they already belong to, and for heterosexual families it is most of our social institutions. Gay people with HIV still do not have that special place. . . . Dehomosexualizing AIDS means that once again gays are being told to keep quiet about their legitimate and undeniable claims, as usual, for the sake of some diffuse mythical, and "general" good. For this faggot with AIDS that price is too much to pay.

Perhaps because of Bell's rallying letter, subsequent meetings of the nascent PLWA coalition were attended mostly by gay men with HIV and AIDS. It was this pattern, despite the cooption of a heterosexual man and a number of uninfected women to the first committee, which set the identity structure of the organization. And Young, after having publicly announced that the theme for the second Living Well conference in Sydney was to be "Dehomosexualizing AIDS," retracted that statement.

ILLNESS CAREERS (2): ORGANIZATIONAL DEVELOPMENTS

Early meetings of PLWA (NSW) during October and November 1988 identified the main structural issues for the organization: membership definition, representation, and administrative structure. The membership issue remained unresolved until the "Living Well II" conference in February 1989. Then, a constitution was adopted that structured the management committee of the new organization, PLWA (NSW), in such a way that it would always be dominated by people with HIV. Those with the virus were given full membership, though there was no requirement to disclose one's status publicly, and those who were uninfected were allocated associate-member status with no right to vote infected members to the committee.

Nevertheless, doubts were being voiced regarding the ability of the currently gay-dominated collective to speak effectively for non-gay members. A woman whose husband had been infected through a blood transfusion, and who was present at the inaugural public meeting, for example, confided to me that transfusion recipients would not be likely to participate in such an organization because they knew that they were infected with blood from homosexuals. She was upset that transfusion recipients were not mentioned as a separate group at any time during the meeting. Meanwhile, Vince signaled his intention not to participate in the organization, in part because he was aware of his conflict with the gay agenda as embodied in Terry Bell's letter to the *Sydney Star Observer*. The committee realized a compromise was necessary, to encourage broader participation in the group while maintaining a priority on gay issues. This was in part achieved by the successful cooption of two uninfected women and an infected heterosexual man onto the committee in early 1989, individuals who nonetheless often felt marginal to the gay core of the group.

The issue of the new group's relationship with ACON, as the over arching community-based AIDS organization, was also a matter for early consideration. Some members saw dependence on ACON as a threat to the new group's autonomy, warning that this relationship threatened the absorption of the group into ACON's own agenda. Final consensus was that some link to ACON was necessary in order to avoid duplication of administrative infrastructure. An ongoing relationship was important and useful, it was argued, at least at this early stage, to secure access to important resources such as communications lines, computers, and up-to-date information. Meanwhile, while the issue of the incorporation of the new body as a legal entity was deemed problematic, it was necessary if funding independent of ACON was to be forthcoming from the government. A draft constitution was designed according to the standard corporate format, with modified membership and committee structure details to fit the particular needs of the organization.

Given that people with HIV and AIDS had already a range of possible places to meet, including in the support groups run by the Albion Street

Clinic, and the "Maitraya" AIDS Day Care Centre, the emergence of another, ostensibly political AIDS group raised some suspicion and comment among the infected. Tom, for example, expressed concern that there was a perception among people with AIDS that PLWA (NSW) was an organization composed of healthy people, those with HIV but not AIDS. Understandably, those in the group who did in fact have AIDS took particular offense to this. A tension thus arose early on between the organization and other established, and less political groups for people with AIDS.

Despite this, illness was an ever-present phenomenon within the new group, fueling concerns about the organization's long-term stability. As one member commented, "We're not going to kill ourselves doing this." Already, before the year was up, one member of the group had become too ill to continue participating, leaving the task of preparing a membership survey incomplete. Another member developed a cancer early in 1989 that left him in hospital undergoing chemotherapy treatment or recovering at home for lengthy periods. In an effort to resolve this problem, a structure was established whereby alternative office bearers could stand in for representatives in the event of illness.

Illness experience was not necessarily only debilitating for the organization, in the emerging environment, it was also potentially political. Another illness episode was significant in setting the agenda of the new group. Tom experienced a minor illness in January that saw him admitted to the casualty section of an inner-city hospital with an HIV/AIDS medicine speciality (St. Vincent's). Tom was kept on a stretcher in the emergency ward for several days waiting for a spare bed to become available in the AIDS ward. This delay was interrupted only when he took action himself and demanded he be transferred to another hospital where beds were available. As a result of his demand, he was transferred and finally received the medical attention he needed. Tom later reported that four other individuals had in this time experienced similar delays in reaching the AIDS ward.

On release, he returned to the PLWA committee angered at the way he and the others had been treated, and proceeded to write a letter to the New South Wales State Minister of Health outlining the inadequacies of the existing AIDS ward and demanding immediate action. PLWA (NSW) also wrote to various agencies urging action on behalf of people with AIDS. ACON responded quickly and put pressure on the NSW State Department of Health to increase the available number of beds in the AIDS ward. This issue of the adequate supply of beds was to engage both organizations for some time until the capacity of the AIDS ward was eventually expanded.

Importantly, this episode helped codify a political relationship between ACON and PLWA (NSW). A key member of ACON confided in me that he felt this kind of activism was exactly the role PLWA could most usefully perform: that of noisemaker, of agitator for change. PLWA was free to engage in more radical action than ACON, even to the extent of individuals chaining themselves to the fence of hospitals if this was necessary. He saw the organization as complementing ACON's more "business-suit" brand of politicking, imposed by the larger body's inextricable reliance on government through funding agreements and political agendas.

The "hospital trolley" episode is a good example of how the establishment of a designated political action group created the conditions for the possibility for organized action against the public health system. Motivation for this action was based on personal experience: the foundations of a "consumer" perspective. The argument that people with the virus were the real "experts" in AIDS rested on an assumption that immediate experience is superior knowledge to an intellectual, objective understanding. Such claims are political acts, suggesting a shift in power relations between patients and hegemonic regimes such as health-care systems.

Members of PLWA clearly experienced powerful emotions of anger, frustration, and a need to sustain dignity under threat from an inadequate and depersonalizing health-care system. It was the anger, with respect to his treatment at the hospital, that motivated Tom to begin to protest via the group. In this manner, emotions such as anger encoded a collective style of being in the world which guided how activists saw themselves and their relation to others. Individuals were effective in the collective because of a powerful nexus of personal experiences: declining health at a young age, the illness of friends and associates, frequent experiences of (gay and   AIDS-related) discrimination, and a privileged (class-related) ability to position the self within a wider social system. It is through this nexus of structure and experience that the transition from tactic to strategy is realized.

ILLNESS CAREERS (3): MEDIA IDENTITIES

With an organizational infrastructure established, the new spokespeople for the HIV-infected could begin to make systematic incursions into the public representation of AIDS. Drawing on his political experience as a gay man, and following the example of Michael Callen from the United States, Paul Young set about deploying the strategy of coming out as a means of re-presenting the public image of the "AIDS victim." His strategy was to offer himself to electronic media, namely television and press, as a person living with AIDS.

Paul's activities as a public representative of people with AIDS illustrate Goffman's notion of an illness career; he was a person who made a profession of his stigma. In situating himself as a representative of people with AIDS, Paul sought to modify public representations of the HIV-infected, and to heighten his own social standing. We will see that this strategy of coming out as a person with AIDS is not unproblematic, and may itself come under processes of regulation.

Paul was an established media identity by the time PLWA (NSW) held its first public meetings in Sydney in late 1988. His brash audacity, eccentricity of personal style, wide and diverse connections and supporters, and determination to reconstruct himself as the "HIV superstar" had won him notoriety within and beyond the gay community.

Paul lived in a house typical of Sydney's inner suburbs, often alone, or accompanied by a lover or, later in his life, a relative or supporting friend. His hobby was an enormous and flourishing vegetable garden and a roost of show-grade bantams for which he regularly won prizes. The final months of 1988 saw regular gatherings in his garden, events he referred to as "glitterati barbeques," which provided him opportunities to recount tales of sexual conquest, brushes with the police or "poofter bashers," and heroic victories against bigotry. Danger seemed to loom over Paul's life, not only in the form of the frequent episodes of debilitating illness which slowly etched away at his body, but in the form of external attacks. One threat that both outraged and amused him most was a scribbled, almost indecipherable letter slipped under his door. It read:

> Mr AIDS. Watch your back. We promise we will get you! A petrol bomb in your front window or back! You are no loss. Die prick! We hate you!

This life of danger was punctuated by rewarding encounters with prominent persons. Paul proudly recalled one such meeting, at a parliamentary function, with a former New South Wales State Premier who expressed a wish to meet "the charming man in the red shoes."

In establishing communications with media reporters, Paul sought to exert greater influence over the manner in which people with HIV were represented in the public space. Paul's "Alive and Thriving Tour" to the New South Wales regional city of Newcastle in October 1988 broadened his public reputation as an outspoken person with AIDS. Local newspaper coverage of his addresses portrayed him as:

> Leading Sydney AIDS activist . . . Mr. Young is 33 years old and was diagnosed as having HIV antibodies 5 years ago. He now has full-blown AIDS and is being treated with the drug AZT. He is one of two people with AIDS on the NSW AIDS Council [ACON], and is a very vocal State representa-

tive for the People Living with AIDS (PLWA) — people he points out, who are living, not dying (*Newcastle Post* 19 October 1988).

Here are the beginnings of a new representation of those with HIV: politically active, busy, socially connected.

Following this report, Paul's face, captioned with his full name, appeared in the November 26 edition of the *Good Weekend*, a magazine supplement to Sydney's leading daily newspaper, the *Sydney Morning Herald*. A number of other men appeared in the same article. "John," also pictured, and four other gay men, not pictured, were all identified only by first names. A recognized AIDS specialist and a nutritionist were also featured. The article was constructed around a theme of irrational desperation, with the title "Sufferers Willing to Try Anything to Stay Alive." All these men are cited as relying, not on "synthetic" drugs such as AZT for their health and survival, rational drugs because of their conventional scientificity, but on regimens of diet, experimental treatments such as Ozone therapy, and "attitude." Illustrating this last point, Paul describes AIDS as "a manageable disease, like diabetes. . . . I'm going to live until I'm ninety-one. I've got too many important things to do to accept that I'm going to lock myself away and die" (*Sydney Morning Herald* 26 November 1988).

The overall representation is of individuals empowered with a philosophy of hope and active intervention. Significantly, self-empowerment is constituted through a break with conventional medicine. Three of these men with HIV are identified as being associated with AIDS organizations such as ACON, "the people Living with AIDS Coalition," "the Australian quilt project, making quilts dedicated to individual AIDS victims," and "the day center for AIDS victims" (Maitraya Day Centre). It is this sociality of various AIDS organization that allows "gay community" to remain unnamed by the newspaper; the sexuality of these men infected with HIV is only indirectly noticeable because they are all male. And as always, the notion of the AIDS victim continues to focus the media account, even with the report's emphasis on self-help organizations and activited.

The limitations of this empowered life with AIDS to those already stigmatized is suggested in the juxtaposition of this article with one about "20 heterosexual AIDS victims" entitled "AIDS Plus Ostracism." This story tells of "transfusion cases," individuals who remain nameless and un-pictured and whose voices are predominantly female. The article deals with the rejection experienced by these individuals from all but immediate family and close friends. Infection is an alienating experience, not empowering, one that marginalizes those who were once securely positioned within a normality. This repositioning brings uncertainty to life, an experience one describes as "living in a time bomb, wondering when it's going to go off." For these "victims," stigma is derived from the association between HIV infection and homosexuality. The stigma of AIDS, driven by this association, spills over to all those with the infection regardless of their sexuality. HIV "homosexualizes" the HIV-infected individual.

On the other hand, homosexual men are empowered through their defiance of conventional medical wisdom and recourse to irrational (that is, non-medical) strategies of survival, and through a reconstructed sociality centered around membership of a new AIDS-industry sector. Their identity is concretized. As a PWA identity, a "homosexual transfusion recipient" is inconceivable. Likewise, "gay community" and the non-gay world, the "general community," are differentiated, bounded and impermeable:

> For these and other heterosexual victims of AIDS, there are no organized support networks. Although they would be welcome in the groups established by the gay community, they say they feel awkward in the gay environment. They have separate and quite different problems which should be recognized (*Sydney Morning Herald* 26 November 1988).

Everything in this emerging discourse of people with AIDS is characterized by a movement toward a fragmentation of identities. The unifying possibilities of a shared biological organism, as envisioned by the speakers of the first Living Well conference, are not being realized. Rather, differentiation of identities is occurring around modes of infection. It is not the objective fact of HIV that is significant in this discourse, but the social identities betrayed in the routes of viral transmission.

The text described presents a partial disruption of previously dominant public representations of people with AIDS, especially those who are gay, as decrepit and pitiful. At the same time these images speak of a deeper cultural logic of the Other built on constructions of both sexuality and illness. The strategy of coming out is not, therefore, unproblematic. Coming out is an essentialist strategy in so far as one is said to reveal that which has been hidden. For gay men, coming out was understood as a defiance of sexual repression and a revealing of the truth of homosexuality. For Paul, coming out as a person with AIDS defied prevailing myths of the AIDS victim and replaced them with the truth of himself. But rather than being a simple process of revealing the unknown or misrepresented, "coming out" is itself implicated in the construction of a social identity. In presenting himself to the media, Paul was not only reconstructing the public image of AIDS, he was simultaneously reconstructing himself. This is an ontological dialectic whereby the positioning of the self in the public space allows what Foucault (1985) called the constitution and recognition of self as a social subject. The truth game of coming out — as gay, as a person with AIDS, as being of a particular ethnicity (the options appear to be expanding) — may be better characterized as *"be-coming out."*

ILLNESS CAREERS (4): DISCIPLINE AND ORGANIZATION

With the progressive formalization of the structure and aims of PLWA (NSW), individuals began to question Paul Young's charismatic style of leadership. Distrust was growing over both his ability to speak on behalf of people with AIDS and his unwillingness to allow others to contribute to the organization's media activities. This issue of leadership came to a head on World AIDS Day (December 1) 1988 at a public rally in Sydney's central business district where Paul addressed several hundred people gathered around the first thirty panels of the new Australian Quilt which had been launched earlier that day. A number of his statements aroused a great deal of resentment. Punctuating the air with his walking stick, Paul told the audience that he was unable to determine how he had been infected, it could have been through gay sex, or prostitution, or intravenous drug use, but this was irrelevant to the fact that he was now living with AIDS and would continue to do so until he was ninety-one. Often-heard threats to incarcerate people with AIDS on an island away from a threatened public, he jested, would not be all that bad. "Can you imagine a thousand PWAs partying on an island?"

Within a week members of PLWA were discussing the need to remove Paul from the position of convenor and replace him with another, more reliable and widely appealing public speaker. Some group members, together with key individuals in ACON, were angry and dismayed at his performance. It was felt by many that he presented a disrespectful image. Cynically it was suggested that he be deposed under the guise that his illness was preventing him from presenting effectively in public. The issue was openly discussed at the group meeting following World AIDS Day where Paul's performance was described as embarrassing and damaging to the group's role as a representative body for people with AIDS. He later confided in me in a very angry tone that he considered the committee to be far too conservative. "Why shouldn't I be able to say in public that I'm a poofter, and an IVDU, and have been a prostitute? Why not say 'fuck' in public?" Efforts to restrain Paul were stepped up as the committee denied him any opportunity to speak at the Living Well II conference in any official capacity.

Paul resigned from the committee of PLWA in mid-August 1989 following his failure to secure the organization's paid administration position. His enthusiasm and vision for the organization was not deemed sufficient compensation for his lack of technical skills. He responded emotionally and angrily to this rejection, interpreting it as a personal attack. Paul's rapid decline in health at that time enhanced his alienation from PLWA and most public political activity. The irony of his alienation from the very organization he established, one that aimed to help people with AIDS, was not lost on some. Friends close to Paul voiced strong criticism of the lack of support PLWA demonstrated to Paul in his final days. He died in May 1990.

Two images of Paul are etched in my memory. Visiting him only days before his death, I found him barely conscious and heavily sedated with painkilling drugs. We hardly recognized each other. More powerful than this memory, however, is a recollection of Paul, draped in 1960s "retro" gear, dancing with thousands of other gay men at the Mardi Gras party only three months previously. He gyrated over to me and screamed over the pounding music, "I think this will be my last Mardi Gras. Isn't it fabulous! I've been waiting for this. Now I can die."

Paul's career as media representative for people with HIV/AIDS was short-circuited by the very process he believed would enhance it. In a Weberian-like transition, PLWA (NSW) had founded itself on the strength of an idiosyncratic and erratic charismatic leader, only to reject that leadership once it had established a coherent structure which allowed others to participate and have some role in its efforts to represent people with AIDS. The progressive refinement of the organization's agenda, decision-making structures, and legal status is consistent with the trend, noted in Chapter Two, to the managerial-style government of AIDS. The structural trajectory that informs both government and non-government organizations, therefore, was also influencing the collectivization process. Paul represented a transitional identity, a charismatic who, because of his individuality and strength of personality, spearheaded the collectivization process. The final irony is that this very achievement destroyed his illness career.

With the employment of a full-time administrator through funds provided by the New South Wales State Department of Health, PLWA underwent a rapid transformation. With a greater deployment of computer assistance, the organization's records and communication structures became systematized. Such systems brought PLWA in line structurally with other AIDS organizations. At the time of this transformation, members who had previously undertaken administration work voluntarily were greatly relieved for such support.

However, the process of organizational rationalization can also alien-
ate those unable to operate within bureaucratic culture. By the end of 1989
signs were appearing that PLWA had in fact lost its initial impetus and was
losing support among people with AIDS themselves. Committee attendance was in decline, faith in the representative structure was failing, and
the public media presence of the organization had fallen off. Critical comments from members increased over time. Some voiced this alienation
through observations that power and decision making were being concentrated into the hands of an elite at the expense of an active membership.
Others claimed that the group was becoming irrelevant to people with
AIDS.

On the other hand, ironically, the organization had become structurally
more sound with the employment of two half-time positions in administration and newsletter production. The newsletter was itself rapidly becoming the most widely read and recognized information source of its kind in
the country. The purchase of new computer equipment for its production
increased efficiency of output and professional appearance. Committee
activity was increasingly taken up with positions on advisory panels and
steering groups for government projects. While the organization had secured its place in the eyes of the health bureaucracy as the representative
organization for people with HIV and AIDS, it had, in the process, somewhat alienated itself from its own membership.

This rationalization of PLWA (NSW) later stimulated a further transformation of activism in the form of a local ACT UP group, a direct-action
group established by some PLWA members in early 1990. It was through
this new group that the person with AIDS was rescued from rationalization
with the deployment of anger as the organizing emotion of protest. I pursue this issue of the deployment of emotion for strategic intent in Chapter
Eleven.

NOTES

1. Gay Men's Health Crisis: the first and now largest gay community-based AIDS
   organization in the United States and the world.
2. This and the following quotes come from the report of the "Living Well" conference, Melbourne 1988.

CHAPTER 9

The Emergence of a New Treatment Activism

TAKING ON THE DOCTORS

Shortly after Paul's departure from PLWA (NSW), a new opportunity arose for the organization to present itself through electronic media, this time through national television. The manner in which the opportunity was taken up suggests a shift in the organization's emerging strategies from *ad hoc* presentations of identities to a focus on institutional targets, in this case the conservative lobby of the Australian medical profession. In that shift, we also detect the emergence of a new patient activist, one who is angry, articulate, and organized, and prepared to take on the medical profession.

In late April 1989, the largest national medical doctors group, the Australian Medical Association (AMA), released a new AIDS policy document at a Summit Conference called by the Australian Doctors Fund (ADF) in Sydney. True to the organization's historical opposition to Labor Party policies, the AMA document challenged the Labor federal government by advocating testing of patients for the safety of health-care workers:

> Some parts of the Federal and State Governments' strategies to control the disease are wrong. Currently the best estimate of the number of Australians infected with HIV is between 0.1 and 0.2 percent of the population. As infection can only be transmitted by contact with an infected person (particularly through blood or secretions), the major focus of the Government's efforts must be in identifying people who are infected, providing them with adequate care and helping to ensure they do not transmit the disease. The prime responsibility for preventing the spread of infection lies with the 0.1 and 0.2 percent of the population who are infected, not with the 99.8 percent who are not infected (AMA 1989).

These statements contradicted the policies of both the federal government and community-based organizations such as ACON and the newly formed PLWA. Members of PLWA reacted with horror at the singling out of the infected as the sole bearers of responsibility for prevention of the spread of the disease. The policy threatened, it was said, to stigmatize the infected further by subjecting "at risk" populations to a regime of mandatory testing. Forced identification of the infected undermined the empowering strategy of testing and disclosing (coming out) of one's own volition, and threatened discrimination in the form of a sanctioned right of health-care workers to refuse treatment.

Significantly, this renewed debate regarding HIV testing originated in the United States. A surgeon from the San Francisco General Hospital, Dr. Lorraine Day, challenged the apparent medical consensus regarding the transmission of HIV and safety of health professionals. For example, she claimed HIV could be transmitted through the aerosol vapors common in operating rooms (Day 1989). Day called for the routine testing of patients for HIV in the interests of both patient and doctor. The AMA had invited Day to present her arguments to the ADF Summit. Clearly Day's position was influential on the AMA policy and was consistent with their historical opposition to the voluntary and confidential testing now recommended by the federal government.

Community organizations began to mount a defense of the established testing policy. The federal government, through the Inter-Governmental Committee on AIDS (IGCA), commissioned a discussion paper that canvased the issues. The paper was written by a gay man and endorsed by the executive of the Australian National Council on AIDS (ANCA), the top advisory body to the federal Minister of Health. The paper strongly refuted Day's arguments as "serious distortions of history" and a "careless use of sources." It concluded:

> The risk of occupational transmission of HIV to health-care workers is a manageable one, and that rigorous application of practical infection control and accident prevention guidelines will greatly reduce the risk. This paper has shown that some recent statements have over stated the risk of HIV infection of health-care workers, and that some of these statements have been based on a dismissal or a misunderstanding of the available evidence.
>
> The HIV epidemic will only be defeated through the cooperative efforts of the medical and scientific communities, other health-care workers, governments, organizations representing the communities affected by the epidemic, and people living with HIV infection and AIDS themselves. The objectives of providing the highest standard of care for people affected by the epidemic and of safeguarding health-care workers from infection are not contradictory, but complementary. They can both be met if the health-

care professions adhere to their traditional commitments to care, compassion, professionalism and responsibility (IGCA 1989:26-7).

Some doctors working in AIDS also positioned themselves in opposition to Day. Professor John Dwyer, for example, prepared a comprehensive critique for the media. This document formed a basis for further media debate and provided the factual data for press releases from ACON and AFAO. There thus came about, under the threat of a common enemy, a significant collaboration between community groups, government agencies, and less conservative members of the medical profession.

On Tuesday April 25, 1989 (the ANZAC Day public holiday, the national day of remembrance of those who fought and died in wars), PLWA's Advocacy Group, a small group of men including Terry Bell and Tom, gathered at ACON's offices to discuss how their organization could respond to Day and the AMA. Bell was suffering from a toothache on this occasion, unable to find a dentist to treat him on this public holiday. The pain and the difficulty he had alleviating it produced a short temper and a determination to formulate an effective challenge to the AMA.

Terry and Tom suggested PLWA produce what was to be its first press release, calling for the deregistration of health-care workers who refuse treatment to people with HIV. Bell, drawing on a history of media work, drafted the release. The forthcoming Summit is described as:

> Little more than a thinly disguised political push by conservative forces in the medical profession . . . promoted by the [New South Wales] AMA President, Dr. Bruce Shepherd, who led the rebel orthopaedic surgeons when they walked out of [New South Wales] public hospitals. Dr. Shepherd was also instrumental in setting up the Australian Doctors Fund which is funding the summit, and which was originally established to pay for a campaign against Medicare.

The statement identified PLWA's political allegiance to the federal government's health policy, concluding with an appeal to scientific reason:

> To continue to discriminate or suggest that special precautions are necessary is ignoring the majority of scientific opinion and may further discredit the medical profession in the eyes of the public.

Response to the release was encouraging. Both commercial radio stations and those belonging to the national, government-funded public radio and television broadcaster, the Australian Broadcasting Corporation (ABC), quoted the press statement and sought further comment for their news reports. The *Sydney Morning Herald* quoted the demand for deregistration in a coverage of the opening of the Summit, together with a review of Day's arguments, the AMA New South Wales Branch President's opening speech which reiterated Day's position, and the Inter-Governmental Committee on AIDS rebuttal. The media successfully covered all aspects of the debate.

A face-to-face confrontation with Day and her supporters came on the day following the Summit. Orchestrated by the Australian Broadcasting Corporation (ABC), this episode of the national television debate program "The Couchman Show" involved all interested parties. The producers had contacted PLWA several weeks earlier asking it to facilitate the presence of people with HIV at the recording. Chris Carter from Melbourne's PLWA group was flown to Sydney by the ABC to attend. A strong non-medical presence was established, with many ACON workers and people with HIV in the audience. Only two spoke as PWAs however: Carter and Bell.

Day presented her argument in formal introductory debate opposite Dr. Ken Donald from the Inter-Governmental Committee for AIDS. Day referred to the infected as "time bombs" who threatened to infect surgeons exposed to blood during operations. Donald refuted the assertions with the arguments set out in the IGCA document (IGCA 1989). Bell launched the audience debate, asking Day if she had herself been tested for HIV. Day replied that she had been tested but refused to disclose if the result was positive or negative, saying she reserved the right not to disclose. Many in the audience erupted into spontaneous acclaim and applause, recognizing the inconsistency of this position.

The debate became more lively and unruly. Interjections from the audience, such as "This is rubbish!" and "She lies!" signaled an increasing anger. Bell forcefully recounted his toothache episode, providing an example of what may happen in the event of the introduction of policies such as Day was advocating (namely, mandatory testing before any treatment). Carter challenged Day's authority as a knowledgeable expert, pointing to her confused interchangeable use of HIV and AIDS as a case in point. People with HIV and AIDS were the real experts, he contended, precisely because they have intimate experience in dealing with the disease on a day-to-day basis.

Despite attempts from the audience to broaden the debate to include issues of discrimination, and alternative methods of education and prevention the discussion was manipulated from the chair to focus almost exclusively on this issue of testing. Representatives from the AMA were vocal in support of Day and, by the conclusion of the telecast, a general opinion settled on the community-based groups that the charismatic force of Day's personality and authority had won the debate for the doctors.

Bell's approach to the media was very different from that of Paul Young. While Paul was optimistic, if not naive, about the ability of the media to represent him faithfully, Bell was far more skeptical of its intentions and effects, and held doubts about his ability to influence media representations. As a result, Bell's approach was far more constrained, calculated, and in line with his insistence on democratic procedures, rehearsed and endorsed by the collective. This was an approach that rested more comfortably with the political culture of the new PLWA organization. The result was a thoroughly different image. Gone was the eccentricity of previous identities. Bell and Carter's media performances announced the arrival of a new patient/activist: articulate, informed, angry, and impatient with political and medical conservatism.

Day and AMA NSW President Shepherd were formidable adversaries and aroused some nervousness among their opponents. PLWA's fear of failure in the face of Day's performance arose from an appreciation of the perceived authority of the opponents: their legitimacy as medical professionals and a society-wide acceptance of doctor expertise. Ironically, it was this rather than the degree of scientific validity of their position that caused concern. For, despite the AMA position, it was already widely recognized among many health professionals that mandatory testing was an ineffective prevention strategy and ethically untenable. The debate, in one sense, thereby formed around competing claims to expertise and the truth value of different interpretations of scientific information.

At the conclusion of this particular conflict, the AMA did backtrack slightly, even if only momentarily, on its position. The collective resistance, in which people with HIV/AIDS were now included as important players, succeeded in deflecting the political agenda of this professional faction. This was not achieved by one group alone, but was the result of a unified effort between the established community AIDS organizations, government agencies, and more progressive sections of the medical profession.

A notable aspect of this media event was the manipulation by the program producers of the identities of the people involved into designated roles. These identities, with identified positions on the issue, were then pitched against each other in the hope of generating the most media-worthy debate. With respect to members of PLWA, this maneuvering was only possible because of a rare confluence of intention on the part of the media and the new organization seeking to influence representations of people with AIDS and the policies and practices of institutions significant to them. The event illustrates a transitional form of PLWA practice intermediate between tactic and strategy. Practices were beginning to be ordered around an institutional location (an organization), and protest was becoming more focused on an identified target (the medical establishment). And yet its discursive and institutional infrastructure was not yet mature enough to allow a fully autonomous response. We see, rather, a subtle manipulation of the nascent PLWA strategic intent by an established and powerful media industry, a manipulation informed by the electronic media's interests for storytelling and conflict enactment, for the presentation of drama for its audience.

FOCUSING ON TREATMENT ISSUES

Having established communication links to the electronic media and having made initial inroads into the prevailing public image of the person with AIDS, PLWA increasingly turned its attention to the issue of medical treatments for AIDS. This developing discourse intruded into the then-established dialogue between the medical establishment and the various state AIDS councils which had, to this time, spoken on behalf of the HIV-infected. With the systematization of a PLWA voice, AIDS treatment discourse was injected with an additional moral dimension, a development that was to drive the campaign for clinical and bureaucratic reform explored in the remainder of this study.

Statements at the above mentioned Hobart and Melbourne conferences in 1988 indicated that existing treatments such as AZT were considered problematic by people with HIV and AIDS, and that an exploration of therapeutic alternatives was desirable. Substantial time was devoted at the Melbourne "Living Well" conference to "Alternative Therapy Models," with three speakers discussing homoeopathy, Chinese medicine, and nutrition. This interest was framed by an insistence on the need to "take absolute personal control and responsibility for our health and well-being" (Living Well Report 1988). Similarly, Paul Young, in his first letter to the *Sydney Star Observer* as an elected representative of People with AIDS Coalition stated:

> Given that approximately 50 percent of PWAs cannot take AZT because of its toxic side effects, one of the Coalition's immediate goals is to strive to non-toxic, affordable and accessible alternative treatments (*Sydney Star Observer* 28 October 1988).

At the first public meeting of the PWA Coalition in September of that year, information sheets on the substances dextran sulphate and AL721 were distributed. These two clinically manufactured substances were generating considerable excitement at the time among both research groups and activists. Within a few weeks of its establishment, the new group began investigating these substances, producing short reports in the first issue of its newsletter, *Talkabout* (PLWA (NSW) 1988). Its response to AL721 positioned PLWA (NSW) as a new voice in the medical discourse on treatment developments for AIDS.

AL721 AND THE CONDUCT OF TRIALS

AL721, a derivative of egg lipids, was developed in the 1960s at Israel's Weitzman Institute as an anticancer therapy. It was first tested on a person with AIDS in 1986 and by early 1988 the institute was conducting an innovative trial with sixty people, comparing the substance with AZT. Results from the trial were encouraging. A small number of trials were also underway in the United States by this time, but the substance received little recognition from most of the medical research institutions undertaking clinical trials of potential HIV treatments and therapies in the United States. Succumbing to public pressure, AL721 was the eventually released as a food supplement instead of a drug (*New York Native* 25 April 1988), opening the way for people with AIDS in Australia to purchase it for personal use.

Terry Bell had immediate access to community-based information sources in the United States, such as *AIDS Treatment News* and Project Inform publications, which delivered to him new treatment developments often months in advance of either workers in community organizations such as ACON or general medical practitioners. Bell's impatience with PLWA in producing its first newsletter motivated him to produce his own newsletter, *AIDS Advocate* (see Chapter Five). Treatments were a priority issue, and one of his first stories was on AL721.

Almost simultaneously, the Albion Street AIDS Clinic announced it was preparing to undertake a three-month trial of AL721 with fifteen HIV-infected people with mildly compromised immune systems. In a statement to the gay press, the director of the clinic, Dr. Julian Gold, warned people with AIDS not to purchase the substance for personal use from the United States until more information was available "after Christmas when the Clinic will be able to advise people on the results of the trial" (*Sydney Star Observer* 11 November 1988). Christmas was then only six weeks away. This statement can be read as an attempt by the medical research establishment to reassert control over treatment information and its interpretation, control that was under threat from a growing patient activism.

Information about treatment developments in the United States was generating a perception among local community groups that such "alternative" therapies were of much more limited availability in Australia than in both the United States and the United Kingdom. AL721 was, for example, already available in the United States as a food substance and in the United Kingdom through prescription. There was a consensus among community-based groups — the Australian Federation of AIDS Organisations (AFAO) nationally, ACON at the state level, and now PLWA — that the time had come to step up political pressure to expand and innovate the treatment development system in this country, to put it in line with developments in the United States.

Soon after, disturbing news reached PLWA that the Albion Street Clinic was to cancel its proposed trial of AL721. Reports were being received from researchers in the United States that the substance was not holding up to initial expectations. This question of efficacy was not, however, the main issue to Bell. In late April 1989, he proposed that PLWA challenge drug-trial facilities such as the Albion Street AIDS Clinic to be more answerable to people with AIDS. They must, he argued, inform people with HIV/AIDS of their intentions, provide information about treatments, and report publicly on trial results. Further to this argument, Bell drafted a press release condemning the clinic, and using the issue as a lever to demand community-based trials of the kind now running in the United States:

> People Living With AIDS, the organization formed to represent the interests of HIV infected people, has expressed its strong disappointment at the decision by the Albion Street AIDS Clinic not to proceed with the long-awaited trial of the egg lecithin product, AL721 . . . Research institutions such as Albion Street have a moral obligation not just to do scientifically interesting research, but to also undertake research which is socially useful . . . We will be approaching the ACON/AFAO Clinical Working Group to develop criteria for the allocation of AL721 to people who wish to try it on a self-treatment basis . . . such community research initiatives have been developed as a way of identifying effective treatment combinations which are of little interest to the high-tech, high profit venture capital research companies which are moving into the field of AIDS research in great numbers. If such an initiative could be established in Sydney, it would be a major step forward in broadening the search for more effective treatments for HIV infection (PLWA (NSW) 27 May 1989).

This statement represents the first organized local claims of patient expertise on this issue of medical treatment. Both the mainstream press and the local gay press failed to report the essence of Bell's critique. Rather, coverage in the national newspaper portrayed PLWAs as foolish in rejecting the scientific evidence against AL721. An article in a national daily, entitled "Sufferers Try 'Useless Treatment' for AIDS," stated:

The director of the Albion St Clinic, Dr Julian Gold, said he was distressed by PLWA claims that the clinic was not being socially responsible by abandoning the trial. Albion St now advised its patients not to use the substance because recent evidence showed it was useless (Allender 1989).

Gold told the press he would delay a final decision on the trial until he heard further information about AL721 at the forthcoming International AIDS Conference in Montreal.

The Australian Broadcasting Corporation's youth radio station, 2JJJ, sought to pursue the issue further and organized a debate between Gold and PLWA (NSW). Points of argument were formulated, by Bell and others, in preparation for the debate, including:

(1) PLWA members had expressed a wish to try the substance through the trial, currently the only means of access in Australia.

(2) The Clinic had made no efforts since its announcement to enroll participants, suggesting its incompetence at efficiently conducting trials.

(3) In the interim PWAs had, in desperation, begun importing the substance at their own expense from the U.S., and were therefore taking it without proper monitoring.

(4) The Clinic is obliged to inform PLWAs of up-to-date information about treatments and had failed to do so in the case of AL721.

(5) The Clinic appears to be only interested in conducting trials with safe and predictable results, rather than running trials which risk failure.

(6) PWA's faith the Clinic has been damaged, threatening the high level of cooperation in Australia between the HIV-infected and trial scientists.

(7) The Clinic had broken faith with the AIDS Trust, a national fund-raising charity for AIDS which had promised to fund the trial.

(8) "Community-based trials" are the solution to the growing disaffection of PWAs in the trial system and the need for quicker development of alternative treatments. Community trials should be conducted outside the traditional research hospital setting, perhaps among medical practitioners or community AIDS organizations, utilizing maximum input from people with HIV/AIDS in their design and execution, in order to ensure trials are responsive to real patient needs.[1]

This embryonic discourse drew heavily on the critique coming from community organizations in the United States, such as Project Inform, the Community Research Initiative, and, of increasing importance, the AIDS Coalition to Unleash Power (ACT UP).

COMMUNITY DRUG TRIAL PROPOSALS

This debate was the first discussion of community trials in a public forum in Australia, representing a direct challenge by patients to scientific research. However, PLWA's critique quickly began to be undermined by developments in a number of sectors.

Following the radio debate, it was brought to PLWA's attention that ACON had in fact been working, in collaboration with key AIDS researchers, on a proposal for a community trial system. PLWA was permitted only limited access to this proposal at a very late stage of its development, a strategy that infuriated Bell. His anger increased after an announcement by ACON to the press in August that the proposed Community HIV/AIDS Trial Network (CHATN) was primarily interested in substances "particularly for use among people who are asymptomatic" (ACON press release 28 August 1989). Bell interpreted this development as illustrative of a developing rift between the asymptomatic and people with AIDS. The well were being "bought off" with the promise of early medical intervention while those more disadvantaged by ill-health were being confined to the conventional hospital system.

Bell himself had rather different views of how community trials should be structured. Bell demanded speed and efficiency with a priority for those who needed treatment most urgently, namely people with AIDS. He stated that any promising substance was worthy of testing, a taunt to the more cautious position of both clinical researchers and ACON, the latter adopting an increasingly conventional position on treatment development.

Bell perceived PLWA to be increasingly under threat of absorption into ACON's agenda and the conflict over the Community AIDS Trial Network strengthened that conviction. He was critical of PLWA's inability to respond quickly and with sufficient force to the slow pace of the research establishment. "Your approach is to die politely," he once angrily accused the organization. Its "managerial style of leadership" modeled in the first instance on ACON, only facilitates its easy incorporation into the AIDS establishment. "PLWA," he warned, "will be indistinguishable from ACON within two years."

As to what PLWA was getting itself into with its close links with ACON, Tom loudly commented one day in the offices of ACON that, "ACON is starting to behave like the medical profession. It's like an intellectual elite deciding for gay people what is good for them and what they should do."

Bell was attacking the very form of organization through which PLWAs were constituting themselves. By duplicating rational forms of power relations, by then so pervasive in the established AIDS sector, complete with a hierarchy and bureaucratic processes of decision making, and PLWA (NSW) was becoming indistinguishable from the establishment, and thereby incapable of changing it. Like Paul Young, Bell had been repositioned outside the orbit of PLWA as the organization progressively rationalized its structure. In that process, radical elements, which so often provide great impetus to such organizations, are purged from the ranks.

I am reminded of a statement by Foucault on political action:

> Those who resist or rebel against a form of power cannot merely be content to denounce violence or criticize an institution. Nor is it enough to cast the blame on reason in general. What has to be questioned is the form of rationality at stake . . . The question is: how are such relations of power rationalized? Asking it is the only way to avoid other institutions, with the same objectives and the same effects, from taking their stead (Foucault 1988:84).

PLWA (NSW), after only one year of operations, was indeed duplicating the very structures that it sought to overcome. Only those, like Bell, who remained outside these structures by choice or otherwise, could retain a radical critique of these forms of power.

As if by some wicked scripting of fate, this early era of the organization was effectively closed, for me at least, with Terry Bell's death on December 15, 1989. His death shocked many who were unaware of the severity of his illness toward the end of that year. Terry was working on a draft of a treatment information news sheet in bed on the day of his death. Terry Bell worked relentlessly to the last day to improve the predicament of people with AIDS.

NOTES

1. The community trial idea was receiving wide publicity in the United States by this time, with the establishment of the Community Research Initiative in New York. In Australia, these developments received their first significant media coverage in the national public affairs weekly, the *Bulletin* (22 August 1989), under the heading "Desperation Drugs: Frustrated AIDS Patients are Spurring the FDA to Relax the Rules of the Game."

CHAPTER 10

Therapeutic Truth Games

Taking a social constructionist approach to science, Latour and Woolgar (1979), in their ethnographic study of a scientific laboratory, argue that scientific "facts," rather then being unproblematic, progressive, revelatory truths, are linguistically constituted within the context of a global political-economic order. They are drawing upon the analytic frameworks developed by the school of the philosophy of science in which Kuhn (1962), Mulkay (1972) and Feyerabend (1978) are notable. This school sought to penetrate the hallowed ground of modern science and subject it to the kinds of social analysis that had been applied to most other areas of social life. Science, it seemed, had remained sacred, untrammelled by the threats of deconstruction, a testimony to its truth value in our societies. Since Kuhn's ground breaking work, a large and diverse body of social research on science has emerged, exploring the political, historical, economic, cultural, and, most recently, gendered dimensions of science.

In this chapter, I draw upon Latour and Woolgar's appraisal that the "facts" of science are encoded social constructs fixed within truth regimes through processes of "the organization of persuasion through literary inscription" (1979:88). Science constructs facts through the use of a hierarchy of "statement types," ranging from pure conjecture to progressively more confident statements ("what might reasonably be thought to be the case") and finally to statements of uncontested "truth" value. Truth may be contested, of course, as the history of science readily reveals. We will see in the short history of AZT a complex matrix of competing truth claims. I refer to the published papers of research scientists together with the statements and actions of government and non-government community-based organizations. This broad approach allows some understanding of the cultural, political, and economic dimensions of scientific research as it is applied to the problem of HIV/AIDS.

ANTIVIRAL RESEARCH: THE DEPLOYMENT OF AZT

AZT was first developed as a potential anticancer agent by the Michigan Cancer Foundation in 1964 and abandoned shortly thereafter because it was ineffective. When HIV was identified in 1984 Burroughs Wellcome, the owner of the AZT patent, began searching for a compound that could be effective against the virus. Burroughs Wellcome is a significant multi-national drug company known for its long-term focus on research and development (Klass 1975:110). With the assistance of the U.S. National Cancer Institute, Burroughs Wellcome demonstrated AZT to be effective against HIV *in vitro*. First experiments on humans began in July 1985 and early results of the Phase One trial, favorable to the drug, were first published in March 1986 (O'Reilly 1990).

While evidence of some efficacy against HIV was known as early as September 1986 when the Phase One trial was terminated, official peer-reviewed information only first appeared in July 1987 in an issue of the *New England Journal of Medicine*. Two reports dealt respectively with the "efficacy" (Fischl et al. 1987) and "toxicity" (Richman et al. 1987) of AZT "in the treatment of patients with AIDS and AIDS-related complex." The summary conclusions of the two reports hinted at the difficulties to come. The summary on "efficacy" stated:

> These data demonstrate that AZT administration can decrease mortality and the frequency of opportunistic infections in a *selected* group of subjects with AIDS or AIDS-related complex, *at least* over the 8 to 24 weeks of observation in this study (Fischl et al. 1987:185, emphasis added).

The key indicator of efficacy used in the study was the comparative rates at which those on the drug progressed to death against those who did not use it. This "end stage" approach disallowed measurement of the quality of that extended life or of the long-term effects of the drug.

The second report, on "toxicity," did discuss this issue.

> Although a subset of patients tolerated AZT for an extended period with few toxic effects, the drug should be administered with caution because of its toxicity and the limited experience with it to date (Richman et al. 1987:192).

These first reports were circumscribed by the limitations of the Phase One trial design. The conclusions suggested a predictable relationship between the drug and its effects only in these restricted circumstances. The narrow parameters of the trial study opened space for a wide contestation of the meaning and implications of the results.

The structure of the trial itself set the nature of the ethical debate that ensued. Some 282 research subjects were enrolled in the double-blind, randomized (placebo-controlled) trial, by then the standard research practice in the development of pharmaceutical drugs. Only thirteen of these, the report states, were not men. Of the subjects, 160 had AIDS and 122 had AIDS-related complex (ARC), a milder stage of the disease. Of these, 145 were randomly assigned AZT at a dose of 1500 milligrams per day. No rationale was offered in the report for the establishment of this dosage or other indicators or variables. The remaining 137 received an inactive placebo. At the conclusion of twenty-four weeks, nineteen from the placebo group had died, and one only from the AZT group had died. In addition to improved mortality rates, the study reported those on AZT experienced decreased frequency of opportunistic infections, weight gain, and improvements in immune function. The cautious tone of the report rested, however, with the observation that those with less-developed illness responded better to the drug than those with AIDS. The reason for this response was hypothesized to be an effect of cumulative toxicity, a toxicity that may be the result of a dosage which was unnecessarily high. The "toxicity" report noted:

> The encouraging reduction in mortality and opportunistic infections and the improvement in the quality of life observed in the controlled clinical trial were often accompanied by toxic effects induced by AZT (Richman et al. 1987:196).

In particular, the occurrence of anemia and neutropenia suggested the risk of toxicity in long-term use of the drug and the need to reduce dosages. Reasons for the observed results were not understood at the time, but one commentator writing eight months after the publication of results suggested that reduced antigenemia (presence of virus in plasma) reflected "diminished virus replication in vivo" (Hirsch 1988). These results led to the early termination of the study by an independent data-safety monitoring board, with those on placebo being offered the active drug. Continued observation supported the argument for beneficial effects of the drug as they were defined by the study design; that is, decreased mortality rate.

In Australia, a trial of the drug was established through the Federal Government National Health and Medical Research Council (NH&MRC) in 1987, providing people with AIDS in Australia access to the drug.

PROFIT VERSUS LIFE: THE FIRST WAVE OF PROTEST

By late 1987 concern was being expressed in Sydney about the inadequate supply of AZT to people with AIDS. On August 21, the *Sydney Star*

Observer reported that AZT availability was now a priority for ACON. It was said that adequate supply of the drug was being hindered as a result of insufficient government funds. The manufacturing pharmaceutical company, Burroughs Wellcome, charged approximately $10,000 for a year's supply of the drug for one patient. Unlike in the United States, where the absence of a comprehensive national health scheme left individuals to pay for the drug themselves, in Australia government paid, in the first instance, through controlled clinical trials, and then through the Pharmaceutical Benefits Scheme when the drug was approved. ACON's president, speaking to the *Sydney Star Observer*, accurately foreshadowed the conflict that was to develop:

> Expensive as this and other potentially beneficial drugs may be, they save lives in the short term, and will also save governments money in the long term. The gay community may need to run vigorous public campaigns to ensure their availability. . . . Different types of health education programs may also have to be developed among antibody positive people so they can monitor their own health status more effectively. . . . Drug trials inherently raise complex ethical and legal issues for participants and organizers. The involvement of community-based representatives in monitoring trials and evaluating results is vital. . . . Future drug trials must also ensure community representation on overseeing bodies (*Sydney Star Observer* 21 August 1987).

Community-based AIDS groups were working to establish their presence in both the public discourses about the treatment of the disease and in influencing government decisions about funding.

In late October, the New South Wales State Minister for Health approved funding for AZT for a further 210 people. The minister simultaneously called for a reduction in the price of the drug, as Burroughs Wellcome had promised. ACON supported this demand and proceeded, despite the Government's action, to stage a protest rally on 24 November outside the State Parliament House calling on the Government to "make AZT available for all who need and want it." An information leaflet, distributed prior to the rally, announced a demand that more government money be made available for the supply of the drug. It presented an analysis of the drug in this way:

> AZT is a frontrunner in the treatment of AIDS — many people here and overseas are experiencing a lessening of symptoms, and feel well enough to go to work and resume a normal lifestyle.
>
> The evidence shows that the earlier people start taking AZT, the better its effects on their health. Any delays can be devastating for those who need and decide they want AZT.

As of 1 November the [New South Wales] Government allows only 20 people to receive AZT per month. But there is already a waiting list and each month 40-60 new people are being diagnosed with AIDS related conditions that make them potential AZT recipients (ACON information leaflet, November 1987).

The confidence of this statement contrasts strikingly with those of clinical researchers. Gone are the uncertainties and cautious warnings regarding the drug's efficacy and long-term effects. While the statement has qualifying phrases such as "the evidence shows that," it invests the utility of AZT with a fact-value well above the contemporary clinical research statements. This is possible using a different logic to that of data-dependent scientific discourse, one grounded in a moral-political liberal philosophy that places a priority on the well-being of the individual and stresses the responsibility of the state in ensuring this well-being. This shift in logic was politically successful. Following discussions with ACON, the New South Wales Minister for Health announced an end to the rationing of AZT (*Sydney Star Observer* 25 December 1987).

Debate regarding the cost of AZT was also occurring in the United States and Europe among medical researchers and gay communities. As early as mid-December 1987, Burroughs Wellcome had reduced the price of AZT by 20 percent in response to demands from U.S. activists (Strubbe 1988), yet this was not a sufficient reduction for people with AIDS in the United States itself who had to bear the cost of the drug directly. In 1988, a comprehensive independent overview of the cost debate as it was presented in the United States was prepared by Thomas and Fox (1988). They linked the high cost of the drug not to an unreasonable profit margin, but to the unusually high dosage of two capsules every four hours, coupled with the long treatment period and "marketing decisions" involving factors such as cost of production and the need to recoup development costs. Their review concludes:

The absence of price regulation in the pharmaceutical industry reflects recognition that the cost to the public of this pricing power is more than offset by the benefits of a flexible market structure that supports innovation.

The review also canvasses a range of moral and policy issues raised by AZT:

Should special funding be provided because of the magnitude of the burden on patients, or the size of the population on which this burden falls? Should special funding be provided to encourage efficiency if AZT is cost-effective, or is cost-effectiveness irrelevant to policy decisions about a life-sustaining therapy?

The ethical difficulty faced by governments is in part a function of the nature of the technology. And:

Controversy over drug costs could become an increasing policy issue during the AIDS epidemic, if AZT is the first of a series of complex new drugs that must be taken over long periods to ameliorate without curing the disease (Thomas and Fox 1988).

This new discursive struggle can be positioned within a debate that has been continuing for some decades now around the cost and benefits associated with high-technology medicine (Jennett 1986). What gave this new struggle its unique character was the historical nexus between high-technology medicine and an articulate patient population with an historically problematic relationship to medicine and government. Any attempt by governments to restrict the development of AIDS treatments was destined to be interpreted by gay and AIDS activists as an expression of "homophobia," the denial of citizen rights to a despised and outcast group (see, for example, Kramer 1989; Shilts 1987).

This struggle over drug costs was beginning to win the attention of the Australian gay press by 1988. An article on demonstrations and political organizations in the United States quoted an American gay man with AIDS:

> Terry [Sutton] believes that in the United States, a country devoid of national health care, where sickness and disease are big business, it's expected for profits to be made from illness and death. In a capitalist society it's natural to make a buck from just about anything — including your wellbeing and your life. A best friend or lover uses AZT, buys a little time, then dies a year or two later — maybe someone on the Burroughs Wellcome board of directors takes a trip to Tahiti or Rome on the blood money. They call it "making a reasonable profit" — he would call it obscene and criminal (Strubbe 1988:23).

The article reported a large and angry demonstration, organized from within the gay community of that city, outside the Burroughs Wellcome building in San Francisco. The protest was organized by a group calling itself AIDS Action Pledge. They demanded the release of all profit figures on AZT from Burroughs Wellcome, a complete and unbiased report on the efficacy of the drug, that the company expedite research, and an explanation for an alleged payment to the National Institute of Health on the day the company was granted permission to market the drug. The observer of the rally noted that T-shirts were worn reading "Action = Life" and "Silence = Death" beneath the gay symbol of the pink triangle. This symbol was designed by a group of six gay men in New York in 1986 calling itself the "Silence = Death Project." The group lent its logo to the newly formed activist group ACT UP (NY) in the northern spring of 1987 (Crimp and Rolston 1990:14). About her first sighting of the symbol on a poster on the streets of New York, Cindy Patton wrote:

> The poster spoke an international closeted language. It was multivocal and polysemic, but also anonymous and with a single, urgent meaning: this was a rallying cry to no place in particular — no march, no meeting, no group. A notice to a community of camouflaged guerrillas that "AIDS" — as a contemporaneous stencil graffito said — "is not over" (Patton 1990:126).

The logo quickly became the icon par excellence of AIDS activism, the symbol of a resistance, stamped on posters, banners, buttons, and T-shirts. It became a ready-made chant for demonstrating activists. The semiology of the icon is undeniably gay: the pink triangle, but inverted as if to signal a reversal of the gay status quo, and the suggestion of "coming out" implied in the denial of silence. The secrecy of the closet now threatens death. With the establishment of ACT UP chapters in many other countries around the world, the same logo may now be seen in many different languages, suggesting the multivalency of this simple but powerful image. It was to be another two years before ACT UP was successfully to be set up in Sydney, yet the activities of the groups in the United States were sooner to exert a powerful influence on the future Australian strategic responses to clinical research on AIDS treatments.

ACON continued its advocacy of AZT into the following years. In February 1988 it released an information statement on the drug's benefits and explained who may be eligible for access, according to clinical definitions. On June 1, in Sydney, ACON staged a public forum at which AIDS researchers were invited to present up-to-date information on AZT. Two representatives of Burroughs Wellcome were present, together with two representatives from the federal government. The forum attracted the interest of a commercial television station that filmed the opening introductions for a news story on the issue. Almost one hundred people attended, mostly gay men. The two researchers described developments in an optimistic framework. Professor David Cooper noted that better results were being observed in trials investigating the use of AZT in combination with other drugs, and Dr. Julian Gold noted the probable benefits of early intervention for successfully prolonging life. He recalled an earlier period when "all we could do was watch people coming in on Friday mornings progressively deteriorating."

At question time, an ACON committee member put the following query to one of the Burroughs Wellcome representatives:

In order to be assured there is no rip-off going on we need information, none of which has been forthcoming. In a situation where Burroughs Wellcome has no competitor and therefore rules of commercial confidentiality don't apply, why can't information on mark-ups be provided?

The representative claimed he had no such information and, regardless, the price of the drug was not exorbitant and would come down "when sales overtake costs." Replies from the audience were angry and forceful. "Why can't the books be thrown open? What *are* gay men meant to think?" The company representative responded to these demands with vague assurances that profits were considerably less than that normally imposed on new drugs.

The following day an increase in the federal AZT budget to $9.4 million was announced. ACON responded by stating, "This will come as a relief to many people affected by AIDS, who have been very worried about gaining access to this vital drug and then being able to continue to receive it" (*Sydney Star Observer* 10 June 1988). The problem of availability had, it appeared, been resolved for the time being.

Meanwhile, just one month after the community forum, Burroughs Wellcome undertook a public relations exercise and announced to the gay press a contribution of $5,000 to the local AIDS-service charity, the Bobby Goldsmith Foundation, with a further $5,000 forthcoming. The exercise was clearly intended to rectify the company's bad image among the gay community. The *Sydney Star Observer* recorded, "Mr Abrahamson [company representative] agreed Wellcome Australia (and its parent company, the multi-national Burroughs Wellcome) had a public relations problem with AZT in the gay community both here and overseas. He said this was unfortunate." He justified the company's sudden action by adding that the company had "'some obligation' to contribute to the wellbeing of AIDS patients" (*Sydney Star Observer* 8 July 1988). Contributions of this kind, while always controversial, were to become more frequent.

The developments in the United States and Australia were parallel in many respects. At issue was the role of the state in checking capitalist forces in the provision of health care and in treatment development. In the United States, the price burden on the consumer revived a debate among the political left about capitalist exploitation and the need for a national health scheme to compensate for market forces. The Australian debate centered on the ability of government to meet its responsibility as provider of equitable health services, a responsibility made problematic by the fact that treatment research was centered in other countries. The broad issue, then, was Australia's relationship to multinational drug companies and foreign governments' drug regulation apparatuses.

THE SHIFT TO TREATMENT FOR PREVENTION OF ILLNESS

Allopathic medicine's ideal is the "cure" of disease; that is, the total eradication of a disease from the body. Its principles of diagnosis and intervention are oriented around this ultimate and ideal objective. Likewise, popular folk belief holds the cure of disease to be medicine's mission, despite the fact that, in practice, modern medicine has eradicated only a small number of diseases (Jennett 1986:15).

Basic science research into the nature of HIV produced growing doubt among scientists that this model of cure could be a reasonable expectation in the case of AIDS. Removal of the virus from the body, it was soon realized, would be technologically impossible given that the virus acts by incorporating itself into the genetic structure of the body. Removing the virus would mean removing or destroying infected cells, for example the cells of the immune system, which are necessary for protection of the body from infection. If by cure one means the permanent cessation of the progression of the disease and the restoration of the immune system, this looked increasingly unlikely, at least with chemotherapeutic antivirals such as AZT. Such drugs appeared to check replication of the virus for a limited period only. Immune function already lost could not be replaced, and very little research appeared to be underway on drugs that would act as "immune boosters" (see ACT UP 1989). This research agenda is a product of the domination of virology over immunology in the field of AIDS research. Hope for a cure for HIV infection rested with the development of vaccines that would either inactivate the virus in those already infected, or that would be useful in preventing initial infection, such as the vaccines for smallpox or hepatitis.

A shift occurred by the end of the decade in the conceptualization of the treatment of AIDS: from cure to preventative "management" of the disease. HIV infection, some researchers were claiming, would soon be definable as a "chronic manageable disease," much like diabetes. The treatment of opportunistic infections experienced by people with late-stage HIV disease had greatly improved and was largely responsible for the improved quality of life and life expectancy of people with AIDS. The place of AZT in the treatment of late-stage disease would continue to be contested. As to those in early stages of HIV infection, hope now focused on the administration of AZT while the immune system was relatively intact.

In the United States a new trial, coded 019, was set up to determine the efficacy of the drug for those with CD4 counts of less than 500. Later, in early 1989, the establishment of a new French/British trial was announced in the medical journal, the Lancet. Named Concorde I, it aimed "to determine whether early treatment with Zidovudine [AZT] in symptomless seropositive patients (CDC group II or III) delays progression to symptomatic disease and whether it reduces case fatality" (Anonymous II 1989).

The Concorde trial (in which Australia was to participate) sought to address a number of problems regarding the early use of AZT:

> It is tempting to use zidovudine early in the course of the disease — i.e. in symptomless patients — in the hope that such treatment will delay or even prevent progression to symptomatic disease and death. However, early use may lead to unnecessary toxicity and the development of Zidovudine resistance. . . . Moreover, the move towards antiviral therapy in symptom-free patients puts considerable psychological pressure on seropositive individuals, who are constantly reminded about the risk of progression at follow-up visits. Nevertheless, the place of zidovudine in such patients must be established in large-scale placebo-controlled trials before the drug is given indiscriminately (Anonymous II 1989:415).

These European researchers were more cautious than North Americans on this issue of early AZT therapy. Caution was advised on using the drug prematurely in early stages of the disease. Interestingly, the Concorde trial results, when finally released in 1993, were less than optimistic and reinvigorated the early treatment debate after a period of little public discussion.

Meanwhile, before Concorde (and Australia's participation in it) was announced, Sydney's AIDS organizations had already begun to translate the hypothesis regarding the possible usefulness of AZT for the asymptomatic into an education campaign encouraging individuals to undertake the HIV-antibody test and thereafter monitor their health if they were infected. ACON adopted a pro-HIV testing policy by September 1988 and produced a pamphlet entitled "Know Your Health Status" bearing this message. ACON's president announced this policy change to the gay community in the *Sydney Star Observer:*

> We're quite rapidly moving towards a situation in which AIDS will be able to be clinically managed. I'm confident medical authorities in San Francisco will announce this year various combination drug therapies which will change AIDS from being a terminal illness to a chronic disease. I don't want to raise false hopes. . . . HIV-infected people will still be vulnerable to episodes of illness. But it's politically vital we understand the importance of knowing our health status. Armed with this knowledge we can begin to demand particular drug treatments and insist particular drug trials be carried out (*Sydney Star Observer* 16 September 1988).

There are no truth statements here. Rather, the statement is one of hope. The rapid development of efficacious drugs for HIV infection is now confidently anticipated. Action has been taken on this anticipation, requiring the reversal of ACON's testing policy and the encouragement of its constituents to consider early treatment.

HIDDEN ILLNESS: SCIENCE GAZES UPON THE WELL

Because the immediacy of death was not an issue, the use of placebo-controlled trials to test AZT's efficacy at early stages of infection raised little controversy. ACON agreed with researchers on this point and endorsed the Concorde trial, in which Australia was playing a part. In April 1989 an ACON spokesperson put it this way:

> We have to be realistic. . . . The only way we're going to get approval and funding for AZT in people without symptoms is on the basis of [placebo] controlled studies.

Difficulties raised in the *Lancet* article cited above were dismissed with a reference to future possible developments:

> I'm not suggesting AZT is the wonder drug or that it doesn't have some sort of downside. But if we can stop damage to the immune system, put people on hold till something better comes along, their chances are vastly improved. There are many other drugs in the offering which may be more effective and with fewer side effects than AZT. But there will be none realistically in use for early stage patients within the next three years (*Sydney Star Observer* 7 April 1989).

This optimism was not limited to gay community representatives. Some Australian clinicians were also excited about the potential for the early use of AZT. For example, the clinical coordinator for the early intervention trial in Australia was quoted in the Sydney daily press as saying:

> Once we can demonstrate that AZT is better than nothing for people without symptoms, we'll only have to show that future drugs are better than AZT (*Sydney Morning Herald* 30 May 1989).

Clinical testing is no longer viewed as a means of identifying the drug's efficacy. The fact of its efficacy is asserted and the trial procedure is simply a necessary step in inevitable approval. In the discourse of clinical research and community-based organizations alike, practical science becomes a hindrance to the confirmation of fact, not a means to its discovery.

Despite this local optimism, caution about the drug was still widespread. Scientific journals continued to debate the wisdom of interrupting trials raising, among other issues, the possibility of resistance to AZT developing in early users (see, for example, Cherfas 1989). In Australia's next most populous state, the Victorian AIDS Council (VAC) maintained a cautious approach to these developments and refused to follow ACON in modifying its testing policy. And one person with AIDS was quoted in the *Sydney Star Observer* as saying: "The medical profession is taking a calculated risk in setting up this trial. We want them to find cures, but also to inform people of the risks" (*Sydney Star Observer* 21 April 1989). Such patient caution was read by clinical practitioners as an impediment: stubborn and even irrational resistance to positive action on one's health. One clinician, for example, was cited in the Sydney daily press in this way:

> The trial nurse Mr Clive Darcy-Evans said there was a lot of apathy among people who are antibody positive and well. "The problem is motivating them to do something about their health while they are still feeling well," he said (*Sydney Morning Herald* 30 May 1989).

Two alternative constructions of health are coming into competition over this issue of early medical intervention. Health for the infected person is a reading of the absence of illness in the body. The bodily experience of wellness confirms health. Health for the clinical researcher, on the other hand, is a deceptive condition hiding progressive bodily decay. To rely on a subjective bodily reading based on a sense of wellness is dangerous. As one physician noted, "It would be very unwise for HIV-infected individuals, or their physicians, to consider themselves healthy because they feel well" (Klein 1990).

In this new medical discourse, the responsible citizen must relinquish the task of reading the body to the medical practitioner. It is the latter who has access to the technological means that can detect approaching illness in advance of visible symptoms or bodily sensitivity. The technological gaze becomes preeminent; bodily experience redundant. The early intervention debate thus extended the authority of medical technology over the independent judgment of its subjects.

Australia was well behind developments in the United States. The U.S. Secretary for Health announced on August 10, 1989, only four months after the Concorde early intervention trial was begun in Australia, the termination of the placebo arm of the American 019 trial:

> I am pleased to announce today the first results from the largest AIDS clinical trial ever conducted. With these results, we are witnessing an additional significant milestone in the battle to change AIDS from a fatal disease to a treatable one. The study showed that Zidovudine (AZT) delays progression of HIV disease in certain people infected with the HIV virus who have not

yet developed symptoms. Only two weeks ago, we announced that this drug slows progression of HIV infection in persons with early AIDS-related complex, or ARC. What we have learned from these two studies provides real hope for the millions of people worldwide who are infected with HIV (Wellcome Foundation 1989).

This announcement significantly raises the fact-value of the efficacy of AZT at early stages of HIV disease. However, it was not until eight months after this public announcement of the termination of the placebo arm of the 019 trial that the results were published in a scientific peer-reviewed journal (see Volberding et al. 1990). The practice of inscription of scientific fact through publication, once central to the policing of rigor in scientific experimentation, appeared to be weakening in response to this new health problem.

As early as December 1989, Gottlieb and Hutman could opine that, "Prior to August, the use of zidovudine in mildly symptomatic or asymptomatic HIV infection was an area of controversy among experts. In the months since the data were made public a new consensus is emerging." While they noted that, "The [NIH asymptomatic] study was inconclusive with respect to the advisability of zidovudine for HIV-positive individuals with greater than 500 T4-cells," they were still confidently able to anticipate that:

> Given zidovudine's track record of benefit in successively earlier HIV populations, it seems likely that efficacy will eventually be demonstrated . . . In my view it is appropriate to offer Zidovudine at 500 mg/day to asymptomatic patients with greater than 500 T4-cells (Gottlieb and Hutman 1989:6).

The authors refer to patient "reluctance to start therapy 'too soon'" for fear of developing resistance to the drug, as no longer a valid concern: "In the asymptomatic patient, the issue of resistance is mainly theoretical." The U.S. Federal Drug Administration (FDA) extended the licence for the use of the drug for asymptomatic patients with fewer than 500 T4-cells in March 1990. A meeting of the NIH at that time recommended to clinicians that AZT be prescribed for early use (Cotton 1990). With the publication of the trial results in April 1990, the fact-value of the drug's efficacy was further strengthened. The issue of the short-term efficacy of early AZT treatment was thereby more or less settled within American therapeutic discourse.

This was far from the end of controversy, however, with the issue of the long-term effects of the drug still open to debate. The uncertainties raised by the U.S. 019 trial left the European coordinators of the Concorde 1 trial unconvinced that their newer study should also be interrupted. The coordinator of the French arm of the trial, for example, stated in *Science*, "The results we have seen do not allow us to give a strict recommendation to give AZT [to asymptomatics]" (Cherfas 1989). The Concorde trial was modified however, to allow physicians to give the drug to patients if they wished to take it. An editorial appeared in the *Annals of Internal Medicine* in May 1990 supporting this caution, saying:

> The available data do not address the question of whether early intervention with zidovudine in persons with CD4 counts between 200 and 500/mm³ prolongs life or improves its quality. Whereas the selective use of zidovudine in such persons should be endorsed for the present (Ruedy et al. 1990).

In reference to the early-use study, Friedland described the natural history of HIV infection as one that presented "a grim vision of the future" where "most of those infected will eventually go on to have a serious and probably fatal outcome." The establishment of AZT's efficacy, at least in the short term, was not sufficient to solve the dilemmas inherent in the practice of early drug use. For one:

> The minimal effective dose has yet to be established. Furthermore, because of the need for early termination of the study, the long-term benefits of this strategy of early intervention to delay clinical progression and prolong survival are not yet known (Friedland 1990:1001).

The question of resistance remains, the author states, as does uncertainty regarding the "golden moment" to begin treatment; that is, the moment "when efficacy may be maximized, toxicity minimized, and the most durable benefit ensured." The decision as to when to start treatment, he concluded, rests with both doctor and patient (Friedland 1990:1001), a position community-based organizations would certainly endorse.

In short, the decision to begin drug use, especially in this case of early intervention with AZT, cannot be guided by scientific fact alone. Rather, doctor and patient should negotiate the available information together, interpreting facts and their implications. Inevitably the doctor will have a predilection one way or the other, as will the patient. Decisions may be reversed as new information becomes available and the patient accumulates experience with the therapy. In this manner, therapeutic practice can still be realized, even amidst a cloud of scientific uncertainty.

THE POLITICAL ECONOMY OF BELIEF

The combined effect of the release of AZT for early use in the United States, and the reluctance of the Europeans to interrupt their trial, was to stimulate a stronger campaign in Australia to broaden access to the drug. While in the United States the debate about the desirability and efficacy of

AZT was continuing among people with AIDS and AIDS organizations,[1] the debate around the benefits and disadvantages of the drug was not as polarized in Australia. Advocates in the United States demonstrated a much stronger skepticism of the motivations and machinations of scientific developments such as AZT. ACT UP New York, for example, described AZT in 1989 as one of a number of "AIDS drug development disasters:"

> Developed largely at public expense, its revenues have been privatized in the hands of Burroughs Wellcome, impoverishing most people who take it. Considered too toxic even for cancer chemotherapy when first discovered in 1964, it was approved for AIDS at a dose so strong most users became transfusion-dependent or stopped taking the drug. In AZT's expedited approval, crucial questions were overlooked: Why was such a toxic drug recommended? Can a drug which drives many people into poverty be considered "safe"? How many other companies will exploit the Orphan Drug Act and profiteer off the bodies of people with life-threatening disease? The FDA revised its Treatment IND program on the basis of its experience with AZT, but no drug since has received the same wide distribution AZT got before marketing approval. The Federal AIDS Program's clinical trial pipeline is still clogged with AZT trials, more than 2 years after approval (ACT UP 1989:14–15).

American activists were far more critical than Australians of the profit incentives that directed drug development, a critique driven, as noted earlier, by the structure of health delivery in that country.

The weakness of a critique of AZT in Australia is a product, I suggest, of the different health economies of the two countries. In Australia, the profit motivation of pharmaceutical companies was indeed recognized. For example, Adam Carr, commenting in the gay press on the potential explosion of the demand for AZT with its approval for early use, described the drug's development as "a gigantic rip-off of people with HIV and of the taxpayers who are subsidizing the cost to patients." Interestingly, however, Carr saw the most probable and effective check to this exploitation in the possible development of competitive new drugs (Carr 1989e). The linkage between drug development and capitalist profit was appreciated but any critique of the industry that went beyond demands for price reduction was short-circuited. The more extreme critique of AZT that was featured widely in New York's gay press was dismissed by the Australian national gay press as "campaigns of disinformation" (Carr 1989a). While this local support of the value of AZT did not deny the toxicity of the drug, and still condemned the manufacturers as "rapacious bloodsuckers who ought to be prosecuted for extortion," the drug was defended as "still the best treatment for AIDS we have" (Carr 1989b). A growing expectation of the future development of effective drugs, and a more-or-less comprehensive and relatively responsive national health delivery system, deflected the Australian critique away from the problematic issues of scientific research practices and capitalist exploitation, toward the role of the state in providing access to potentially life-saving drugs.

NOTES

1. For the argument against AZT see for example: "Sins of omission: the AZT scandal," *Spin* (January 1990); M. Callen, "Challenging AZT myths," *AIDS Forum* 1(2) (March 1989). For the argument in favour of AZT see, for example, R. Schick, "The Crazy Case Against AZT," *PWA Coalition Newsline* 49 (November 1989).

CHAPTER 11

Getting Angry: Emotional Expression as Strategic Intent

End in anger, I say, because it is only sane to rage against the dying of the light, because strategically anger is a political response, because psychologically anger replaces despondency and because existentially anger lightens the solitude of frightened individuals.

– Edmund White (1987)

ACT UP SYDNEY-STYLE

When access to AZT in the United States greatly improved with the expansion of the number and type of trials conducted with the drug, AIDS treatment activists in that country turned their attention to new developments in antivirals and other drugs. In Australia on the other hand, a major campaign was about to begin to convince the Australian authorities to approve early use of AZT just as had occurred in the United States. With the announcement of the U.S. 019 trial results in August 1989, the various state AIDS councils quickly moved to assess the situation in Australia. The move in the United States to grant early use of the drug was taken as evidence for the drug's efficacy and justification for equivalent access to be granted here.

A discussion paper prepared by the peak community-based body, the Australian Federation of AIDS Organisations (AFAO), in August 1989 argued that "the results of these U.S. trials strongly suggest early intervention will delay progression to disease." The paper recommended that the local authority, the Australian Drug Evaluation Committee (ADEC), discontinue the Australian arm of the early intervention AZT trials; that Burroughs Wellcome determine the lowest effective dose rate and reconsider its pricing policy in the light of expanded use; and that the Australian federal government investigate the cost implications of wider use in this country (AFAO 1989b). The report's recommendations reached the federal government, through the Inter-Governmental Committee on AIDS (IGCA) and the Australian National Council on AIDS (ANCA) early in March.

As AFAO began its lobby campaign through the gay and mainstream press and television, Adam Carr in the national gay press again made brief mention of the inconclusiveness of early treatment. "The ethics of prescribing a drug of zidovudine's toxicity to asymptomatic people in the absence of decisive evidence of protection from illness will now need to be debated" (Carr 1989d). Such a debate was not forthcoming, however, as efforts were directed toward persuading an obdurate government to grant access to the drug at early stages of the disease.

In late 1989 a small group of gay men with HIV issued an anonymous press release announcing the establishment of a new group "OZ ACT UP." The statement, informed by the discourse of moral outrage of ACT UP (AIDS Coalition To Unleash Power) groups in the United States, equally condemned community organizations and government for not moving quickly enough on this issue of early access to AZT:

> We are angry that AZT is not yet freely available to people infected with the AIDS virus whose immune system shows signs of being compromised. It is over 3 months since early intervention trials in the United States were cancelled for humane reasons. The evidence is clear — early intervention with AZT will prevent people from progressing to full AIDS (ACT UP Australia 1990).

The faltering formation of the group, later reconstituted as ACT UP Sydney in mid-1990, indicated that the time had arrived for a radical activism positioned outside the established lobby channels of community-based AIDS organizations. The statement was not written by new personnel but by a handful of individuals already positioned within the existing AIDS sector. The formation of new groups does not necessarily signal new actors in the game, but rather efforts by the same players to constitute new strategies of protest.

By early 1990, when it became clear that ADEC was not going to expedite approval for the use of drug at early stages of HIV disease, the campaign was broadened to include more AIDS groups and intensified with increasingly strong demands. ACON and PLWA (NSW) both issued statements condemning the federal government's inaction. ACON interpreted the U.S. scientific evidence as "overwhelmingly clear" in showing "that the drug is dramatically effective" (ACON press release 31 January 1990). PLWA (NSW) took a more dramatic approach, describing the government's failure to act as "an early death sentence for people with HIV" (PLWA (NSW) press release 1 February 1990; see also *Sydney Star Observer* 9 February and 9 March 1990). Broader political support had been won from the center-left political party, the Australian Democrats, who joined the call for the release of AZT for early use. Their statement deployed an economic rationalist argument appealing to "the preservation of life by society as worthy," pointing out the potential cost effectiveness of early drug intervention (*Sydney Star Observer* 23 February 1990). Attempts by ACON to win the support of another health lobby organization, the Consumer's Health Forum, failed however, with that group expressing a strong preference for strengthened drug regulatory systems (ACON 1990a).

On March 22, PLWA (NSW) staged a public forum at which representatives of Australia's AIDS research establishment, Burroughs Wellcome, and the federal government were questioned by members of the organization. At the meeting Professor David Cooper, principle investigator for AIDS drug trials in Australia, stated his belief that placebo-based trials were still the most rigorous method for determining the efficacy of a drug, and intimated that moves in the United States to reorganize such trials on "parallel track" structures, in response to pressure from activists there, had curtailed the progress of knowledge of the drug. Activist interference had, in short, threatened scientific integrity. Cooper had been under increasing pressure by this time to cancel the placebo arm of the Australian trial. He had stated his reluctance to do so for this reason of scientific integrity. In support of his actions he added a cautious remark that the long-term effects of the drug in early use were still unknown.

On the other hand, Cooper acknowledged the inadequacy of the government's drug approval system, and suggested activist groups had a constructive role to play in helping to bring about change. The comment deflected criticism away from medical research itself and toward the federal government's administrative apparatus. It also suggested a common enemy that researchers and activists could mutually identify and target.

When the public forum concluded, thirty-one people gathered in an adjacent room to consider the situation further. One individual present argued that ADEC was the appropriate target for protest. (The Australian Drug Regulatory Authority of which ADEC is the evaluatory arm, reviews the marketing application and approval for all new therapeutics in Australia.) "It's run by people who are quite crazy and incapable." "We need a revolution in the present drug approval system if we are going to speed up the decision-making process," was another man's comment. "We now have a major task in stepping up pressure to make these changes happen." Others stated that the established AIDS organizations, such as ACON and PLWA (NSW), would be ineffective in initiating changes because they were "in effect behaving like branches of the Health Department." Thus a decision was made to establish ACT UP Sydney, an activist group that could be unrestrained in its criticism and action against government bureaucracy. The following morning on the Australian Broadcasting Corporation's youth radio network, JJJ, a member of the new group announced the formation of ACT UP in Australia, anticipating a campaign that would press for major changes to the drug approval system in Australia.

Two weeks later, on April 10, 1990, PLWA (NSW) staged the inaugural meeting of ACT UP Sydney in the meeting space of the newly established gay "Pride" center in Darlinghurst. Of the sixty who were present only four were women, the remainder gay men. Many present were unknown to those who already worked in the AIDS sector. Many had been recruited to the meeting by some enthusiastic individuals who had attended the treatments forum and subsequent meeting. For these newcomers to AIDS activism, ACT UP presented an opportunity to participate in action that the existing organizational infrastructure did not provide. These were individuals who, for whatever reason, had been excluded from that organizational infrastructure.

The staging of this inaugural meeting suggested an innovative style of organizing for Australian AIDS activism. For example, a chairperson was not required, as the group was to resist the reproduction of oppressive hierarchies of the kind that were said to characterize established AIDS organizations. Instead, four individuals volunteered to act as "facilitators" for the evening's proceedings. The gathering was staged in a circular seating arrangement, reproducing this ideology of egalitarianism in a spatial form.

The manifesto of North American ACT UP groups was read as an opening statement:

> The AIDS Coalition to Unleash Power is a diverse, non-partisan group, united in anger and committed to direct action to end the AIDS crisis. We distribute the latest HIV/AIDS treatments information. We protest and demonstrate. We are not silent.

This statement identified an affinity between this nascent group and the established groups of North America. To reinforce the linkage, a fax from ACT UP New York was read that expressed support for the new group. The communication concluded by stating, in rhetoric reminiscent of gay liberation, that only when the epidemic had finally been defeated could activists return to the greater agenda of smashing the heterosexism that allowed the epidemic to go unchecked in the first instance. This statement discloses the ideological roots and underpinning of ACT UP, with its historical origins in the gay and women's movements of the 1970s.

Opening the discussion, one man spoke of his recent attendance at ACT UP New York meetings. He described with enthusiasm the energy at such meetings. People queue for hours, he claimed, just to get into the meetings, which eventually see "thousands" engage in heated and angry debate until three in the morning.[1] Throughout the evening's discussion this man implored the group to become more angry and enthusiastic like those at the New York meetings. "For God's sake, get angry, you lot!" he proclaimed. "We should all be screaming at each other and jumping out of our seats. Our friends are dying. What are we doing about it?"

Many in the room found these proclamations disturbing and several individuals left the meeting as a result. One man's rejoinder, that "lecturing to people about how they should feel and behave is not going to help us," received a loud applause from the group. Another man contrasted this meeting's structure with his recent experience with ACT UP London, where, he said, elected committees carefully control proceedings. "We should not blindly follow the American example," he stated. After the meeting one participant commented to me that he was worried that ACT UP meetings could become an avenue for people simply to express their anger, "to cathart," and risk losing their potential effectiveness as forum for developing strategies for action.

We see at this inaugural meeting an attempt to generate and harness the anger, so characteristic of North American AIDS activist protests, as an appropriate emotion with which to drive the Australian campaign for treatment access. However, many of those present resisted this emotional engineering, felt uncomfortable with the demands, and advocated different procedures. Anger was not spontaneously forthcoming. It would require a degree of preparation and rehearsal before it could be effectively and publicly deployed.

Yet many at the meeting were indeed angry. For example, one woman expressed her anger at her sense of isolation as a person who cares for people with AIDS. A man expressed his anger at losing friends because of AIDS. Such anger, however, is not necessarily expressed in the form of spontaneous verbal outbursts. Once having acknowledged their anger, participants then proceeded to a careful and considered debate of the perceived problems and the means of addressing them. It was argued that the issues under consideration were extremely complex and individuals expressed a desire to be better informed before they be called upon to contibute to decisions on further plans. This led to a small number of individuals from established groups explaining details of the predicament to the majority of the meeting. Final resolutions saw the scheduling of a further meeting to discuss the details of a demonstration to target ADEC.

AGAINST GOVERNMENT

On April 27,1990, ACT UP Sydney staged its first demonstration outside the Sydney offices of the Commonwealth (i.e. federal) Department of Community Services and Health (CDCSH), demanding release of AZT for early use. Extensive television coverage captured images of a "grim reaper" labelled "I am ADEC," withholding AZT capsules from the grasping hands of patients. A "die in" on the pavement was immediately followed by attempts to enter the CDCSH offices, without success. The imagery of the demonstration was a deliberate redeployment of the iconography that the CDCSH has used in its first television AIDS information campaign, portraying AIDS as the "grim reaper," in 1987. That campaign is widely despised by activists for the short-term hysteria it generated and the resultant demand it placed on their education organizations. Inverting the imagery of that campaign represented a revenge attack on a government bureaucracy perceived to be the source of much distress. Newspaper reportage of the event presented images of "vocal" and "angry protesters" demanding access to AZT. "People are very angry," a spokesperson was quoted as saying. "They are very tired of sitting back and looking at the polite political channels" (*The Advertiser* [Adelaide] 28 April 1990).

Through this iconographic style of communication, compatible with the evocative and truncated language of mass media, ACT UP was highly successful in generating considerable media attention in the United States and then in Australia. The first images of North American ACT UP to reach the Australian press were of the group's "hijack" of the opening ceremony of the Fifth International Conference on AIDS in Montreal.[2] The action was greatly admired by some Australians who witnessed it at the Montreal conference, as by some at home who learned about it through the media. Such conferences became a favorite forum of ACT UP for staging large and disruptive protests, in part because the presence of international media at such events provides ready access to a global audience.

In June 1990, ACT UP demonstrations at the Sixth International Conference on AIDS in San Francisco again captured media attention, this time dominating the international media reportage of the event. This success was due to the construction of a sophisticated "media center" in a hotel near the conference site. From there, protests were planned, communications orchestrated between groups across the country and internationally, and information was fed to the media. Large meetings of several hundreds in the local gay and lesbian community center led to the planning and staging of many protests throughout the week, sometimes several in one day. These protests ranged over issues such as the U.S. government's entry restrictions for people with HIV, the neglect of women's educational and treatment needs, the state of decay of the celebrated San Francisco AIDS response, treatment development issues, and the need for a comprehensive national U.S. health policy and program. The campaign received sensational coverage in the Australian press. Among the headlines were: "Militants Sabotage AIDS Conference" (*The Advertiser* [Adelaide] 26 June 1990), "AIDS Protesters Drown out Speech" (*The Daily Mirror* [Sydney] 25 June 1990) and "AIDS Furore over Visa Ban" (*The Australian* [National] 22 June 1990).

*   *   *

A decision to approve the early use of AZT in Australia was expected in August 1990 in time for a scheduled Australian National AIDS Conference in the national capital, Canberra. The federal administration's failure to meet this promise further fueled the determination of activists. At the Canberra conference, a number of people with HIV and AIDS, backed by other community activists, made their strongest demands for the approval of the drug. In what appeared to be a well orchestrated and collaborative effort, activists from ACT UP demonstrating at the opening of the conference were supported in their demands by invited speakers within the conference program (see ACON 1990b; ACT UP Australia 1990).

ACT UP captured the conference's opening ceremony in an action that reproduced the "hijack" of the international conference in Montreal in 1989. Unlike the action at Montreal, however, this action was anticipated by conference organizers and participants, and thereby had more the air of a dramatic performance than a spontaneous outburst of anger. Media coverage of the event presented images of a new Federal Minister of Health, Brian Howe, humbled before a crowd of shouting men and women sporting T-shirts demanding, "Cut the Red Tape."

The rhetoric of the group's statement was constructed around the anger of people with AIDS at the federal bureaucracy. In the eye of the national media, and before a plenary gathering of Australian AIDS health professionals, researchers, community educators, and people with HIV/AIDS, an Australian-resident North American gay man with AIDS, acting as spokesperson, stated:

> We are angry because our voices are not being heard. We are angry because the Australian Government is ignoring its responsibilities to its citizens with HIV and AIDS. We are angry because lack of action is destroying our hope and our lives.
>
> We are angry because people are dying and all Brian Howe does is to appoint more committees!

We are here to express our outrage that Government bureaucrats, pharmaceutical executives, researchers, doctors and the media, including those
participating in this conference, have locked us out of decisions affecting
our lives. We demand access to all information and a strong voice in all decisions affecting our lives. We demand that our Government begin to behave responsibly towards its citizens with HIV and AIDS.

Following a chant of "Silence = Death, Action = Life," the demonstra-
tors then quietly vacated the platform for the scheduled opening address
by the federal minister. His prepared speech revealed that the preceding
action had been fully anticipated by the Government:

As we face the start of the second decade of AIDS in Australia, there is simultaneously both growing maturity in the community's response to the
virus and a second and more militant wave of activism amongst some
people living with AIDS. An important aspect of the conference will be to
address the causes and challenges of this latter development.

The minister's ten-minute speech repeatedly acknowledged the importance
of consulting "people living with AIDS" as part of the Australian response to
the epidemic, and in it he announced his initiative of establishing a special
working party to investigate delays in the drug approval process in this
country and to put recommendations for the system's overhaul. He noted,
also, his government's intention to "fast-track Wellcome Australia's application to extend the availability of AZT."[3]

Thus, the ACT UP demonstration was more performative than informa-
tive. The demands expressed were not new to the government. Rather the
performance functioned to emphasize the urgency of the demands, an urgency articulated through the public display of anger. In response, the government capitalized on the situation by announcing its initiatives designed
to resolve the problem.

TRANSLATING ANGER: THE ADMINISTRATION REFORMS ITSELF

Shortly after the conference, ADEC indeed announced its decision to approve early use of AZT. However, the larger battle for the streamlining of
the drug-approval bureaucracy had only just begun.

In December 1990, the Federal Minister of Health's special working
party tabled its report at a meeting of his peak AIDS advisory body, the
Australian National Council on AIDS (ANCA). The report made thirty-
seven recommendations for streamlining the process for making new
therapeutic drugs available in Australia. Causes for the significant delays

in the availability of treatments already accessible overseas (in the U.S., the U.K., and Europe) were identified to lie in:

(1) The unique format requirements of the authorities for marketing applications.
(2) The attempts by Australian authorities to undertake independent evaluations without adequate resources.
(3) Inadequate links to overseas drug companies and clinical trial networks.
(4) Limitations of trials to a small number of institutions.
(5) Limited human and financial resources.
(6) Poorly developed administrative system.

Significantly, these impediments to the drug-evaluation and marketing process were not unique to HIV/AIDS therapies, but were "symptomatic of difficulties in drug availability as a whole" (ANCA 1990:3).

ANCA endorsed the thrust of the report but had reservations over the working party's recommendation 16 which suggested that:

Marketing approval granted by designated overseas regulatory authorities (for example those in the U.S.A., U.K.) should be accepted in Australia. The Product Information should be identical with that granted overseas (ANCA 1990).

This particular recommendation was considered by activists to be crucial to the streamlining process. However, objections were raised within the Department of Health and by key medical researchers that it would threaten Australia's "self-determination" on issues of drug evaluation by submitting to decisions made overseas.

The federal government responded to the ANCA report by setting up another inquiry, chaired by Peter Baume, with the brief to make specific recommendations as to how the existing drug evaluation system could be streamlined. Meanwhile, activists and community organizations were determined to keep up the pressure. The next Sydney Gay and Lesbian Mardi Gras parade, on February 16, 1991, saw a new group, the AIDS Treatment Action Committee (ATAC) lead a contingent of one hundred people dressed in black T-shirts inscribed with a pair of red lips ingesting an AZT-like capsule. ATAC was a coalition of several AIDS lobby groups, including ACON, PLWA (NSW) and ACT UP, a dramatic and forbidding presence in what is otherwise a highly extravagant and flamboyant procession. The intention of the contingent was to consolidate public support for the campaign and further demonstrate activist resolve to the government.

This shift to public spaces is a strategy fundamental to contemporary protest. The presence of an audience is critical in this strategy. Conference delegates, television viewers, pedestrians, or Mardi Gras participants constitute large audiences to which protesters perform. Anger in this sense, is itself performative, and takes on its transformative potential through its acting out before an audience. Through performance, the problem and proffered solution are placed in the public domain, generalizing the issues, rendering them "everyone's problem."

Meetings of ATAC continued through to the release of the federal government's next initiative, the Baume Report (named after the committee's chairperson) in July 1991. Baume and his colleagues made wide-ranging recommendations, along the lines of those in the 1990 ANCA Report, with one significant exception. The original working party's recommendation 16 was rejected by Baume on the grounds that:

> The Australian public is entitled to a sovereign evaluation and decision-making process which takes proper account of Australian interests. Those interests are not always the same as the interests of other countries, and Australia's ability to respond to problems arising with marketing products would be impaired if it had not had access to the data on which the decision to allow marketing was based (Baume 1991:xiv).

Exactly what those unique interests were, beyond "sovereign authority," are not spelled out in the report.

The bureaucratic structure singled out by the Baume Report for major reform was the Therapeutic Goods Administration (TGA). The Report notes that, under its present brief, the bureaucracy operated only to guarantee safety and efficacy of therapeutic goods. What was necessary in the current health crisis (i.e. the HIV epidemic) was a consideration of "a crucial aspect which has forced its way to prominence in recent years, that of 'timely availability' of therapeutic goods" (Baume 1991:xiv). The report also links cancer and AIDS, noting the importance to both of the "timely" accessibility of experimental drugs. In its recommendation 94 it generalizes to those with life-threatening conditions:

> Arrangements for access to drugs for the terminally ill and those for whom no conventional therapy exists should be as compassionate and flexible as possible without sacrificing broader community interests, or facilitating the exposure of terminally ill people to commercial quacks (Baume 1991:103).

Any facilitation of availability of drugs by the government should not, the report notes, "compromise the high standard of safety currently enjoyed by Australians" (Baume 1991:xiv).

The federal minister responded to the report with a promise to implement all the recommendations. At time of writing that process of implementation was underway.

The Baume Report represents the translation of the demands and expectations of people with HIV/AIDS into a discourse comprehensible to government administration. This discursive translation, a routinization of activist discourse, was necessary in the first instance for the new social category of "people with HIV/AIDS" to gain full recognition of their status as citizens of the state. The process thereby constructed this newly identified sub-population as a legitimate recipient of state protection. Secondly, the routinization of activist discourse was necessary in order for the administration to recognize those very demands put by activists and to translate them into processes of self-reform.

The acceptance of the report's recommendations signals a shift in the role of the state in the management of its citizens' health. As a direct response to the agitation of people with HIV/AIDS, and of the community-based agencies developed in response to AIDS, the federal government has undertaken to improve access to pharmaceutical products for people defined as having a "life-threatening illness." Thus, in the new environment of the AIDS epidemic, government has been called upon to expand its function in this area from simply one of guaranteeing the safety of its citizens, to guaranteeing right of access to experimental therapies for those with life-threatening illnesses.

What is required of government is a new balance of responsibilities between, on the one hand, conventional "public health" concerns, the benevolent supervision of citizens in their own interests, and, on the other hand, the rights of citizens to define for themselves their own health strategies, to define for themselves the acceptable levels of personal risk in the use of experimental therapeutic agents. The shift brings this area of government policy into alignment with the contemporary ideological pursuit of the "empowered," autonomous, self-creating individual.

Within this matrix of interests lie the profit pursuits of international pharmaceutical companies. Pharmaceutical industries have an interest in government regulatory processes in that, through them, they gain marketing approval for their products. In this way, government colludes with capitalist interests in a way that meets both the responsibilities of government to protect its citizens and the requirements of the industry to make profits. On the other hand, overly restrictive regulatory mechanisms are a disincentive to companies to seek marketing approval. Restrictive regulations, together with the small consumer market in Australia were identified in the ANCA report and Baume Report as major causes of delay in the availability of new treatments in Australia. The restrictive powers of the Australian government are in direct contrast to those of the United States where capitalist interests are more actively encouraged through government-driven incentives. In the United States, this configuration has resulted in the vastly greater array of therapeutic options so envied by people with HIV/AIDS in Australia. Acknowledging this, the Baume Report recommended that Australia seek closer relations with both pharmaceutical companies and drug regulatory apparatus in countries such as the United States, in order to encourage drug company enterprise in this country.

While the pharmaceutical industry stands to benefit from a deregulation of safety and efficacy controls, it also relies on such mechanisms to facilitate the approval of its products. The Baume Report embodied a balance of capitalist and governmental interests, while rejecting some of the demands of people with AIDS. It suggested means by which unapproved treatments may be trialed and approved more quickly, but failed to address the demand to make available those treatments already approved in other countries.

REINVENTING OUR SELVES

> Anger is a kind of interpretation, not of a feeling but *of the world*. It is, one might say, not an "inner" phenomenon so much as a way of being-in-the-world, a relationship between oneself and one's situation . . . Anger, in other words, is essentially a *judgmental* emotion, a perception of an offence. It consists of a series of concepts and judgments that among other ingredients, involve the concept of *blame*. Getting angry is making an indictment.
>
> – R. C. Solomon, "Getting Angry" (1984:250)

At the height of the ATAC campaign, at a point when the release of the Baume report was imminent, I had one of those key "Aha!" experiences that anthropologists often speak of when recalling the experience of fieldwork. A gay journalist was seeking views from those who had been active in the treatment campaign about the intransigence of the government bureaucracy in responding to the demands of people with AIDS. "I want you to tell me," he said, thrusting a microphone into my face, "about how angry you are." "But I don't feel angry," I confessed with some embarrassment. He looked rather disconcerted, and after a few more futile attempts to encourage me to answer his question, packed up his equipment and continued on his quest for a vocal angry activist.

This brief encounter provoked a realization that my role as AIDS activist had become so overdetermining in this period of my fieldwork, that even my emotional state was assumed by others. In admitting my failure to feel anger I had failed, as it were, the test of a good activist. More important, I then understood exactly how salient emotional states had become in the representation of AIDS activists and people with HIV/AIDS. Electronic media had responded to the cues provided by AIDS activists and were now collaborating in the active construction of an angry AIDS subject. Concomitantly, activists themselves were expected to conform to this emotional state of being.

It is often lamented that AIDS is an "emotional issue." The conventional explanation of this emotionality — as one which emerges from the conflation of sexuality and death — fails to appreciate that emotion is itself constitutive of the phenomenon under discussion. Pleas by policy makers for "rational" responses renders emotion as a force that obstructs appropriate action. Emotion is constructed in this discourse as dysfunctional, within the realm of the irrational, and a force to be purged through processes of rationalization.

This conceptualization of emotion as a dysfunctional residue has been the subject of recent critique. Social theorists are repositioning emotion as a phenomenon that is structured, realized, and interpreted in social contexts. Emotion is seen in this framework as circumstantial, often moral, and strategic in that it serves individual and collective objectives (see, for example, Harre 1986). It is thus with a view to its intent that the anthropologist Rosaldo (1984) came to speak of "the cultural force of emotions."

I have attempted to demonstrate in this account the centrality of the emotion of anger in the construction, by AIDS activists, of strategic responses to their predicament. While the numbers of individuals involved is numerically small, the impact of their strategic discourse is disproportionately significant. Through the organizing emotion of anger, activists have been able to effect change at an institutional level far removed from their original sphere of influence. Emotion here has been a democratizing force in Australian political relations.

While the strategy of anger originated in the United States, the experience and expression of the emotion of anger by AIDS activists in that country and in Australia differ. These differences, I would suggest, are linked to the different structures of power extant in the two countries, structures that developed as a result of each country's respective AIDS epidemic.

*   *   *

The United States lacks the structures of consultation and shared decision-making which in Australia constitute the celebrated "tripartite" structural relations between government, medicine, and the community sector (Altman 1988). This "tripartite" power structure, while in no way rendering each sector an equivalent status, is preserved in a national AIDS strategy, and does provide forms of communication and lobbying to the AIDS-affected that are progressive by international standards.

In the United States, on the other hand, people with HIV and AIDS, gay men, lesbians, ethnic minorities, and others who constitute the membership of activist groups like ACT UP, are individuals who have been excluded from formal decision-making structures. The community-based AIDS sector is largely a self-funded, welfare-oriented one, with limited links to government. Political channels between the community sector and government are restricted, and, generally speaking, the political climate is less conducive to arguments for change. This set of power relations requires and generates non-institutional forms of protest such as ACT UP, protest organized around the emotion of anger in order to accentuate the predicament of exclusion. Anger is the emotion of the powerless.

When translated into the Australian context, this emotion-based strategy takes on a different style. Structurally, ACT UP was not excluded from the power grid, as its practitioners contended, but was included by being positioned on the periphery of the tripartite power structure. From this position, anger could be deployed to augment a more broadly based campaign for government reform. The net effect was to radicalize the organizational field within which AIDS is managed in Australia.

With a radical and non-institutional organization like ACT UP positioned on the periphery of the power relations, the legitimacy of established AIDS organizations was enhanced in the eyes of the state, in turn permitting those established organizations to pursue more ambitious strategies to reform government. While activists positioned their issues in the public domain through conference and street demonstrations, ACON quietly set aside resources to research the mechanics of the government drug regulatory bureaucracy and lobbied for political support at the federal level. In this total strategy, street activism linked with government-supported community-based organizations to problematize government regulatory bureaucracies.

The groups involved shared this single strategic objective, and each group's specific strategy was designed to complement the other's. Each lobby group distinguished itself through its own style of communication, and a rhetorical style informed its position within the organizational field. Thus, as established AIDS organizations moved closer to the center of power, those emergent on the margins of the political field were granted more extreme rhetorical possibilities. With increasing distance from the center of power, rhetoric and activity became more angry and militant. We thus begin to appreciate emotion as being institutionally organized.

During the period under discussion, anger, more than any other emotion, came to organize the experience of having AIDS. This anger is not one.that all people with HIV felt at all times. Nor is it a condition that erupts spontaneously from the state of being HIV-infected. Emotions are culturally mediated, shaped, and made meaningful within the broader cultural environment in which an individual "feels" a particular emotion. This is not to say that emotions are not real, or transparent, and that a more true state lies beneath. They are experienced as valid and real by those who embody them. The point is that emotions take shape within the grids of power through which they are rendered meaningful and find expression.

Being angry, particularly for those who position themselves as political activists in AIDS, is an essential condition of being in the world. Activists themselves see this emotion as naturally erupting from their predicament. What I have attempted to reveal here, however, is the strategic invention of this emotion at a particular moment in the history of the AIDS epidemic. In the formative years of AIDS activism, in the early 1980s, anger was not frequently evoked in spoken or written discourse as a necessarily appropriate response. In time, however, anger was increasingly evoked and experienced by AIDS activists, particularly those who are infected, as a condition contingent on having AIDS, and as a state of being that is threatening to the political status quo.

In this way, anger became an "outlaw emotion" (Jagger 1989:160), potentially subversive of the dominant regime. Unlike the positivist derailment of female or ethnic emotion observed by Jagger, however, in the case of AIDS we have in fact seen the *effective* deployment of emotion to influence some state agencies.

Why was this strategy of anger a successful one? Why could not some other emotion effectively underpin a strategy for social change?

I refer to the work of June Crawford and her colleagues on the gendering of emotion in seeking an explanation. They observed how Australian women experience and express anger differently than men. This difference of emotional structure is a function, they suggest, of power. Anger is an expression of powerlessness, and is not necessarily empowering, particularly when it is female anger, because it defers to the powerful who do not need to feel or express (or understand) anger. The anger of a powerless person has a strong element of victimization, they suggest. It is a response to a perceived circumstance of injustice (Crawford et al. 1990). Anger functions in this situation to convey the conviction of the protester's sense of unfairness.

On the other hand, they note that male anger is equated, in a male-dominated society, with aggression. AIDS activism became, over the period under consideration, increasingly aggressive. Not surprisingly, in Australia AIDS activists are predominantly male. This form of anger, I would suggest, is therefore, comprehensible to the prevailing power regime. It is because AIDS activism became male, angry, and aggressive, that it was eventually successful in transforming a masculine regime. The "outlaw emotion" of AIDS-activist anger successfully legitimized the perceived injustices brought by AIDS.

NOTES

1. This description contrasts with my own experience of ACT UP New York meetings in June 1990. Then, I observed meetings of about 600-700, run rather tightly by an elected chair, and generally of very good humor, even at times very entertaining. These disparate experiences suggest that the style and emotional atmosphere of such gatherings can change, sometimes over very short periods of time, according to political developments.
2. "AIDS is Spreading Faster and Faster" (*SMH* 6 June 1989:2). This coverage of the Montreal conference was accompanied by a photograph of the ACT UP demonstration, captioned: "AIDS activists disrupt the conference's opening speech by Canada's Prime Minister, Mr Mulroney."
3. The working party was established in direct response to pressure from community groups, and included a representative from the AIDS councils. The Minister had requested an investigative report on the drug approval system by December 1990.

CHAPTER 12

Conclusion

Through the intervention of patient groups in the development of AIDS clinical trials and treatment access, the role of government as the protector of its citizens has been slightly modified. Through the construction of a new class of citizens, those with "life-threatening illnesses," the state has codified a new responsibility in response to an old predicament. The acknowledgment, by government, of the peculiar rights of those diagnosed with terminal illnesses such as cancer or AIDS, suggests a weakening of the grip of the state on diseased bodies. The demand by people with HIV/ AIDS to take responsibility for their own treatment necessitates overriding the privilege of government in determining who shall receive the products of medical research, when that will occur, and where.

On the surface it appears that all participants in this drama of disease stand to gain. People with HIV/AIDS gain wider access to previously restricted drugs. Local medical research establishments increase their standing at home by appearing, at least in the short term, to be coming up with effective methods of fighting off death. And internationally, Australian science increases its reputation through an expansion of research programs. The state wins credit for facilitating important scientific breakthroughs, and pharmaceutical companies stand to increase their profits through expanded patient markets.

But let us reconsider these outcomes, in the light of Foucault, feminism, and the critique of science, in terms of the implications these transformations have for the overall distribution of power in our society. The threat to the legitimacy and power of scientific medicine has been deflected. The early threat by people with AIDS to resist science through noncompliance has been met with a restructuring of scientific method that has rescued the docility of the gay subject. Gay men are recognized as the most accessible and compliant of all AIDS research subjects. Gay men, because of gender and class compatibility with the brokers of sci-

ence, form the easiest alliance with the scientific project. It is because of
this alliance that transformations within clinical AIDS research have
not, in the final analysis, threatened the principles of science themselves. In feminist terms, the masculinist project of positivist science has
been upheld.

For example, one area where this transformation of scientific practice
is evident is in the structuring and practice of AIDS clinical trials. This
restructuring is one that New York ACT UP first championed at the
Montreal AIDS conference in 1989. Their statement (ACT UP 1989) argued for a number of significant changes in the practice of such trials, including:

(1) Patient participation in the design and execution of trials
(2) Effective and rapid drug development which does not sacrifice safety
    and access to those in need of some form of therapeutic intervention
(3) The expansion of eligibility criteria beyond the previous strict range of
    requirements in the interest of homogenizing study populations
(4) An end to placebo controls
(5) The permission of use of other infection control drugs while on a trial.
(6) The end of the use of inhumane endpoints such as disease progression
    or death
(7) Alternative economic strategies which will not deny therapy to the
    poor
(8) Federal government support to community-run trials

Initially, scientists were reluctant to explore these proposals because such
modifications threatened to undermine the scientific validity of clinical
research. By weakening their control on the variables of a research environment, scientists faced greater challenges in measuring the effects of interventions in accordance with their narrow epistemological parameters.
Survival, for example, is a traditional measure of a drug's efficacy in the
case of a terminal illness. Death as an objective measure leads to arguments bordering on the absurd. Take for example, the following discussion
of changes brought by activists' demands:

> Survival is one of the most important end points in trials comparing treat-
> ments for a disease that is usually fatal, like AIDS, especially when the
> treatments have potentially life-threatening toxicity. Survival has the ad-
> vantage of being objective, easy to measure, and not liable to bias in assess-
> ment (Byar et al. 1990:1346).

Toward the end of the first decade of the crisis, however, many of the demands of activists were beginning to be acknowledged, not just as realizable, but to be in the very interests of clinical science. Thus in mid-1990,
one medical researcher in the United States was able to comment favor-

ably on "changes promoted by a partnership of patients, their advocates, and clinical investigators in the AIDS Clinical Trials Group" (Merigan 1990:1341). In conclusion he recommends:

> We encourage patients and their organizations to participate in the planning of clinical trials. Such participation is likely to ensure greater agreement with the objectives and design of the trial and to make people with AIDS more aware of the opportunities to enter trials.

Central to these changes is a shift in medical science's approach to clinical trials, from one that sees trials as means of determining a substance's therapeutic efficacy, to one in which trials are seen as a form of therapy for patients with life-threatening illnesses for which no therapies are actually yet proven.

While debate continues over the danger to scientific integrity through the loss of placebo-controlling mechanisms, in practice new trials are now being designed that eliminate the use of placebo arms while expanding eligibility criteria to those who may be in need of some form of therapy. These changes have reached Australian clinical research practice also. In 1990, after much delay and controversy, a new trial was underway for the antiviral ddI, a derivative drug of AZT. The trial included a placebo arm as optional, with a second arm randomizing patients to different doses of the drug. This is a method originally proposed by ACT UP (NY). Because the drug was available to those who were no longer responsive to AZT, and were therefore at the chronic stage of illness, no one enrolling in the trial chose to enter the placebo arm, much to the disappointment of researchers. This was a clear message to researchers that participation was contingent on protocols providing real benefits to participants.

This new alliance between medical researchers and affected communities is best illustrated in the inclusion, particularly in the United States, of people with HIV/AIDS on decision-making bodies. While no studies have been undertaken to measure the rate of compliance among trial participants, it is a safe bet that the growing collaboration between activists and scientists will continue to generate protocols that satisfy, to some extent, the demands of activists. This collaboration has rescued positivist science from the threat of noncompliance. Through a process of negotiation, largely headed intellectually by ACT UP New York's "Treatment and Data Group," new scientific procedures have been arrived at that recognize both the demands of people with AIDS and those of positivism.

Such changes signal a fundamental shift in the design of clinical science drug trials. The central organizing principle is no longer the determination of drug efficacy regardless of patient experience. After the social organization of patient experience into effective political lobby groups, clinical *research* practice is shifting to incorporate a dimension of clinical *treatment*, a practice that attempts both to advance therapeutic science and to care humanely for chronically ill patients. It could be said, therefore, that AIDS activism has transformed the practice of clinical science from one that prioritizes the demands of science itself, to one that is more responsive to the needs of human beings. However, there is a price for this enhanced answerability. People with AIDS, through the force of their own expectations, are more than ever a reliable and obedient reservoir of experimental subjects. AIDS science has returned the gay body, to borrow Foucault's phrase, to docility. Anger, in the final analysis, has served the interests of science well.

In responding to the demands of activists, science has shown a responsiveness for which it is not often credited. That responsiveness will ultimately pay off, however, and the brokers of science are beginning to recognize this fact. The rescuing of patient compliance from the threat of angry anarchy has served to build the prestige and power of the medical research establishment. An increase in prestige necessarily implies an increased efficacy in managing human bodies and human populations more generally. This is a power trajectory identified by Foucault (1976) as broadly characteristic of human societies at this historical moment, a configuration he characterized as "bio-power."

As Foucault hypothesized, bio-power is not operationalized through the heavy-handed imposition of authority. Rather, power is articulated through the complex interrelations of social subjects positioned at multiple sites. I have attempted to move beyond these Foucaultian characterizations of power, an approach centered on the structures of discourse, by focusing on the subjects under contestation. By positioning the subject within this contemporary and shifting apparatus of management, the hegemony of structure is revealed as unstable and subject to modification through strategic resistance. In discussing both tactical and strategic resistances, I have attempted to return the issue of historical agency to a more central position within the discussion of the postmodern condition. The focus on subjects has revealed shifts in power relations: between patient and doctor, and between a subordinate sexual community and government. These shifts have been effected through a complex interplay between emergent social subjects and key sites of power. And emergent social subjects, in this case AIDS activists, constituted through a discourse of anger, transformed the organizational field through which the AIDS epidemic is understood and managed in Australia. In the process of engaging in struggle, subjects are themselves transformed. Indeed, new subjectivities have emerged; social beings that function as sites for the contestation of power. In the process of attempting to transform our enemies, we have remade ourselves.

As I have attempted to show, this remaking is a project full of ironies. The gay community's ongoing struggles against the "dehomosexualization" of AIDS by state bureaucracies and the medical profession seem, in Australia, to have been moderately effective to date. AIDS activist claims that men (in Australia, at least) bear the greatest burden of the disease are irrefutable, and lend credence to the concomitant claims that they therefore deserve the largest slice of the clinical and research funding pie. Yet here is a prime example of the adherence by homosexual men to the enlightenment model of science. And, as I noted in Chapter Two, given the tensions that structure the relations between homosexuality and biomedicine, the development of a vast funded research establishment in AIDS which positions homosexuality as a central problematic should not necessarily be seen as unqualified progress. Perhaps Paul Young's warning back in 1988, that "If we attempt to hang onto AIDS as the 'gay plague,' the vital contributions of the gay community . . . will be lost," does not — in this one respect at least — ring quite so hollow.

This experience of AIDS leaves me with a sense of a society structured through opposing centripetal and centrifugal forces. The will to collectivize, to gather in communities, struggles against this continual process of identity fragmentation and proliferation. The argument replaces the social metaphors of center and periphery (state and community, heterosexual and homosexual, discipline and liberation) with one in which society oscillates between periods of identity fission and collective fusion. And in this endless specialization of identity and reformulation of community we glimpse the significance of de Certeau's observation that, in productivist/consumerist societies such as ours, marginality is fast becoming a universal predicament. But this marginality is more optimistic than Orwell's vacant alienation or Durkheim's anomie. For, like Foucault's reversal of the oppressive metaphors of power, de Certeau sought the creative dimension of marginality. Indeed, I have attempted to illustrate, through a documentation and analysis of the tactical and strategic responses of people with HIV and AIDS, the creative potential of this modern condition. It may be that this contemporary predicament brings with it a vision of modes of being in the world that are the reciprocal of Foucault's panoptic administrative regimes — lives that are creative, subversive, and, when sufficiently systematic in their marginality, transformative of the received social order.

BIBLIOGRAPHY

Abrams, D. I. 1990. "Alternative Therapies in HIV Infection." *AIDS* 4:1179–87.

ACT UP 1989. A National AIDS Treatment Research Agenda. Paper presented at the Fifth International Conference on AIDS, Montreal. June.

ACT UP Australia 1989. Press release.

ACT UP Australia 1990. Canberra manifesto.

ACON [AIDS Council of NSW] 1987. Annual Report 1986/87.

ACON [AIDS Council of NSW] 1988. *Frontline* September.

ACON [AIDS Council of NSW] 1990a. The Trialing, Approval and Marketing of Treatments and Therapies for HIV/AIDS and Related Illnesses. Policy document. September.

ACON [AIDS Council of NSW] 1990b. View of the National HIV/AIDS Strategy. *Frontline*.

AFAO [Australian Federation of AIDS Organisations] 1989a. Participating in Drug Trials. *HIV Brief* 1

AFAO [Australian Federation of AIDS Organisations] 1989b. Implications of the Termination of the US AZT Trials on Asymptomatic People with HIV and People with "Early ARC": A Discussion Paper. 24 August. Canberra.

Allender, J. 1989. "Sufferers Try 'Useless Treatment' for AIDS." *The Australian* 30 May:3.

Altman, D. 1975. Article in *Gay Lib Press* 6 (Jan–Feb): 35.

Altman, D. 1978. "Oz Movement 1971–1978." *Campaign* 36:18.

Altman, D. 1979. *Rehearsals for Change: Politics and Culture in Australia.* Melbourne: Dominion Press.

Altman, D. 1988. "Legitimation Through Disaster: AIDS and the Gay Movement." In E. Fee and D. M. Fox (eds), *AIDS: The Burdens of History.* Berkeley: University of California Press.

AMA [Australian Medical Association] 1989. Policy on AIDS. 10 September.

ANCA [Australian National Council on AIDS] 1990. Report of the ANCA Working Party on Trials and Treatments. Canberra.

Anderson, W. 1991. Recourse to Alternative Therapy for HIV Infection by Patients Attending Conventional Medical Clinics. Paper presented at the Seventh International Conference on AIDS. Florence. 17–21 June.

Andrews, D. 1988. Living With AIDS, Session 14(c). *National AIDS Bulletin* 2(8):38.

Anonymous I 1988. "Update: Serologic Testing for Antibody to Human Immunodeficiency Virus". *Mobidity and Mortality Weekly Report* 36(52):833–45.

Anonymous II 1989. "Zidovudine in Symptomless HIV Infection". *Lancet* 25 February:415–16.

Ariès, P. 1974. *Western Attitudes Toward Death from the Middle Ages to the Present*. Baltimore: Johns Hopkins University Press.

Ariss, R., Carrigan, T., and Dowsett, G. 1992. "Sexual Identities of HIV-Positive Men: Some Implications for AIDS Service Organisations." *National AIDS Bulletin* 6(7):20–24.

Armstrong, D. 1979. "The Emancipation of Biographical Medicine." *Social Science and Medicine* 13(A):1–8.

Armstrong, D. 1984. "The Patient's View." *Social Science and Medicine* 18(9):737–44.

Aronowitz, S. 1987/88. "Postmodernism and Politics". *Social Text* (Winter): 99–113.

Arras, J. D. 1990. Noncompliance in AIDS Research. Hastings Centre Report. September/October.

Aver, J. 1990. "Encounters with the State: Cooption and Reform. A case Study from Women's Health." In S. Watson (ed.), *Playing the State. Australian Feminist Interventions*. Sydney: Allen and Unwin.

Balshem, M. 1991. "Cancer, Control, and Causality: Talking About Cancer in a Working-Class Community." *American Ethnologist* 18(1):152–72.

Barr, R. F. and Catts, S. V. 1974. "Psychiatric Opinion and Homosexuality: A Short Report." *Journal of Homosexuality* 1(2):213–15.

Bates, E. and Lapsley, H. 1985. *The Health Machine: The Impact of Medical Technology*. Ringwood: Penguin.

Baum, M. 1989. "Rationalism Verses Irrationalism in the Care of the Sick." *Medical Journal of Australia* 151:607–8.

Baume, P. 1991. A Question of Balance: Report on the Future of Drug Evaluation in Australia. Canberra: Commonwealth of Australia.

Berman, R. 1989. "From Aristotle's Dualism to Materialist Dialectics: Feminist Transformation of Science and Society." In A. M. Jagger and S. R. Bordo (eds), *Gender / Body / Knowledge*. New Brunswick: Rutgers University Press.

Browning, B. 1993. "The Gay Network." *Quadrant* March: 77–81.

Byer, D. P., Schoenfeld, D. A., Green, S. B., Amato, D. A., Davis, R., DeGruttola, V., Finkelstein, D. M., Gatsonis, C., Gelber, R. D., Lagakos, S., Lefkopoulou, M., Tsiatis, A. A., Zelen, M., Peto, J., Freedman, L. S., Gail, M., Simon, R., Ellenberg, S. S., Anderson, J. R., Collins, R., Peto, R., and Peto, T. 1990. "Design Consideration for AIDS Trials." *New England Journal of Medicine* 323(19):1343–48.

Callen, M. 1983. *How to Have Sex in an Epidemic*. Pamphlet. New York: News From the Front Publications.

Callen, M. 1990. *Surviving AIDS*. New York: Harper Collins.

Callen, M. and Turner, D. 1988. "A History of the PWA Self-Empowerment Movement." In M. Callen (ed.) *Surviving and Thriving with AIDS: Collected Wisdom, Vol. 2.* New York: PWA Coalition Inc..

Calnan, M. 1984. "Clinical Uncertainty: Is it a Problem in the Doctor-Patient Relationship?" *Sociology of Health and Illness* 6(1):74–84.

CAMP [Campaign Against Moral Persecution] 1979. Newsletter 49.

Carr, A. 1985. "We Deserve to Live." *Outrage* 21:20–21.

Carr, A. 1986a. "The National Gay Conference: Still Searching for a Role." *Outrage* 37:14.

Carr, A. 1986b. "Goodbye to the Politics of Self-Indulgence". *Outrage* 43:18–19,71.

Carr, A. 1989a. "Antibody." *Outrage* 70:18–19.

Carr, A. 1989b. "Antibody." *Outrage* 72:20.

Carr, A. 1989c. "Time for Some Good News." *Outrage* 73:21–24.

Carr, A. 1989d. "Antibody." *Outrage* 75:64.

Carr, A. 1989e. "Antibody." *Outrage* 77:50–51.

Carter, C. 1988. "Living Well: A Personal Perspective." *National AIDS bulletin* 2(9):39–43.

Catania, J. A., Turner, H. A., Choi, K.-H., and Coates, T. J. 1992. "Coping with Death Anxiety: Help-Seeking and Social Support Among Gay Men with Various HIV Diagnoses." *AIDS* 6(9):999–1005.

Charmaz, K. 1983. "Loss of Self: A Fundamental Form of Suffering in the Chronically Ill." *Sociology of Health and Illness* 5(2):168–95.

Cherfas, J. 1989. "AZT Still on Trial." *Science* 246(4932):882.

Comaroff, J. 1978. "Medicine and Culture: Some Anthropological Perspectives." *Social Science and Medicine* 12(B):247–54.

Comaroff, J. 1982. "Medicine: Symbol and Ideology." In P. Wright and A. Treacher (eds), *The Problem of Medical Knowledge.* Edinburgh: Edinburgh University Press.

Comaroff, J. and Maguire, P. 1981. "Ambiguity and the Search for Meaning: Childhood Leukaemia in the Modern Clinical Context." *Social Science and Medicine* 15(B):115–23.

Commonwealth of Australia 1989. National HIV/AIDS Strategy. Canberra: Australian Government Publishing Service.

Connell, R. W. 1990. "The State, Gender, and Sexual Politics: Theory and Appraisal." *Theory and Society* 19:507–44.

Connell, R. W., Crawford, J., Kippax, S., Dowsett, G. W., Baxter, D., Watson, L., and Berg, R. 1989. "Facing the Epidemic: Changes in the Sexual Lives of Gay and Bisexual Men in Australia and their Implications for AIDS Prevention Strategies." *Social Problems* 36(4):384–402.

Connell, R. W., Dowsett, G. W., Rodden, P., Davis, M. D., Watson, L., and Baxter, D. 1991. "Social Class, Gay Men and AIDS Prevention." *Australian Journal of Public Health* 15(3):178–89.

Connor, L. H. 1982. "Ships of Fools and Vessels of the Divine: Mental Hospitals and Madness. A Case Study." *Social Science and Medicine* 16:783–94.

Cotton, P. 1990. "Controversy continues as experts ponder Zidovudine's role in early HIV infection. *Journal of the American Medical Association* 263(12): 1605–09.

Cozijn, J. 1982. "Sydney 1981: A Community Taking Shape." *Gay Information* 9/ 10:4–10.

Crawford, J., Kippax, S., Onyx, J., Gault, U., and Benton, P. 1990. "Women Theorising Their Experiences of Anger: A Study Using Memory Work." *Australian Psychologist* 25(3):338–421.

Crimp, D. and Rolston, A. 1990. *AIDS Demo/Graphics*. Seattle: Bay Press.

Crooks, L. 1992. "Mourning and Celebration: Grief and Loss and HIV." *National AIDS Bulletin* 6(7):11–13.

Davis, M., Klemmer, U., and Dowsett, G. W. 1991. Bisexually Active Men and Beats: Theoretical and Educational Implications. Monograph. Sydney: Macquarie University AIDS Research Unit.

Davison, G. C. 1978. "Not Can But Ought: The Treatment of Homosexuality." *Journal of Consulting and Clinical Psychology* 46(1):170–72.

de Certeau, M. 1984. *The Practice of Everyday Life*. Berkeley: University of California Press.

Delaney, M. 1990. "Significant Advances in AIDS Treatment". *Talkabout* 1(12): 22–24.

d'Emilio, J. 1983. *Sexual Politics, Sexual Communities*. Chicago: University of Chicago Press.

Douglas, M. and Calvez, M. 1990. "The Self as Risk Taker: A Cultural Theory of Contagion in Relation to AIDS." *Sociological Review* 38(3):445–63.

Dowsett, G. W. 1990. "Reaching Men Who Have Sex With Men in Australia. An Overview of AIDS Education: Community Intervention and Community Attachment Strategies." *Australian Journal of Social Issues* 25(3):186–98.

Duckett, S. J. 1984. "Structural Interests and Australian Health Policy." *Social Science and Medicine* 18(11):959–66.

Duesberg, P. 1989. "Human Immunodeficiency Virus and Acquired Immunodeficiency Syndrome: Correlation but not Causation." *Proceedings of the National Acadamy of Science* 86:755–64.

Dwyer, J. 1993. *The Body at War: The Story of Our Immune System*. Sydney: Allen and Unwin.

Elias, N. 1985. *The Loneliness of Dying*. Oxford: Basil Blackwell.

Farmer, P. and Kleinman, A. 1990. "AIDS as Human Suffering." In S. R. Graubard (ed.), *Living With AIDS*. Cambridge, Mass.: MIT Press.

Feyerabend, P. 1978. *Science in a Free Society*. London: NLB.

Finkler, K. 1986. "The Social Consequences of Wellness: A View of Healing Outcomes from Micro and Macro Perspectives." *International Journal of Health Services* 16(4):627–42.

Finkler, K. 1991. *Physicians at Work, Patients in Pain: Biomedical Practice and Patient Response in Mexico*. Boulder, Col.: Westview Press.

Fischl, M. A., Richman, D. D., Grieco, M. H., Gottlieb, M. S., Volberding, P. A., Laskin, O. L., Leedom, J. M., Groopman, J. E., Mildvan, D., Schooley, R. T., Jackson, G. G., Durack, D. T., and King, D. 1987. "The Efficacy of Azidothymidine (AZT) in the Treatment of Patients with AIDS or AIDS-Related Complex." *New England Journal of Medicine* 317(4):185–91.

Foucault, M. 1973. *The Birth of the Clinic*. London: Tavistock.

Foucault, M. 1978. *The History of Sexuality*. Harmondsworth: Penguin.

Foucault, M. 1985. *The Use of Pleasure*. New York: Pantheon.

Foucault, M. 1988. *Michel Foucault: Politics, Philosophy, Culture*, L. D. Kritzman (ed.). New York: Routledge.

Freeman, H. E., Brim, O. G., and Williams, G. 1970. "New Dimensions of Dying." In O. G. Brim (Jun.), H. E. Freeman, S. Levine, and N. A. Scotch (eds), *The Dying Patient*. New York: Russell Sage Foundation.

French, R. 1986. *Gays Between the Broadsheets: An Annotated List of Australian Media References on Homosexuality, 1948–1980*. Sydney: Gay History Project.

Friedland, G. H. 1990. "Early Treatment for HIV: The Time Has Come." *New England Journal of Medicine* 322(14):1000–02.

Galbraith, L. 1992. "AIDS: How the Gay Press Told the Story." *National AIDS Bulletin* 6(6):18–22.

Gambe, R. and Getzel, G. S. 1989. "Group Work with Gay Men with AIDS." *Social Casework* 70(3):172–79.

Game, A. and Pringle, R. 1977. "The Feminist Movement, the State and the Labor Party." *Intervention* 8:45–62.

Gamson, J. 1989. "Silence, Death and the Invisible Enemy: AIDS Activism and Social Movement 'Newness'". *Social Problems* 36(4):351–67.

Gardner, H. 1989a. "Political Parties: Ideology, Structure and Practice." In H. Gardner (ed.), *The Politics of Health*. Melbourne: Churchhill Livingstone.

Gardner, H. 1989b "A Pluralist Democracy?: Interest Groups and the Political Process." In H. Gardner (ed.), *The Politics of Health*. Melbourne: Churchill Livingstone.

Getzel, G. S. and Mahony, K. F. 1990. "Confronting Human Finitude: Group Work with People with AIDS (PWAs)." *Journal of Gay and Lesbian Psychotherapy* 1(3):105–20.

Goddard, M. 1994. "Shunning Treatment." *Outrage* 129(Feb):10–11.

Godwin, J., Hamblin, J., and Patterson, D. 1991. Australian HIV/AIDS Legal Guide. Canberra: Australian Federation of AIDS Organisations.

Goffman, E. 1963. *Stigma: Notes on the Management of Spoiled Identity.* Hardmondsworth: Pelican.

Gottlieb, M. S. and Hutman, S. 1989. "The Challenge of Timing Antiviral Therapy." *AIDS Patient Care* December: 5–6.

Grimshaw, J. M. 1989. "The Individual Challenge." In E. Carter and S. Watney (eds), *Taking Liberties: AIDS and Cultural Politics.* London: Serpent's Tail.

Harre, R. 1986. *The Social Construction of Emotions.* Oxford: Basil Blackwell.

Hay, B. 1979. Editorial. CAMP (NSW) Newsletter 50:1.

Hay, L. L. 1988. *The AIDS Book: Creating a Positive Approach.* np: Hay Louise Inc.

Hirsch, M. S. 1988. "AIDS Commentary: Azidothymidine." *The Journal of Infectious Diseases* 157(3):427–31.

Hoff, C. C., McKusick, L., Hilliard, B., and Coates, T.J. 1992. "Impact of HIV Antibody Status on Gay Men's Partner Preferences: A Community Perspective." *AIDS Education and Prevention* 4(3):197–204.

Imrie, A., Best, S., Penny, R., and Cooper, D. A. 1987. "False-Negative ELISA Result for HIV Antibody Due to an Apparent Protozone Phenomenon." Letter to *Medical Journal of Australia* 147:42.

ICGA (Inter-Governmental Committee on AIDS) 1989. A Discussion Paper: Health Care Workers and the Risk of HIV Infection.

Jagger, A. M. 1989. "Love and Knowledge: Emotion in Feminist Epistemology." In A. M. Jagger and S. R. Bordo (eds), *Gender/Body/Knowledge.* New Brunswick: Rutgers University Press.

James, J. S. (ed.) 1989. *AIDS Treatment News* (Issues 1–75 reissued as a bound volume). Berkeley, Cal.: Celestial Arts.

Jennett, B. J. 1986. *High Technology Medicine: Benefits and Burdens.* Oxford: Oxford University Press.

Johnson, T. M. and Sargent, C. F. (eds) 1990. *Medical Anthropology: A Handbook of Theory and Method.* New York: Greenwood Press.

Johnston, C. 1981. Articles in *Gay Information* 4 & 5.

Katoff, L., Rabkin, J., and Remein, R. 1991. "A Psychological Study of Long Term Survivors of AIDS." *National AIDS Bulletin* 5(11):14–15.

King, P. 1992. *Quest for Life.*

Kippax, S., Connell, R. W., Dowsett, G. W., and Crawford, J. 1993. *Sustaining Safe Sex: Gay Communities Respond to AIDS.* London: Falmer Press.

Klass, A. 1975. *There's Gold in Them Thar Pills: An Inquiry into the Medical Industrial Complex.* Harmondsworth: Penguin.

Klein, R. S. 1990. "Zidovudine for HIV Infection without Symptoms." *Lancet* 19 May: 1228.

Kramer, L. 1989. *Reports from the Holocaust: The Making of an AIDS Activist.* New York: St Martin's Press.

Kübler-Ross, E. 1969. *On Death and Dying*. New York: Macmillan.

Kübler-Ross, E. 1989. *AIDS: The Ultimate Challenge*. New York: Collier Books.

Kuhn, T. S. 1962. *The Structure of Scientific Revolutions*. Chicago: University of Chicago Press.

Laffan, J. 1992. HIV/AIDS National Counselling Guidelines. Canberra: Australian Government Printing Service.

Latour, B and Woolgar, S. 1986. *Laboratory Life: The Social Construction of Scientific Facts*. Beverly Hills: Sage.

Lauritsen, J. 1990. *Poison by Prescription: The AZT Story*. New York: Afklepios.

Lee, J. 1972. Gay Liberation Newsletter. November.

Lee, J. 1973. *Gay Lib News* August.

Le Vay, S. 1993. *The Sexual Brain*. Boston, Mass.: MIT Press.

Lévi-Strauss, C. 1979. *Structural Anthropology*. Harmondsworth: Penguin.

Lowenthal, R. M. 1989. "Can Cancer be Cured by Meditation and 'Natural Therapy'?" *Medical Journal of Australia* 151:710–15.

McKegney, F. P. and O'Dowd, M. A. 1992. "Suicidality and HIV Status." *American Journal of Psychiatry* 149(3):396–98.

MDW 1985. "AIDS Antibody Screening Test." *Analytic Chemistry* 57(7):773–76.

Mechanic, D. 1974. *Politics, Medicine, and Social Science*. New York: John Wiley and Sons.

Menon, J. 1989. "Removing Obstacles for Homosexuals." *Australian Doctor's Weekly* 4 August.

Merigan, T. C. 1990. "You Can Teach an Old Dog New Tricks: How AIDS Trials are Pioneering New Strategies." *New England Journal of Medicine* 323(19):1341–43.

Meyer-Bahlburg, H. F. L., Exner, T. M., Lorenzo, G., Gruen, R. S., Gorman, J. M., and Ehrhardt, A. A. 1991. "Sexual Risk Behaviors, Sexual Functioning and HIV-Disease Progression in Gay Men." *Journal of Sex Research* 28(1):13–27.

Michaels, E. 1990. *Unbecoming: An AIDS Diary*. Rose Bay: Empress.

Morgan, A. 1990. Issues Surrounding Sexuality for People with HIV Infection. Discussion paper. Sydney: ACON [AIDS Council of NSW]. 6 July.

Mulkay, M. J. 1972. *The Social Process of Innovation: A Study in the Sociology of Science*. London: Macmillan.

Navarre, M. 1988. "Fighting the Victim Label." In D. Crimp (ed.), *AIDS: Cultural Analysis, Cultural Activism*. Cambridge, Mass.: MIT Press.

NCHECR [National Centre in HIV Epidemiology and Clinical Research] 1992. National Working Group on HIV Projections: Estimates and Projections 1981–1994. Sydney.

Nungesser, L. G. 1986. *Epidemic of Courage*. New York: St Martin's Press.

O'Brien, M. E. 1992. *Living with HIV: Experiment in Courage*. New York and Westport, Connecticut, np.

O'Connor, B. B. 1990. Vernacular Health Belief Systems and their Implications for Clinical Care. Unpublished Ph.D. dissertation. University of Pennsylvania.

O'Connor, B. B. 1991. PWA Use and Evaluation of Alternative Therapies in Philadelphia. Paper presented at the Seventh International Conference on AIDS. Florence. 17–21 June.

O'Conner, B. B., Anderson, W., Schwartz, J. S., and MacGregor, R. R. 1991. Recourse to Alternative Therapy for HIV Infection by Patients Attending Conventional Medical Clinics. Unpublished paper.

O'Reilly, B. 1990. "The Inside Story of the AIDS Drug." *Fortune* 5 Nov: 60–68.

Patton, C. 1990. *Inventing AIDS.* New York: Routledge.

Phoenix, P. 1989. "Alive with AIDS." In S. Graubard (ed.), *Living with AIDS.* Cambridge, Mass.: MIT Press.

PLWA (NSW) [People Living with AIDS Inc. (NSW)] 1988. "AZT and Beyond." *Talkabout* 1(1):8–10.

PLWA (NSW) [People Living with AIDS Inc. (NSW)] 1991a. "HIV Support Groups: Your Questions Answered." *Talkabout* 1(12):8–9.

PLWA (NSW) [People Living with AIDS Inc. (NSW)] 1991b. "Positive Sex." *Talkabout* 2(2):7–27.

Priestley, J. 1991. Information pack. Center for 21st Century Medicine. Los Angeles.

Richman, D. D., Fischl, M. A., Grieco, M. H., Gottlieb, M. S., Volberding, P. A., Laskin, O. L., Leedom, J. M., Groopman, J. E., Mildvan, D., Hirsch, M. S., Jackson, G. G., Durack, D. T,. and Nusinoff-Lehrman, S. 1987. "The Toxicity of Azidothymidine (AZT) in the Treatment of Patients with AIDS and AIDS-Related Complex." *New England Journal of Medicine* 317(4):192–97.

Roy, S., Portnoy, J., and Wainberg, M. A. 1987. "Need for Caution in Interpretation of Western Blot Test for HIV." Letter in *Journal of the American Medical Association* 257(8):1047.

Ruedy, J., Schechter, M., and Montaner, J. S. G. 1990. "Zidovudine for Early Human Immunodeficiency Virus (HIV) Infection: Who, When, and How." *Annals of Internal Medicine* 112(10):721–22.

Russo, V. 1989. In *PWA Coalition Newsline* March.

Saillant, F. 1990. "Discourse, Knowledge and Experience of Cancer: A Life Story." *Culture, Medicine and Psychiatry* 14:81–104.

Salzman, B. 1991. "Howling at the Moon." *PWA Coalition Newsline* 69:28–29.

Sax, S. 1984. *A Strife of Interest.* Sydney: Allen and Unwin.

Scheper-Hughes, N. 1990. "Three Propositions for a Critically Applied Medical Anthropology." *Social Science and Medicine* 30(2):189–97.

Schwartz, J. S., Dans, P. E., and Kinosian, B. P. 1988. "Human Immunodeficiency Virus Test Evaluation, Performance, and Use." *Journal of the American Medical Association* 259(17):2574–79.

Scott-Hartland, B. 1991. "Is There Sex after Diagnosis?" *PWA Coalition Newsline* 69:23–24.

Shernoff, M. and Bloom, D. J. 1991. "Designing Effective AIDS Prevention Workshops for Gay and Bisexual Men." *AIDS Education and Prevention* 3(1):31–46.

Shilts, R. 1987. *And the Band Played On*. New York: St Martin's Press.

Siegal, K., Levine, M. P., Brooks, C., and Kern, R. 1989. "The Motives of Gay Men for Taking or Not Taking the HIV Antibody Test." *Social Problems* 36(4):368–83.

Silverman, D. 1989. "Making Sense of a Precipice: Constituting Identity in an HIV Clinic." In P. Aggleton, G. Hart, and P. Davies (eds), *Social Representations, Social Practices*. New York: Falmer Press.

Simms, M. (ed.) 1984. *Australian Women and the Political System*. Melbourne: Longman Cheshire.

Singer, M. 1990. "Reinventing Medical Anthropology: Toward a Critical Reallignment." *Social Science and Medicine* 30(2):179–87.

Singer, M., Baer, H. A., and Lazarus, E. 1990. "Critical Medical Anthropology in Question." *Social Science and Medicine* 30(2):v–viii.

Slome, L. R. and Moulton, J. 1991. "Physician-Assisted Suicide." *Focus* 6(9):3.

Solomon, R. C. 1984. "Getting Angry: The Jamesian Theory of Emotion in Anthropology." In R. A. Shweder and R. A. LeVine (eds), *Culture Theory: Essays on Mind, Self, and Emotion*. Cambridge: Cambridge University Press.

Stall, R. D., Coates, T., and Hoff, C. 1988. "Behavioural Risk Reduction for HIV Infection among Gay and Bisexual Men." *American Psychologist* 43(11):878–85.

Strubbe, B. 1988. "A Bitter Pill." *Outrage* 59:22–24.

Sturgis, E. T. and Adams, H. E. 1978. "The Right to Treatment: Issues in the Treatment of Homosexuality." *Journal of Consulting and Clinical Psychology* 46(1):165–69.

Taussig, M. 1980. "Reification and the Consciousness of the Patient." *Social Science and Medicine* 14B:3–13.

Thomas, E. H. and Fox, D. M. 1988. *The Cost of AZT*. Maryland: University Publishing Group.

Thompson, D. 1985. *Flaws in the Social Fabric: Homosexuals and Society in Sydney*. Sydney: Allen and Unwin.

Tindall, B., Swanson, C., Donovan, B., and Cooper, D. A. 1989. "Sexual Practices and Condom Usage in a Cohort of Homosexual Men in Relation to Human Immunodeficiency Virus Status." *Medical Journal of Australia* 151:318–22.

Volberding, P. A., Lagakos, S. W., Koch, M. A., Pettinelli, C., Myers, M. W., Booth, D. K., Balfour, H. H., Reichman, R. C., Bartlett, J. A., Hirsch, M. S., Murphy, R. L., Hardy, W. D., Soeiro, R., Fischl, M. A., Bartlett, J. G., Merigan, T. C., Hyslop, N. E., Richman, D. D., Valentine, C., and Corey, L. 1990.

"Zidovudine in Asymptomatic Human Immunodeficiency Virus Infection." *New England Journal of Medicine* 322(14):941–49.

Waitzkin, H. 1979. "Medicine, Superstructure and Micropolitics." *Social Science and Medicine* 13(A):601–09.

Wajcman, J. 1991. *Feminism Confronts Technology.* Sydney: Allen and Unwin.

Watson, L. 1984. "It is Time to Talk about Money." *Outrage* 18:8–9.

Watson, L. 1986. "Three Years of AIDS, Sydney and Australia Style." *Campaign* 125:17.

Weeks, J. 1977. *Coming Out: Homosexual Politics in Britain, From the Nineteenth Century to the Present.* London: Quartet Books.

White, E. 1987. "The Artist and AIDS." *Harpers Magazine* 274(1644):22–25.

Williams, G. 1984. "The Genesis of Chronic Illness: Narrative Reconstruction." *Sociology of Health and Illness* 6(2):175–200.

Wotherspoon, G. 1988 Letter in *Sydney Star Observer* 74.

Wotherspoon, G. 1991. *City of the Plain.* Sydney: Hale and Iremonger.

Wotherspoon, G. (ed.) 1986. *Being Different.* Sydney: Hale and Iremonger.

Yeatman, A. 1990. *Bureaucrats, Technocrats, Femocrats: Essays on the Contemporary Australian State.* Sydney: Allen and Unwin.

Young, P. 1981. "Better Out and Gay than Home and Dull." *Gay Community News* 3(1):13.

Young, P. 1990. "Boo and Hiss." Letter in *Talkabout* 6:12–13

INDEX